Douglas Gomery

THE HOLLYWOOD STUDIO SYSTEM

© Douglas Gomery 1986

All rights reserved. No reproduction, copy or transmission of this publication may be made without written permission.

No paragraph of this publication may be reproduced, copied or transmitted save with written permission or in accordance with the provisions of the Copyright Act 1956 (as amended).

Any person who does any unauthorised act in relation to this publication may be liable to criminal prosecution and civil claims for damages.

First published 1986

Published by
Higher and Further Education Division
MACMILLAN PUBLISHERS LTD
Houndmills, Basingstoke, Hampshire RG21 2XS
and London
Companies and representatives
throughout the world

Printed in Hong Kong

British Library Cataloguing in Publication Data
Gomery, Douglas
The Hollywood studio system.— (BFI film series)
1. Moving-picture industry — California —
Los Angeles — History   2. Hollywood
(Los Angeles, Calif.) — Industries —
History   3. Los Angeles (Calif.)
— Industries — History
I. Title   II. Series
384′.8′0979494   PN1993.5.U65
ISBN 0–333–32547–8
ISBN 0–333–32548–6 Pbk

Contents

Contents

List of Illustrations

viii

List of Tables and Figures

Preface

This book is an examination of the workings of the
Hollywood studio system between 1930 and 1949, the so-called
'Golden Age' (hereafter referred to as the studio era). During this
period the US motion picture industry dominated the North
American (indeed the world) mass entertainment business. Many
other institutions have supported film-making (educational and
religious organizations provide but two examples), but it was the
profit motive which dictated the nature of film production,
distribution and exhibition in the United States during the studio
era. Eight corporations (narrowly labelled studios) acted jointly
to produce profits for one and all. They competed for the
maximum possible share of box-office dollars, subject to a
complicated set of constraints which effectively blocked entry of
significant competitiors. These oligopolists defined how Americans understood the movies. The movie industry has changed
since 1949 but all these corporations except RKO continue, albeit
under different owners.

After a survey of the functions of the system as a whole,
individual chapters will analyze the structure and conduct of each
of the major corporations. These chapters will deal with management, finance, labor and production (features, shorts and newsreels), distribution and exhibition. In short **The Hollywood Studio
System** strives to be a one-volume guide to the economics of the
studio era, incorporating significant reinterpretations of the
history of the US film industry at present found only in specialized
journals or books.

Douglas Gomery

Acknowledgements

I wish to thank the many friends, colleagues, editors of journals, and former industry hands who have contributed to my understanding of the motion picture industry. Special thanks go to Ed Buscombe for suggesting and setting up the project. Jill Bury did a first-rate job typing the manuscript. I dedicate this book to Marilyn Moon, who has put up with a great deal, and given much of herself. Her own work and writings provided me with a model of clear thinking. Thank you Marilyn.

Douglas Gomery

1:

The Hollywood Studio System: 1930-49

The American film industry – Hollywood in the common parlance – has long been one of the most visible institutions in the United States, indeed the world. Before the coming of television to the US in the 1950s, no industry received more publicity. Newspapers, magazines, and radio alike continually spilled forth gossip, reviews, and advertisements. Specialized fan magazines lined news-stands. Movie houses stood in every downtown, from New York City to Augusta, Kansas to Los Angeles. But despite this presence, precious little was actually known about the handful of companies which created and marketed nearly all available feature films, newsreels, and short-subjects. Even today, with libraries brimming with surveys of film history and specialized film journals, our accumulated knowledge of these giant corporations hardly fills one bookshelf. There are understandable reasons for this. Study of the film industry requires complex frameworks for analysis, and seemingly endless interpretations of complicated data. Economists have had a hard time with the movie business because products seem so ephemeral, not quite a manufactured good, but not a traditional service either.

In one sense the American film industry has always been like other industries. All have had a common goal: making the highest possible profits. Since the turn into the twentieth century, the US film industry has striven for profits from the production, distribution and exhibition of films. Production companies create the films. Rightly, Hollywood has come to symbolize this particular industrial arena, with its cavernous sound stages, multi-acre lots and secret special-effects. The distributor wholesales films from a producer to an exhibitor. Exhibitors, in turn, present the films to paying customers. Specifically, they trade entertainment for money. In the studio era, exhibitors traded shows (in elaborately decorated, air-conditioned surroundings) for fees ranging from 10¢ to $2.00. The film industry, then as now, was a collection of producers, distributors and exhibitors, all trying to make as much money as possible.

The fundamental point for understanding the studio era is that there were only eight corporations which dominated the three functions. Control of an industry by a small number of firms is termed an oligopoly (literally, control by a few). During the first three decades of the twentieth century, the American film industry evolved a complicated system for handling film production, distribution, and exhibition. This particular system guaranteed its major participants enormous profits, while maintaining effective barriers to keep potential competitors out. The so-called majors, Paramount Pictures, Loew's Inc. (parent company of its more famous production subsidiary Metro-Goldwyn-Mayer or MGM), 20th Century-Fox, Warner Bros. and Radio-Keith-Orpheum (RKO), fully integrated production, distribution and exhibition. Universal and Columbia concentrated on production and distribution. United Artists only handled distribution for independent producers, but for a time, like Universal, was affiliated with a small chain of theaters.

These eight corporations controlled the American motion picture industry throughout the 1930s and 1940s. Whether measured by volume of business, cost of films produced, or amount of invested capital, corporations aside from the aforementioned eight pale into insignificance. There were others; for example, Disney, Monogram and Republic were noted producers, but though the last two did own nationwide distribution networks, they were unable to seize a sizeable portion of the market. Instead they had to be satisfied with low returns available in specialized markets: Disney in animated shorts and features, and Monogram and Republic in cheap westerns and serials.

But it was not Hollywood production which provided the majors with the fundamental source of their power. Rather, their wordwide distribution networks afforded them enormous cost advantages, and their theater circuits provided them direct access to the box office. The five fully-integrated majors (Paramount, Loew's, Fox, Warners and RKO) did not own all the theaters in the United States, only the ones which consistently delivered three-quarters of the revenues. Affiliated theaters received the most popular films first, and for exclusive runs in any community or neighbourhood of a large city. By owning these 2600 first-run theaters (16 per cent of the total) the five fully-integrated majors skimmed off the bulk of movie revenues, allowing rivals only what was left over.

2

The Rise of the Studio System

Oligopoly control through ownership of production, distribution and exhibition represented the full-grown Hollywood studio system. This system was so profitable that throughout the studio era members were continually being sued for violation of anti-trust laws. Success, however, did not come overnight. It took thirty years for a fairly competitive industry to turn into a tightly-held trust. A projected motion picture show was first commercially exhibited in 1896. This initial exchange of money for filmed entertainment gave rise to an industry quite different from the studio system of the 1930s and 1940s. Even with certain corporations vying for control of basic patents, a relatively competitive situation prevailed. For the first dozen years of this new industry, it was easy to go into (and out of) business. Films, treated more or less as a novelty, were sold by the foot. There were lots of small producers. Historians have concentrated on those which survived (Biograph or Vitagraph, for example) but the records show there were hundreds, possibly thousands, of others. A like number of distributors – operating in a large city and its surrounding environs – and exhibitors also flourished. Numerous biographies of famous executives tell how easy it was to enter the industry. For example, Marcus Loew and the brothers Warner began as exhibitors and went on to give their names to two of Hollywood's five majors. Neither patent problems nor cost mounted significant long-run barriers to entry in any sector. Profits accumulated rapidly. It was the era in which to try to break into the movie business. It has not been as easy since.

This period of relative competition did not last into the second decade of the century. In 1908, ten leading equipment manufacturers banded together to form the Motion Picture Patents Company (hereafter MPPC). As a cartel, the MPPC tried to use its monopoly over equipment to extort fees from producers and exhibitors. To extract additional revenues the MPPC in 1910 formed its own distribution arm, the General Film Company. This corporation, the first nationwide distributor in the United States, actively sought to acquire (or drive out of business) all possible competitors. In 1910 it looked as if one fully-integrated motion picture corporation could control filmed entertainment in the USA. But the embryonic monopoly failed. As with many other cartels, certain members, thinking they could make more profits, broke with MPPC policies. The US federal government initiated a suit for anti-trust violations. Independents flooded into the market. Scores of films from Europe – Denmark and Italy in particular – appeared on US screens. By 1914 the MPPC was finished as a formidable economic force.

As the MPPC floundered, other film industry enterprises, epitomized by Famous Players-Lasky (later Paramount), innovated a more flexible way to dominate the US movie industry. This three-part strategy enabled this one company, by 1921, to dominate as no company ever had or would. Famous Players secured its position by (i) differentiating its products (ii) distributing on a national, then international level, and (iii) dominating exhibition through ownership of a small number of first-run theaters. Famous Players' executives did not think up the complete strategy in one day. Rather, as soon as they perceived a successful business technique, from one source or another, they took up that tool. Competitors imitated Famous Players' ploys. In the end, Famous Players achieved the most power, not always by being first, but by being forceful enough to mold a system, and then wring out all possible extra profits.

For production, Famous Players differentiated its films using stars. Gone were the days of films being sold by the foot. Each motion picture became a unique good. Early producers (including the MPPC) did not exploit actors' and actresses' images. In contrast, Famous Players heralded certain players who seemed to guarantee high box office revenues. One of the most successful was Mary Pickford, a 'superstar' to her adoring fans, who ascended the salary ladder from $100 per week to $15,000 per week in less than one decade. By 1920, Famous Players (and its competitors) had regularized the issuance of features with stars. Famous Players, true to its name, raided the legitimate stage for potential 'kings and queens' of the screen. Other studios attempted to create indigenous stars by testing potential luminaries in cheaper productions or shorts. Studios linked stars to exclusive, long-run contracts so that the player could not seek a higher salary from a rival company. Fans may not have known they were going to see a Famous Players' product, but they would stand in line for hours to see a vehicle with Mary Pickford or Douglas Fairbanks, two of the studio's most popular attractions.

The second aspect of Famous Players' strategy focussed on national, and later, worldwide distribution. Any time operations in any business reach a certain threshold, costs level off and begin to fall. Adam Smith, the founder of modern economics, outlined more than three hundred years ago the cost savings from division and specialization of labor. In movie distribution there were savings through division and specialization in advertising, sales promotion, and service. During and immediately after the First World War, Famous Players extended its sales territory to include the entire world. By 1925 its far-reaching sales network was firmly in place, and few possible entrants into the movie business had the resources to challenge Famous Players. Only the eight oligopolists were able to construct effective world distribution networks.

Finally, Famous Players learned that it need not own all movie theaters to gain a measure of economic power in exhibition. By owning first- and some second-run picture palaces in major metropolitan areas, it could gather in the bulk of film revenue in any single region. By 1930, Famous Players (now renamed Paramount) controlled over 1000 houses, with more than two million patrons per week.

The coming of sound did not alter the fundamental strategy pioneered by Famous Players. 'Talkies' seemed to come overnight, but speed of transformation should not be taken for chaos or confusion. Warner Bros. and Fox pioneered the conversion. All corporations eventually changed over so that by 1930 the US movie industry produced sound, not silent films. Movie-going audiences of the late 1920s flocked to the new talkies. The profits of the major companies soared. The larger companies and successful innovators used their profits to buy out competitors. Warners, needing theaters, took over First National in 1929. (In 1925, Warners' assets totalled $5 million; in 1930 they topped $230 million.) Fox for a time acquired a controlling interest in Loew's. The Radio Corporation of America created a new, fully integrated firm, Radio-Keith-Orpheum (RKO). There was talk and almost agreement of a Paramount merger with Warners during the fall of 1929, but the US Department of Justice squelched the deal. So the Big Five (temporarily the Big Four) were set: Paramount, Warner Bros, RKO and Fox-Loew's. Universal and Columbia did well enough to stride into the 1930s, though well behind their rivals. United Artists, the third member of the Little Three (with Universal and Columbia) occupied a special niche in the market-place, the distribution of features for independent producers.

The coming of sound did create one new corporation, the fifth member of the Big Five, Radio-Keith-Orpheum (RKO). This firm emerged from the Radio Corporation of America's interest in talkies. In 1919, General Electric and Westinghouse Electric had created RCA to monopolize in radio broadcasting in America. Like its rival AT&T, RCA experimented with sound recording. It developed a sound-on-film recording system, but

5

failed to secure contracts with any major company. (AT&T signed up Paramount and Loew's.) RCA reacted by forming its own movie company. First, it purchased a very small producer-distributor, the Film Booking Office. To develop a chain of theaters, RCA took over the Keith-Albee-Orpheum vaudeville circuit, and gradually wired these well-situated first-run locations. Other small companies were drawn in, and the newly titled Radio-Keith-Orpheum was established in 1928.

In 1929 the structure of the American film industry was clear. Five firms dominated: Paramount, Loew's, Warner Bros., Fox, and RKO. Each of the 'Big Five' owned substantial production facilities in Southern California, a worldwide distribution network and a sizeable theater chain. The Little Three (Universal, Columbia and United Artists) maintained only production and distribution units. A mere handful of specialized producers remained in existence. There were some 15,000 non-affiliated theaters, but collectively they took in less revenues than the 3000 owned by the Big Five, usually far less. Paramount (the former Famous Players) and its seven allies had successfully turned the US movie industry into a smooth-running, profitable trust. The 'Big Five' succeeded where the MPPC failed. Gone were the days of easy entry into the movie business. Artificial restraints loomed everywhere. Giant companies colluded to keep out the competition. And the products featured unique stars, controlled through contractual servitude to one studio. Structurally, the film industry consisted of a few firms whose conduct only served to remind all who looked closely that they were quite willing to take full advantage of their oligopolistic, vertically-integrated power.

The Structure of the Studio System

The US motion picture industry has never produced much in the way of real economic activity. In 1946 the industry reached its peak, yet produced only 0.5 per cent of the national income of the US. In terms of labor, the industry's employees also made up only 0.5 per cent of the US total. Following the industry's own public relations proclamations, some historians have placed the industry in the top ten (or top four) US industries in the 1930s and 1940s. But if size is measured by sales, the film industry never reached the top thirty. For 1937 it placed forty-fifth in sales, ranking with Bituminous Coal, and Life Insurance. Classic manufacturing industries like motor vehicles, iron and steel, electric power, and printing and publishing, generated sales from three to five times the amount of motion pictures. It is only when compared with other forms of recreation available at the time that the motion picture industry dominated. In 1937 movies accounted for three-quarters of America's gross income spent on amusements. It was indeed a golden age relative to the competition, much as broadcast television was in the 1960s and 1970s. But for business historians, motion pictures have always been a relatively small industry.

By one measure – profits – the motion picture industry did do exceptionally well in the studio era. In 1946 when the industry produced a little over 0.5 per cent of the US national income, and the same percentage of total wages, it was able to generate nearly 1.5 per cent of all US corporate profits. That is, the industry generated three times the expected share of profit. It is with this measure that the industry may have moved into the top ten US industries, especially during its most prosperous years, 1941-6 – the so-called Second World War boom. Still, others did far better. For example, before the Second World War restrictions, the automobile and cigarette industries generated profits at twice the rate (and many times the absolute amount) of the motion picture industry. Thus, despite all the glamour and hype, the movie industry could never be considered more than a moderately successful industry, one affected by the usual booms and busts of twentieth-century US capitalism.

With profits high, stockholders of the Big Five and Little Three did well. But these oligopolists also rewarded their executives far in excess of the normal standards of far larger corporations. Through the two decades of the studio era, corporate presidents and a few production bosses consistently earned hundreds of thousands of dollars annually. Loew's, Paramount, Warner Bros. and 20th Century-Fox, the most profitable corporations, all had elaborate management bonus systems. Indeed, throughout the studio era Loew's executives – production boss Louis B. Mayer, counsel J. Robert Rubin and president Nicholas Schenck – were ranked among the highest salaried persons in the United States. The brothers Warner, Fox's Joseph M. Schenck and Darryl F. Zanuck, and Paramount's Barney Balaban and Y. Frank Freeman did nearly as well. These men, as a rule unknown to the general public, wielded enormous power in the industry. In contrast, stars received a large amount of publicity for their high salaries, but few earned enormous amounts for very long. Stars, producers, crafts people all came and went, while their bosses remained, guiding the profit-making destinies of the corporations which put together motion pictures for the US and most of the rest of the world.

If publicity (or even historical study) is any criterion, the bulk of the movie industry was found in the Hollywood studios. Distribution, like much of the wholesaling trade, was 'invisible'. Exhibition had a greater presence, but in most minds never matched the importance of the well-guarded, enormous California production plants. Yet in terms of invested dollars, production accounted for only 5 per cent of total assets. Speaking correctly, distribution, despite its enormous leverage, totalled even less – about 1 per cent. Throughout the 1930s and 1940s by and large most investment took place on the exhibition side – some 94 per cent. The amount of capital required for production paled when compared with the cost of financing a chain of several hundred theaters. Thus, although we know a great deal about the glories of Metro-Goldwyn-Mayer, properly that company was simply one subsidiary of a much larger theater corporation, Loew's Inc. All the highly-paid executives of the period knew where corporate revenues originated. Nearly all had started their careers in the theater end. For a clear picture of the studio era one has to characterize the Big Five as diversified theater chains, producing features, shorts, cartoons, and newsreels to fill their houses. The term 'studio' is a misnomer which has stuck. This book will use the term motion picture corporation. Studio era will be used to represent the 1930–49 era, the latter date being when the Big Five began to split off from ownership of theaters.

The five major companies in the US movie industry during the 1930s and 1940s were Loew's Inc., Radio-Keith-Orpheum, Paramount, 20th Century-Fox and Warner Bros. In terms of total assets, the Big Five corporations were about four times larger than their Little Three rivals. Paramount, Loew's, 20th Century-Fox and Warners were all about the same size. RKO, which continually struggled throughout the studio era, was 25 per cent smaller. Each mirrored the entire industry, with the bulk of invested corporate capital in theaters, not production. With most corporate assets held in, and revenues coming through, the theater division corporate decisions were aimed in that direction. For example, Paramount's vast holdings in theaters dragged the corporation into receivership in the 1930s, but then pushed the corporation to extraordinarily high profits during the boom period of the Second World War. In contrast, Loew's relatively small theater holdings assisted it in the early 1930s. By owning only one-eighth of Paramount's total, Loew's sailed through the Great Depression. But in the 1940s it could not take full advantage of the extraordinary demand for movie entertainment. During the prosperous Second World War period, Loew's was forced to continue to book its features into theaters owned by others, and thus contribute to the profits of competitors with larger chains. In poor times Loew's had, of course, booked MGM films in theaters of others, but then did not have to share in the costs of the upkeep (and mortgages). With such debts a thing of the past by 1946, whenever Loew's created a popular feature film, it only added to the profits of the owners of much larger chains of theaters, rivals Warner Bros., Fox and Paramount.

During the studio era, the Big Five created the bulk of the high budget, so-called 'A' films. Universal, Columbia, and United Artists added their share of features to bring the total of the eight oligopolists to about three-quarters of all features made. Films by marginal, small producers (Monogram or Republic, for example) consisted almost entirely of low budget features, cheap westerns and serials. Such low-cost fare played in small neighborhood theaters and houses in rural America, rarely in the first-run urban operations of the Big Five. Consequently the oligopolists' features helped generate some 90 per cent of the box-office revenues, while marginal producers had to scramble for the rest, faced with the high selling costs associated with dealing with thousands of 200-seat theaters. In addition, the Big Five controlled vital inputs into the process of production, including film processing, music publishing, sponsorship of Broadway plays (to be turned into films) and forays into television. In general, the Big Five rarely took on investments not related to film production, distribution or exhibition. The Little Three stuck to film production and distribution, making few moves into ancillary fields.

Still the majors found no totally effective way to exclude independent producers. United Artists serviced an array of independents, including Sam Goldwyn from 1926 to 1941, when RKO agreed to distribute his films. David O. Selznick created **Gone With the Wind** within his independent shop. In fact, two independent operations were able to merge with and revitalize important production units: Twentieth Century with Fox in 1935, and International with Universal in 1945. The boom in theater attendance in the Second World War plus a restricted use of stars and film stock created a profitable pull to independent entrepreneurs in the 1940s. Leading stars, producers, and directors set up production shops to make one or two films and take advantage of favorable capital gains tax rates. The rigid star system, with its binding seven year contracts, broke down in the face of this thrust. By 1945, of the 1054 members of the Screen Actors Guild who received feature billing, only 261 were under exclusive contract to a major studio. In the 1950s, nearly all important stars would form their own production companies.

A second force for creative independence in film production came with the rise of powerful Hollywood unions. As the American film industry was forming, the open-shop tradition of the Los Angeles labor market prevailed. During the First World War trade unionism began to make inroads among skilled construction crafts, but not among other motion picture workers. As was true in the United States in general during the 1920s, little progress in unionization was made before the Great Depression. The Hollywood producers, in fact, developed their own company union in the form of the Academy of Motion Picture Arts and Sciences. Effective union representation came about during the 1930s, especially under the aegis of the federal government through the National Recovery and the Wagner Acts. By the outbreak of the Second World War, most Hollywood studio labor, even the highly-paid actors and actresses, was unionized. Entrenchment took place during the Second World War; strikes after the war solidified that power. By the close of the studio era, motion picture production in Hollywood was a completely unionized operation.

With unions to support them, creative personnel of all kinds began to free-lance during the 1940s. In 1945, there were 952 active members of the Screen Writers Guild, but only 174 were under long-term contract to one of the Big Five or Little Three. Of the 222 feature motion picture directors in their particular Guild, only 75 were under long-term contract. Since the majors provided employment for all the noted writers, directors, and stars, a number sought the security of a guaranteed income through a studio contract. Still, by the end of the Second World War more and more creative personnel chose to venture into independent work, seeking the best possible offer. Consequently the major film companies were able to extract less and less profit from control over stars, directors, producers and other vital creative personnel. In turn, after the Second World War the Big Five focussed an increasing amount of corporate attention on boosting their power in distribution (especially overseas) and exhibition (forcing the issue on the Paramount anti-trust case as discussed later).

For one aspect of the production process, the Big Five and Little Three openly colluded to protect their joint interests.

Through their trade association, the Motion Picture Producers and Distributors of America Inc. (the MPPDA), they organized self-censorship. Originally, the MPPDA was set in motion in 1922 to fight off a rising tide of state and municipal censorship restrictions. In 1934, after twelve years of informal controls, the MPPDA set up formal enforcement machinery, complete with $25,000 fines. Member producers (the Big Five and Little Three) were obliged to submit all scripts and films for approval. Since the majors controlled the theaters in which all films sought to play, non-approved films were denied access to significant sources of revenue. Indeed, MPPDA disapproval guaranteed – in all but a few cases – box office failure. Effectively, in this manner, the Big Five and Little Three exercised prior-restraint over the entire industry. Controversial films (in terms of sex, violence, religion and politics) simply were never made, stymied early on at the script stage. The MPPDA code would gradually break down during the 1950s as the Big Five corporations spun off their theaters and relinquished a certain amount of their power in the mass entertainment business.

Far less glamorous than production, but far more important for profit-making, was distribution. Agents – in thirty-two major cities spread throughout the United States and in all countries of the world (except the USSR) – negotiated licenses and delivered films to theaters. Only the Big Five and Little Three maintained complete national and international distribution networks. The most powerful marginal producers, Monogram and Republic, had to make do with limited access to markets outside the United States. All the important producers, to ensure reasonable costs, had to work with a member of the Big Five or Little Three. If an independent producer could not negotiate such a contract, he or she stood little chance of making a profit – however promising the film might be. United Artists was set up so independent producers had at least one such outlet, and because RKO did so poorly with its own products, by the beginning of the Second World War it also regularly picked up independently-made works. In particular, Disney and Goldwyn distributed through RKO throughout the 1940s. After the Second World War the situation began to change: the remainder of the Big Five and Little Three began to handle independent deals. Universal and Columbia in particular were able to make great strides by becoming havens for independent producers.

The advantages of a national and international distribution network were considerable. Even though in 1945 it cost Loew's or Paramount about $5 million per year to operate a distribution network in the US, they could spread these costs over numerous features, shorts and newsreels, reaping *low per unit costs*. No outsider could afford to start an international organization for only a handful of films. It was far easier (and cheaper) simply to work through one of the established corporations. In addition, control over key theaters gave the Big Five the power effectively to exclude other distributors from a large share of the potential market. Theaters owned by the Big Five rarely accepted non-UA, non-RKO independent products, and in as many cases as possible independent theater-owners also gave preference to films from the major studios because they contained the most popular stars and promised to make the most money.

Distribution hegemony forced all mainstream producers to go through the Big Five and Little Three. States-rights distributors, each operating in one or two regions of the United States, handled cheap westerns, 'quickies' and exploitation films. Thus during the 1943-4 movie season, for example, the Big Five collected just about 75 per cent of all film rentals paid in the United States. The Little Three took in 20 per cent. That left only 5 per cent of the pie for everyone else. Within the Big Five relative shares did change as one year Paramount would do better, another year Loew's, but the total share taken in by the Big Five and Little Three remained remarkably consistent. The total for the Big Five and Little Three added up, year-after-year, to about 95 per cent of the US box-office takings.

The distribution power of the Big Five and Little Three extended to other countries. After the First World War these eight corporations completed their distribution networks throughout the world. By 1925 (and throughout the 1930s and 1940s) overseas rentals accounted for approximately one half an average feature film's takings. Hollywood dominated Britain as well as France, Italy and even Japan. The coming of sound did not hinder control. Foreign taxes, tariffs and quotas did – to a degree. The United States Department of State helped to neutralize the effects of foreign governments by working with the MPPDA to mute as much as possible foreign constraints. Problems arose during the Second World War because of the loss of markets in Axis countries. After that war the industry set up a formal equivalent of MPPDA – the Motion Picture Export Association – to handle foreign matters. There were constant battles and disagreements, but the Big Five and Little Three never lost their significant comparative advantage.

However, in the end, any consideration of the motion picture industry in the studio era has to return to exhibition. A survey of the theaters in the United States in 1945 is shown in Table 1.1. Although there were relatively few large theaters (picture palaces of 1200 seats or more) these few could hold more than all the other 10,000 small theaters (0–500 seats) in the US. Most of the smaller theaters were in rural towns or in neighborhood shopping areas of major cities. Larger theaters were found downtown, or in regional outlying shopping areas in the fifty largest US cities in terms of population. The Big Five concentrated their ownership in larger theaters, thereby controlling approximately 25 per cent of the total seats in US theaters. Collectively, the majors controlled more than 70 per cent of all the first-run theaters in the ninety-two largest cities in the US, those cities in 1940 with 100,000 people or more. All the statistics point to a system where the majors, through the ownership of large picture palaces in cities of 100,000 or more, were able effectively to harness the market for exhibition in the United States during the studio era. For the most part the Big Five neatly divided the US, with Paramount dominating the South, New England, and the upper Midwest, Fox controlling the Far West, RKO and Loew's splitting New York, New Jersey, and Ohio, and Warners staking out the mid-Atlantic states. In the few areas where the Big Five 'competed', pooling arrangements and/or joint ownership were undertaken to spread the risk.

Table 1.1: Theaters in the United States by Seating Capacity, 1945

Capacity	Theaters	Percentage of Theaters	Percentage of Seats
1500+	996	5.4	21.7
1201–1500	732	4.0	8.6
1001–1200	801	4.4	7.7
751–1000	2687	11.3	15.8
501–750	2979	16.2	16.2
351–500	4311	23.4	15.9
0–350	6507	35.3	14.1
Total	18413	100	100

The control of key theaters by the Big Five had far-reaching consequences. The Little Three and other producer-distributors had to accede to the Big Five's marketing plan in order even to place films in first-run situations, a necessity if profits were to be made. Independent exhibitors also had to toe the line. Otherwise, the Big Five would not rent to them. Then the independent exhibitors would have to turn to poor-quality, low-profit motion pictures. In practice, in first-run houses, the need would be for 100 films per year. That would be filled from the affiliated Big Five studios plus the best from the other four. A subsequent-run house (with three different billings per week) required more than 300 features a year, and so turned to Universal, Columbia, and United Artists.

It was through the theatrical end of the industry, constituting some 90 per cent of all their assets, that the Big Five operated as a collusive unit, protecting each other, shutting out all potential competitors, and guaranteeing profits for even the worst performer, usually RKO. The relationship of the Big Five throughout the studio era was like a chronically quarrelsome but closely knit family. Theatrical inter-dependencies guaranteed that if anyone produced a popular film, all members of the Big Five benefitted. Distribution economies of scale brought forth significant cost savings. Production units corralled valuable stars, producers, directors and other creative personnel and put together variations of certain narrative forms. The Big Five and Little Three co-operated to regularize the movie business, and take out as much risk as possible. Then, subject to those rigid constraints, they competed for a small number of marginal dollars. Rarely publicized, but more forceful, was the struggle within the corporate apparatus of the Big Five. Selling at the theater level, a purely commercial process, demanded one set of skills; making films, a creative endeavour, even in Hollywood's factory days of the 1930s and 1940s, necessitated far different ones. Producers wanted to experiment and try new things to gain an edge on their competitors. If they continued with the same stories and stars, others would surge past them, but exhibitors wanted predictable box office attractions, and tended to support forms and personae that had worked best in the recent past. Consequently, the Big Five and Little Three struggled more within than without, creating a multitude of anecdotes for future biographers. Details of management decision processes will be described and analyzed in the succeeding chapters on individual corporations.

The Conduct of Firms Within the Studio System

The structure of the film industry described and analyzed above set in motion certain forms of business behavior. All companies attempted to maximize profits within a system designed to allocate the bulk of that profit to the vertically-integrated Big Five. Production decisions of the Big Five were based on information generated by their theater divisions. In general the production process began with a corporate decision establishing the number of films needed for the following season. Then, the chief executive of Big Five firm would allocate a budget for production of features (designated 'A' and 'B' by cost) and shorts (including cartoons and newsreels). At the same time, a detailed release schedule was also handed to the executives at the west coast studio. Once these decisions were made – always by the corporate president and his staff in the New York office – the Hollywood staff was relatively free to decide how to produce the most popular products. Throughout the total production process, continuing conferences and negotiation would take place between the New York and Hollywood offices concerning budgets, release schedules, wages and investments. In the end, all final decisions rested with the chief operating officer of the corporation based in New York, not Hollywood.

To produce films as efficiently as possible and still create a stream of 'new-and-different' products, Hollywood utilized a factory system of production based on extreme specialization of labor. Generally, a studio chief co-ordinated the desires and budgets issued by the New York office with the materials and labor at hand. Below the studio chief would be a set of producers who would each be responsible for six to eight of the necessary feature films, shorts and cartoons. (Newsreels were usually handled separately.) The producer in turn would then organize writing, shooting and editing within defined budget constraints. This form of decentralized manufacturing process was innovated during the 1920s at the General Motors Automobile Corporation. Hollywood fully adopted it by 1930. The given studio situation dictated how much relative power producers had. The process of actual film production was divided into specialized units. From finding appropriate stories to writing scripts to actual shooting to cutting, workers handled only their own tasks. Unionization solidified specific jurisdictions. Details on the practices of specific studios are outlined later in individual chapters.

To make the most from their productions and to maximize profits from their theaters, the Big Five developed a complex set of distribution practices. By manipulating trade arrangements they were able to reduce risk and ensure continuity of control. To affect bargaining relations, practices based on the

15

economics of price discrimination were developed. Price discrimination allows the seller (or co-operating sellers) to generate larger revenues (see Figure 1.1). Under typical marketing conditions, the demand for a good or service is expressed by the schedule DD. That is, if the price (P) goes up, consumers will be at a higher point on the curve (DD) and demand less. If the price falls, consumers demand more – all other things being equal. In most situations there is but one price offered, here P_1. Using the curve then, consumers demand Q_1. The seller makes P_1 times Q_1 in revenues. This is represented by the light gray area. However, some people may have strong preferences and be willing to pay prices higher than P_1. If somehow a seller could find those people and charge them those higher prices, additional revenues could be gained. Assuming no one is willing to pay higher than P_2, additional revenues equal to the amount shown by the dark gray area could be added to the basic revenues (light gray area). It is difficult and costly to segment consumers to charge them different prices, however. The US movie industry accomplished the task in a cost-effective straightforward fashion through the use of runs, zones and clearances (a temporal and spatial separation of markets). This pushed the Big Five away from the revenues in the light area, toward but not precisely to the light area plus darker area.

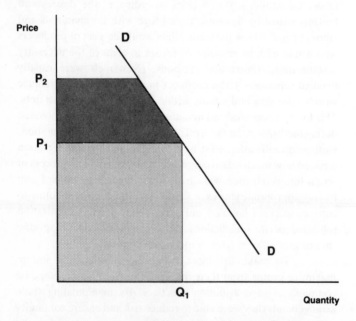

Figure 1.1: Admission Price Discrimination

The distribution exchanges of the Big Five co-operated to establish runs, zones and clearances for all cities and towns in the US. All first-runs were followed by a period of time (the clearance) of seven to thirty days before the film could play second-run – all within certain geographical limits (the zone). Then the film would play second-run. A clearance would follow before the third-run, and so on down the line. In some large cities there might be up to eleven runs requiring more than a year to complete. In smaller communities there might only be a first-run downtown and a final run at a neighborhood theater. Different admission prices were charged for each run, the highest in first-run and so on down the line. Keen movie fans paid up to a dollar to see their favorites. Casual movie-goers waited, and paid as little as 10¢. Wide-scale advertising tried to line up potential patrons to attend a first-run showing rather than some later one. Distribution executives could juggle run status, zone size, clearance time and admission price to milk the most from any market. In actual practice, through a trial-and-error method of experimentation, runs, zones, and clearances were established during the 1920s, and fixed in place for the next twenty years. With few shifts in US population during the 1930s and 1940s, the run-zone-clearance system served to maximise the revenues of the Big Five, regardless of differences in the qualities of the films produced.

Actual bargaining between distributors and exhibitors was not a complicated affair. Each theater had a fixed run-zone-clearance status. Contracts stipulated admission prices. A rivalry did exist among the Big Five to sell their films to the best of the non-affiliated theaters. With block-booking and blind buying the Big Five attempted to force independent theaters to take groups of films, sight unseen. These tactics kept selling costs low and helped to guarantee a base of revenues, even for the most mediocre film. In effect distributors shifted a part of their risk to powerless exhibitors, guaranteeing that even films accepted poorly in first-run houses would receive a sub-run play-off. Block-booking and blind buying helped Columbia and Universal most, enabling them to secure better rates of financing for production, and assuring a cost-effective utilization of their plant and equipment, but even at their peak use in the 1930s these two tactics affected only a small portion of total revenues of the industry.

The admission price discrimination and run-zone-clearance system had far-reaching implications for the motion picture industry. First, this system minimized the number of theaters the Big Five needed to own to effect a measure of control.

In actual practice, with approximately 15 per cent of all US theaters (but the majority of first-run) the Big Five could easily gather in 50–75 per cent of the box-office revenues. Second, it kept Big Five theaters fully utilized. Year-in and year-out, despite depressions, wars, poor films, aging stars and changes in public taste, the Big Five could count on a steady flow of revenues at its box-offices. Finally, this process of selling kept transaction costs low. With fixed agreement as to the status of run, zone, clearance and admission prices, bargaining and negotiation costs were minimal. Distribution staffs were small. Costs of required prints never mounted up. If all theaters showed the same film simultaneously, it would have necessitated nearly 20,000 prints. (At that time prints cost an average of $250 and lasted 200 screenings.) But with a limited number of theaters in each run, only 400 prints were needed. If prints wore out prematurely, later runs were simply canceled since striking a new print and shipping it cost more than expected revenues.

The actual practice of running large theater chains was modeled on retailing techniques developed by chain operations like Woolworths and Sears. In the 1920s Paramount's theater division, Publix Theaters, led the way. Others – Loew's, Fox, Warners and RKO – quickly imitated. Publix regularized costs, booked from a central office and made a science of national advertising. Publix carefully controlled all expenditures at its theaters. Each theater had a weekly budget detailing all costs. All figures were carefully scrutinized by accountants in the home office and any excess had to be explained in a written report. In addition local managers also recorded all non-financial aspects of their operations and forwarded such information to the New York office where experts constructed elaborate charts to serve as guides for future decision-making. For example, all assistant managers of Publix houses recorded the temperature and humidity from the orchestra floor, balcony, lobby and outside, every hour on the hour, for the complete operating day. Publix experts then used this data to issue orders concerning use of the heating and air-conditioning. Other specialists calculated traffic patterns, population densities, income distributions and recreation habits before a theater was built or purchased.

All booking was done from New York. Since Paramount did not make enough films to fill Publix screen-time, Publix bargained with and obtained favorable terms from the other major producer-distributors. Publix's central buyer relied on data from previous years, which had been compiled in massive detail, and suggestions from managers at all levels. The actual scheduling began six to eight weeks in advance. Regional managers prepared master booking sheets and then sent them down the line to be commented upon at each level. The divisional, district and local managers added the 'local' touch, eliminated regionally offensive films and returned the sheets to New York for final approval. Executive managers, recruited from the areas they supervised, visited their territories several times a year. Publix promoted experienced local managers since they had first-hand knowledge of the 'needs' of communities where Publix houses were located.

In a national market Publix could not rely on so-called 'word-of-mouth'. Advertising and publicity became vital inputs. Experts formulated numerous ambitious advertising programs in order to sell the 'Publix' name. The central slogan became *'You don't need to know what's playing at a Publix House. It's bound to be the best show in town.'* All advertising copy was prepared by specialists at the New York office and sent down the line in the form of a manual which contained sketches, model advertisements, suggestions on how to place them, descriptions of 'stunts' to promote the theater's program and even publicity stories to be planted in the newspaper. The major Hollywood producers supplied a similar press kit, but the New York office required managers to use the in-house manual. Each local manager simply selected the material appropriate to his or her market, and then executed the advertising campaign within a budget specified from New York. Since each local advertising budget was balanced only once a month, the local manager had some flexibility in advertising appropriations, but to conduct any elaborate advertising, the local manager had to secure permission from the Publix New York office.

Publix also helped make the 1920s the era of the presentation-cinema. Deluxe, ornate picture palaces served up elaborate shows made up of one-third live performance (a stage show presentation) and two-thirds motion pictures (feature, shorts, and newsreels). Ornate auditoriums housed these spectacles; lighting displays and performers turned each show into a unique theatrical event. A presentation-cinema show opened with a five-minute overture from a house orchestra of twenty-five to one hundred members. Next came the stage show, lasting from fifteen to thirty minutes. A newsreel (five to ten minutes), shorts (ten to twenty minutes), and the feature film (sixty to eighty minutes) followed. Exhibitors tried to limit the complete show to 150 minutes, sometimes cutting the feature by several minutes rather than restricting the number of shows. Big Five theaters mounted the most expensive presentation shows. Independent theaters imitated as well as costs would allow.

The coming of sound changed little. Expensive live shows were systematically replaced by vaudeville shorts. The presentation-cinema became all-movies by 1930. The Great Depression – with its attendant sharp decrease in revenues – forced exhibitors to differentiate their offerings and seek out new sources of revenues. To attract more patrons, small theater owners initiated double, even triple bills. A two-for-one policy, which had been tried as early as 1915, seemed to give the potential patron more for his or her money. In 1931, theater owners also began to tempt customers with give-aways (pillows, chinaware, bicycles, silk stockings, lamps and watches) and games (bingo, races or screeno). However, in August 1933 the US federal government's National Recovery Administration (NRA) prohibited all giveaways and games as 'unfair competition'. Consequently, more and more theater owners turned to double bills. The US Supreme Court delcared the NRA unconstitutional in May 1935, and quickly exhibitors reinstituted give-aways and games. But by then the double-feature strategy had become institutionalized, and would function as the dominant US exhibition strategy well into the 1950s. Even Big Five theaters offered double bills, but not in the numbers of their non-affiliated rivals. The mix varied. Some exhibitors tendered two 'A' films, others an 'A' and 'B', still others two or three 'B's. Theater owners costantly varied combinations in order to gain an edge on nearby competitors.

Exhibitors effected other changes in order to attract more customers, the most important of which was air-conditioning, first offered in Balaban and Katz houses in Chicago in 1917. Only the Big Five could afford this sizeable investment during the 1920s. During the 1930s, with Carrier's development of a compact, relatively inexpensive apparatus, many more exhibitors installed a system for air-cooling and humidity control. Extensive use of Carrier's new inventions at the Chicago World Fair during the summers of 1933 and 1934 generated familiarity and favorable publicity. Big Five movie houses functioned as the sole institution offering such service at prices affordable to middle- and lower-income US citizens. Generally throughout the studio era Big Five theaters offered complete air conditioning – air-cooling plus dehumidification. Independent theaters more often than not only cooled the air, often with indifferent results.

Exhibitors also sought out additional sources of revenue in the 1930s, and so began to sell food directly to patrons rather than let them continue to shop at nearby confectionary stores or popcorn wagons. During the 1920s few exhibitors sold candy. Since at that time theater owners kept their auditoriums very dark and had ushers lead patrons to their seats, only a pre-packaged product could be accommodated, but in any case sales of food did not fit the 'high class' image such operations sought. With the coming of the Great Depression theater owners fired their ushers, turned up the auditorium lights and let patrons find their own seats. Nearly all added candy sales and began to experiment with the marketing of other foods. Popcorn soon emerged as the cornerstone of refreshment operations. Unlike candy, it possessed a seemingly addictive aroma which filled lobbies as customers paused before the movies and between features. Popcorn was easy to manufacture and seemed to appeal to movie-goers of all ages. To complement the salty popcorn, exhibitors introduced an array of cold, soft drinks. Soon suppliers developed beverage-dispensing equipment to solve the problem of individual glass bottles rolling and breaking in the auditorium.

Sales of refreshments skyrocketed. The Big Five purchased popcorn by the railcar load thereby obtaining substantial discounts. A box retailing at 15¢ cost only 3¢ for raw materials – container, oil and corn. Even with wages, equipment and overhead, the profit rate usually soared past 100 per cent. Thus it was not surprising that by 1947 nearly 90 per cent of US movie houses sold popcorn. The lone Big Five holdout was the conservative Loew's Inc. During slow days, sales of refreshments often matched or exceeded box-office revenues. Popcorn soon became a major US crop. In 1920 there were 60,000 US acres devoted to popcorn; by 1948 over 300,000 US acres were planted with this movie-house favorite. Sales of soft drinks (Coca Cola dominated here) and, after 1948, buttered popcorn added to the revenues and profits of the Big Five.

As part of this new strategy (multiple features, air-conditioning and in-house refreshments) exhibitors ritualized the intermission. The first feature would end, the house lights would go up, and the patrons would rush to the lobby to purchase popcorn, candy and colas. 'Coming attractions' would signal a return to more entertainment. The form became narrative, food, narrative in a continuous pattern. Other services, standard during the presentation era, were eliminated. Theater lobbies and auditoriums (as well as exteriors) were left to rundown. Less was spent on upkeep, most potential light sources were covered up or unused, and fewer and fewer ushers were employed. The decorative displays of Oriental, Egyptian, French or Spanish architecture gradually came to represent a bygone presentation-cinema era.

External Shocks

The studio system already analyzed was so successful that only forces outside its control could significantly disrupt it. There were three such outside shocks in the studio era. The first was the decrease in demand caused by the decline in incomes during the Great Depression. Although accurate statistics are hard to come by, box office revenues seem to have declined by 25 per cent. Consumers turned to cheaper substitutes (radio) or simply cut the number of screenings attended each month. The Big Five cut wages, sought new revenues in refreshments and finessed bulging mortgages as best they could. All survived intact. The US federal government through the National Recovery Act (NRA) of 1933 helped by openly sanctioning the monopolistic behavior of the Big Five. Instead of the informal co-operation which had existed throughout the 1920s, open and explicit collusion and exploitation took place, free from any threat of anti-trust action. The Big Five immediately codified the run-zone-clearance system, and boosted revenues. The NRA, as noted above, outlawed all give-aways by exhibitors. Such a sanction helped the Big Five at the expensive of independent exhibitors.

The second outside shock came in 1938 when the administration of President Franklin Roosevelt shifted gears and filed an anti-trust suit against the Big Five and Little Three. The defendants were charged with conspiring to fix distribution contract terms of runs, clearances and admission prices. In 1940 all parties signed a consent decree which set up a broad system of rules for bargaining and settling disputes similar to the pro-Big Five 'self-government' which had operated under the NRA. Little changed. In August 1944, the government reactivated the case, and pressed for divorcement of theaters of the Big Five. This solution was agreed to by the US Supreme Court on 25 July 1949, signaling the end of the twenty-year period of the studio era. Although the full force of this decision would not come about until the early 1950s, continuous pressure did exist beginning in 1938. The Big Five, logically, fought to save their valuable run-zone-clearance system, but for a variety of social and political reasons lost their case.

The final external shock felt prior to 1949 also involved the US federal government – the Second World War. As hostilities spread in Europe and the Orient during the late 1930s the Big Five and Little Three saw revenues from overseas decline. Gradually, they lost markets in Europe and the Far East, which together had accounted for 33–50 per cent of traditional revenues from abroad. When Britain declared war in September 1939 and the Germans began to bomb, some theaters closed, but once the British adjusted, revenues from the United Kingdom soared to twice pre-war levels. Britain clamped on currency restrictions. The Big Five and Little Three had great difficulty taking out all they earned, and so secured a number of investments in British studios and theater chains. Elsewhere the Second World War did what all the earlier quotas, taxes, and tariffs could not do – partially shut down the overseas distribution of Hollywood movies. To offset the loss of European and Far Eastern markets, the Big Five and Little Three turned to South and Central America. The Department of State through the Office of the Co-ordinator of Inter-American Affairs assisted their efforts. Motion pictures were a good way to promote the Good Neighbor Policy. The State Department shipped hundreds of US newsreels south, but demand for other products never followed. Hollywood had fully exploited Latin American markets prior to the war; there was little else to extract.

The market for motion pictures in the US during the Second World War offered a very different prospect. Domestically, the war period provided the best five years in movie history, and these increases more than compensated for any losses from overseas markets. As incomes rose, few durables were available for purchase. Business, especially in large cities with war-related industries, prospered as never before. Revenues in real dollars peaked in 1946; so did movie attendance. With restrictions on production, the number of features fell. No matter, revenues per film rose faster than costs. Even independent producers, usually working through RKO and United Artists, prospered. (Favorable tax benefits also helped.) The year 1946 saw the highest profits during Hollywood's studio era: Paramount – $39 million; Fox – $25 million; Warners – $22 million; Loew's – $18 million; even 'poor cousin' RKO – $12 million. In real dollar terms all these were corporate records, not approached again until the 1970s. The US motion picture industry would have loved the Second World War to go on, at least on the home front, forever.

Conclusion

In sum, the studio era represented a stable twenty-year epoch in the history of American film. Eight major corporations – Paramount, Loew's, 20th Century-Fox, Warner Bros., Radio-

Keith-Orpheum, Universal, Columbia and United Artists – dominated all phases of industry operation. In their quest for profits, these eight regularized film production with standardized products including features, animation and live short subjects, serials and newsreels. All embraced now well-known narrative structures and then actively sought to convince potential movie patrons of the differences in their products. Through widespread advertising, all the majors heralded new stars, interesting stories and stunning special effects. In so doing, these eight corporations worked to define how Americans understood what was an acceptable (natural) use of motion picture technology.

With all the glamour and razzmatazz associated with the launching and promotion of feature films, we have come to associate the economic power of the film industry with its control over film production. Anecdote after anecdote is regularly trotted out to illustrate how movie mogul production bosses such as Louis B. Mayer, Harry Cohn and Darryl F. Zanuck controlled American movie screens. We learn how ruthlessly they dealt with the biggest stars and the smallest extras, a set of medieval lords running their manors to produce guaranteed safe mass entertainment, week after week, year after year.

But if Hollywood production was so predictable, why did others not attempt to enter film production? The answer lies with the barriers to entry created by the eight major movie corporations. Anyone during the 1930s and 1940s could have invested the necessary millions in film production, but then any new corporation would somehow have had to get the films onto theater screens. It was through these two functions – distribution and exhibition – that the eight major corporations co-operated to keep out potential competitors. In other words, it was the mundane worlds of movie wholesaling and retailing which provided the Big Five with the necessary muscle to erect and maintain barriers to entry to keep away all serious competitors for two decades.

Consequently though there were clear corporate distinctions in terms of film production (depending on stars under contract and genres utilized), there were few corporate differences in terms of distribution and exhibition. Indeed, all eight majors co-operated for the common good. There was no competition *per se*. The greatest differences lay in theater style only because, as already described, each corporation dominated one particular region of the USA. As such Paramount might publicize a film in the deep South differently from Loew's in New York City, but all corporations embraced the run-zone-clearance pattern of release, because it was in everyone's best interest to co-operate rather than compete. This constancy of distribution and exhibition made motion pictures a true national mass medium. In the end, corporate and regional differences were smoothed over in favor of the common goal of profit-maximization.

Consequently, in the chapters which follow on the individual corporations there will be little analysis of distribution and exhibition. That is not to say that these functions were not important. Indeed they were vital. My omissions underline the fact that there were few differences to note. All followed the practices described in this introductory chapter.

Also omitted from later discussion are the multitude of external problems which the industry faced through the 1930s and 1940s. The Great Depression, the Second World War, a ten-year anti-trust suit and the coming of unions and independent producers were issues with which all industry participants had to deal. However, with some historical perspective it seems fair to conclude that the studio system was able to surmount all these difficulties. All the corporations survived the Great Depression and went on to thrive during the war years. The US federal government was held at bay for a decade. Unions were able to secure their place in the system and independent producers became commonplace by 1945. Such was the resilience and power of the studio system as a profit-making business institution.

Since the major corporations so benefitted from co-operation, it is important first to analyze them as a group, as has been done in this chapter. The following chapters take up the three-part structure set forth here. Each begins with an historical analysis of how a corporation reached its place in the industry hierarchy. The second part of each chapter then examines the structure of the corporation during the studio era, focussing on ownership, finance and composition of assets. Some corporations experienced significant changes in structure (Paramount, 20th Century-Fox, RKO, Universal); others did not (Loew's, Warner Bros., Columbia). The final part of each chapter will analyze how the corporation operated. Important changes in ownership usually precipitated changes in types of films produced, while little was varied in distribution and exhibition. New owners and managers alike recognized the source of industry power and profit. The order of the following chapters reflects the rank of the corporations in terms of profit and power, moving from strongest to weakest.

2:

Paramount

The most powerful motion picture corporation coming out of the 1920s into the studio era was Paramount. President Adolph Zukor and his management team had built a movie colossus which included studios in Los Angeles, New York and Paris, a worldwide network of distribution exchanges and the world's largest theater chain (Publix theaters). The Great Depression would help topple Paramount from its perch, reducing it to simply another member of the Big Five. On all fronts during the 1930s change was the order of the day for Paramount. Theater circuits were reorganized; studio production chiefs continually turned over, but Paramount was able to return to its former glory with the boom of the Second World War. Under President Barney Balaban and production boss Y. Frank Freeman, Paramount again became the most profitable corporation in the American film industry. The studio produced few classics in the 1940s, but lots of money. Stars from other media, especially Bing Crosby and Bob Hope, formed the core of a group of the most powerful (and profitable) box-office attractions of the second decade of the studio era.

The origins of Paramount went back to the beginning of the American film industry. Founder Adolph Zukor embarked on show business with a penny arcade in 1903; the following year he opened his first theater in New York. To counter the Motion Picture Patents trust, Zukor went into production in 1912. The modest success of the imported feature **Queen Elizabeth** (with Sarah Bernhardt) convinced Zukor there was a place for films longer than the prescribed two-reel maximum of the Patents Company and featuring stars from other media, notably the legitimate theater. Zukor did not invent the feature film or star

1. Adolph Zukor

system, but he exploited those concepts more fully than others. With Broadway producer Daniel Frohman, Zukor formed the Famous Players Company with Broadway stars James O'Neil (Eugene O'Neil's father), James K. Hackett, Lillie Langtry, John Barrymore, Fanny Ward and Geraldine Farrar. But Famous Players' most famous players would be developed as screen stars. None matched the instant success of Mary Pickford. Zukor signed her from the stage in 1913 for $20,000 per year, and soon 'Little Mary' became a national sensation, a true movie star.

Famous Players used Paramount to distribute its feature-length films – a highly cost-effective strategy. William H. Hodkinson had formed Paramount in 1914 from a combine of nine regional companies. Joining forces, Famous Players supplied half of the one hundred films Paramount distributed nationally. Paramount secured the rest from producers such as the successful Jesse L. Lasky Production Company. Zukor realized that Paramount's ability to sell films on a nationwide basis provided a mighty comparative advantage, and so he executed a series of mergers to unite Famous Players and Paramount. In December 1916, he was able to announce the successful formation of the world's largest producer–distributor with himself as president and partner Jesse Lasky as vice-president in charge of production. The

27

new Famous Players–Lasky (hereafter Famous Players) signed new stars including Douglas Fairbanks, Gloria Swanson, William S. Hart, Fatty Arbuckle, Pauline Frederick and Blanche Sweet. A stable of important directors and producers was also assembled including Mack Sennett, Thomas Ince and Cecil B. De Mille.

In 1920, Famous Players stood at the acme of the US movie industry. Others – particularly First National – attempted to block Famous Players' progress by assembling powerful theater circuits. Famous Players fought back. With a $10 million line of credit from the Wall Street investment house Kuhn Loeb, Famous Players was able in only four years to assemble the largest theater circuit in the business. The major investments made were:

1. 30 April 1919   purchase of Lynch Enterprises controlling theaters in eleven southern states;
2. 7 May 1919   acquisition of controlling interest in two first-run theaters in New York's Times Square, the Rialto and Rivoli;
3. 27 January 1920   purchase of half interest in New England Theaters Inc;
4. 5 February 1920   acquisition of controlling interest in theater chain in Canada, renamed Famous Players Canadian.

The buying spree then slowed down, but did not stop. By the mid-1920s the Famous Players-Lasky chain held interests in 368 theaters in the United States, but the most significant merger was still to take place. In the mid-1920s, two American cities constituted nearly 20 per cent of the US population. The New York market was locked up by arch-rivals, Loew's and Fox. Chicago, America's second city, was not yet linked up with a producer-distributor. Balaban and Katz offered control of Chicago plus the most skilled motion-picture theater-managers in the business. In 1925 a deal was struck, and with it a corporate name change to Paramount-Famous-Lasky with Publix theaters as a subsidiary.

In November 1925, Sam Katz, co-founder of Balaban and Katz, brought his management team to New York to institute the Balaban and Katz system for the Publix chain. Immediately, Katz set out to run Publix like a 'legitimate business'. Wanting to create a logo as famous as that of Woolworths, Katz changed the name of many theaters to Paramount. In order to maximize the cost-savings which accrued to chain operations, Katz pushed for rapid growth. In five years Publix expanded to nearly 1200 theaters. Some were constructed but a majority of the growth

2. Sam Katz

came from merger or direct takeover. By 1930, Publix dominated film exhibition in the South from North Carolina to Texas as well as Michigan, Illinois, Minnesota, Iowa, the Dakotas, Nebraska and New England. In addition, through Famous Players Canadian, Publix also controlled Canada. At its peak during the 1930–1 movie season, Publix was the largest motion-picture circuit in film history.

Katz took to New York the methods which worked so well in Chicago and would be copied by all members of the Big Five before 1930. First, all booking was done from a central office, based on information and suggestions from all parts of the organization. Local managers lost all power: under the Publix system they became glorified janitors. All first-run houses presented Publix stage shows. These units toured the USA like small Broadway road companies. The central office formulated all advertising and sent it down to the local manager to set in motion. Even though producers supplied suggestions, Big Five theater-chains used in-house plans. Finally, Publix kept careful control over all expenditures, weekly tabulating and balancing the books from New York. If theaters ran over or under prescribed financial limits, specific orders were issued on how to change. In short, Publix was the first theater chain in the US to embrace business practices widespread in other industries of the day.

By 1928 Sam Katz had fashioned Publix into an efficient

modern retailing operation – the Ford or Woolworths of the motion picture industry. From such a strong base Paramount racked up the profits. With this position, Paramount saw no reason to disrupt continuity by pioneering sound. It left that to others – Warner Bros. and Fox in particular – but in 1928 when it became clear that sound films could make even more profit than silent films, Paramount banded together with Loew's and United Artists to select the industry standard. After much deliberation and bargaining, these three selected Western Electric, and signed identical contracts on 11 May 1928. Quickly Paramount converted to all-talkies, and by 1929 was making more money than before. The Publix theaters had little trouble showing talkies. Most had previously presented live stage-shows, and simply substituted filmed vaudeville shorts in already acoustically perfect auditoriums.

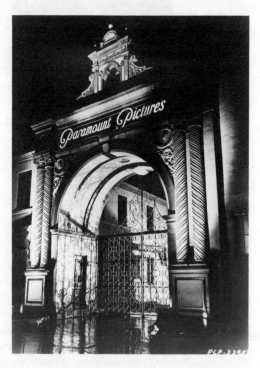

3. The entrance to Paramount Studios

With the profits made from talkies, Paramount began to diversify and expand. It set up a music division to supply songs for its new musicals and the studio signed up twenty-two songwriters, including Irving Berlin. Paramount also became heavily involved in radio. In August 1928 it began broadcasting from its Hollywood studio, but the biggest deal came in June 1929 when Paramount acquired one-half of the new Columbia Broadcasting System (CBS). No cash changed hands because Paramount simply engineered an exchange of common stock. The CBS radio network with fifty-four affiliates could employ Paramount film stars and publicize new films. Paramount also wanted more economic power in the motion picture industry, so late in the summer of 1928 it sought to take over a major film rival. Deals were considered with Fox, Loew's and RKO, but could not be settled. In September 1929 Paramount finally came to an agreement to merge with Warner Bros. to form a new corporation 'Paramount-Vitaphone'. This enterprise would have resulted in America's largest entertainment corporation with over 1400 theaters, six movie studios, CBS radio, and Warners' and Paramount's vast music publishing resources. The Paramount–Warner Bros. merger never took place. The US Attorney-General in the recently inaugurated Herbert Hoover administration promised to sue for anti-trust violations, and members of the US Senate threatened to hold investigative hearings. Paramount had already been through two Federal Trade Commission investigations during the prior decade so it reluctantly backed off.

Instead, Paramount moved to buy up independent theater circuits. Between September 1929 and May 1930 it acquired some 500 theaters. As revenues continued to grow well into 1930, whatever investments Paramount made seemed to turn to gold. With the coming of the Depression, however, Paramount found it harder and harder to cover its enormous mortgage payments. Drastic action was required. John Hertz (of rent-a-car fame), a partner in Wall Street's Lehman Brothers, agreed to help. Hertz became chair of the finance committee of Paramount's board in November 1931. Immediately he directed a 33.3 per cent cut in budgets for feature films, an across-the-board reduction in salaries and consolidation of distribution efforts. Under Hertz, Paramount sold its share in CBS for a $41.2 million capital gain. The core of Zukor's management team (producer Jesse Lasky, distribution expert Sidney Kent and exhibition mogul Sam Katz) moved on to other corporations. However, cost-cutting could not make more people attend Publix theaters. Theater grosses dropped by $25 million in 1932 alone. Despite all his efforts, all Hertz was able to do was administer the transition from an $8 million annual profit (in 1931) to a staggering deficit of more than $20 million in 1933.

Frustrated, Hertz resigned in 1933, leaving a corporation with theaters and real estate valued on the books at some $150 million. But what were all these actually worth? That question would have to be answered because Paramount could not generate enough cash to meet its debts to its mortgage holders. In 1932 Hertz had tried several maneuvers to head off receivership, but failed. In March 1933 the company turned its debts over to court-appointed trustees. It was a complicated financial mess, adjudicated in hundreds of court decisions. A plan for reorganization was finally approved in July 1935. Only $5 million in cash ever changed hands; most debts were covered through payments in bonds and stock in the reorganized company. Paramount Pictures Inc. emerged with shares in over 1000 theaters, valued now at a much more realistic $61 million. The new board of directors was led by former debtors and bankers, including the Royal Insurance Company of Great Britain, Wall Street bankers Lehman Bros. (Hertz's firm) and Electrical Research Products, Inc. (AT&T's subsidiary for the sale of motion-picture sound equipment). Only two of the board's fifteen members, sales manager George Schaefer and founder Adolph Zukor, had any experience in the movie business.

4. The Paramount Building in New York

Seeking a solid businessman to run the new company, the board selected ERPI president John Otterson, whose management experience included stints in the US Navy and at the

Winchester Repeating Arms Corporation. Otterson tried to run Paramount like a public utility, regularizing all decisions. He only succeeded in creating further losses. The board was perplexed, and so turned to Joseph P. Kennedy, founder of RKO and former Securities and Exchange Commission head, to recommend a solution. Throughout May 1936 Kennedy plunged into Paramount's corporate records and talked to current and former employees. On 10 June 1936 he submitted his report, arguing that it would be 'senseless' to study further. New management had to be found immediately. Production schedules were not being met; stars were not being re-signed; negative costs were exceeding budgets (by $7 million so far). Unless Otterson left, Paramount would face yet another set of receivership proceedings.

Action came swiftly. Otterson, in office only one year at $150,000, was let go with four years remaining on his contract. The board was shaken up, with ten new appointments to the board before the end of 1936. Barney Balaban, head of Balaban and Katz's operations in Chicago since Sam Katz's departure to New York, became the new president. Balaban, the long-term financial brains of Balaban and Katz, combined business acumen with experience in the important exhibition end of the motion-picture industry. Balaban moved quickly, consolidating numerous overlapping departments and cutting home-office expenses to effect savings of nearly $1 million. He set up detailed long-term plans. Surprisingly, in 1936 the corporation actually turned a $4 million profit (see Table 2.1).

In 1936, Paramount Pictures Inc. was a vast multinational corporation holding ownership in 194 listed subsidiaries, the bulk of which were theater companies. It owned a 26-acre studio in Hollywood, the Astoria studio on Long Island, a studio near Paris in Joinville, film-processing laboratories in Hollywood, London, Astoria and New York City, and approximately 2700 acres in California used for location productions. In New York there were also facilities for production of shorts and newsreels. Paramount controlled forty-two film exchanges in the United States and Canada, six of which owned the buildings in which they operated. Through forty-three separate subsidiaries, included in the total shown, Paramount distributed films throughout the world. Subsidiaries were also engaged in publishing music and, from time to time, the underwriting of plays on Broadway.

From October 1936, Paramount owned, leased and/or operated approximately 1200 theaters. This number changed regularly as receivership and bankruptcy proceedings were finalized. Two principal subsidiaries handled the more significant

Table 2.1: Paramount's Balance Sheet

Year	Net Profit (millions of dollars)	Assets (millions of dollars)
1930	25.0	306.27
1931	8.7	298.30
1932	–	–
1933	–	–
1934	–	–
1935	–	–
1936	4.0	116.90
1937	6.0	120.20
1938	2.8	118.20
1939	2.8	109.60
1940	6.4	108.80
1941	9.2	116.00
1942	13.1	133.50
1943	14.6	139.20
1944	14.7	148.40
1945	15.4	149.00
1946	39.2	170.40
1947	28.2	185.60
1948	22.6	*
1949	20.8	*

– In receivership.
* Spun-off.

theater holdings: Balaban and Katz in Chicago; Sarenger Theaters in the Deep South. In many cities, Paramount held only one or two first-run properties. In New York City it owned the thirty-one story Paramount building which housed the world headquarters of the corporation. Valued at $12 million (about 10 per cent of the corporation's total assets) this building also housed the corporation's flagship theater, the Paramount.

Paramount controlled the broadest-based theater-chain of all the major companies, operating houses in all but five (Delaware, Montana, Wyoming, Washington and Oregon) of the then forty-eight states. Of the ninety-two cities in the United States with populations of 100,000 or more in the 1940 census, Paramount held a measure of control in the following cities (rank in population in parenthesis): Chicago (2 in population), Detroit (4), Boston (9), New Orleans (15), Minneapolis (16), Houston (21), Atlanta (29), Dallas (31), Memphis (32), St Paul (33), Birmingham (35), San Antonio (37), Omaha (39), Oklahoma City (42), Worcester, Massachusetts (44), Forth Worth (46), Jacksonville, Florida (47), Miami (48), Hartford (50), Grand Rapids (52), New Haven (54), Des Moines (55), Flint, Michigan (56), Salt Lake City (57), Springfield, Massachusetts (58), Scranton (63), Chattanooga (66), Knoxville (75), Tampa (83), Peoria (86), South Bend, Indiana (88), Lowell (89), Charlotte, North Carolina (91) and Duluth, Minnesota (92). Through Famous Players Canadian Corporation, Paramount owned and/or operated 277 theaters and held dominion north of the US border. Other significant foreign theater holdings were in England (the Plaza theater in London, Paramount theaters in Leeds, Newcastle and Manchester and Astoria theaters in Finsbury Park, Streatham, Old Kent Road and Brixton, London), and Paris (the Paramount).

5. (l. to r.) Adolph Zukor, Jane Russell, Barney Balaban

From 1936 to 1964, Barney Balaban ran Paramount. All significant expenditures and decisions required his approval. He paid strict attention to financial data, trying to keep costs in line and approving only 'prudent' business decisions. One report suggests Balaban had to sign off in writing for all expenditures, made on either coast, of $3000 or more. Reports flowed in on a daily basis concerning stories, budgets, schedules and personnel decisions. He began each morning by reviewing daily box-office reports from all Paramount theaters throughout the world and throughout the day attempted to line up production costs with box-office returns. After 1938, although he had strong opinions on what films ought to be made, Balaban usually left such matters up to west coast chief, Y. Frank Freeman. The Balaban-Freeman relationship went back to their days as heads of the two major units in Paramount's theater empire (Balaban and Katz and Sarenger). Georgia-born, Young (his real first name) Frank Freeman supervised Paramount's west-coast operations from 1938 until 1959. Three other men made up the set of Balaban's trusted advisers. George Weltner, long-time Paramount executive, handled foreign operations. Adolph Zukor offered his advice. But it was Paul Raibourn, a university-trained engineer and economist, who was closest to the boss. Raibourn, an expert in statistical analysis, provided Balaban with the data to make daily decisions. This five member group presided over all Paramount's affairs from 1936 until well into the era of television.

Though conservative in its management approach to the motion picture business, the Balaban management group pushed Paramount into television far ahead of all Big Five rivals. Raibourn, with Balaban's full support, took charge of television operations when in 1938 Paramount invested nearly $400,000 in the DuMont Corporation, a pioneer manufacturer of television sets. Paramount pressed DuMont to develop applications of television which could be used in motion-picture theaters. In turn, DuMont tried to utilize Paramount's production knowledge to help to gain a competitive edge on the most significant innovator in television, the Radio Corporation of America (RCA).

Paramount's investment in television went beyond Du-Mont. In August 1940, through Balaban and Katz, it established W9XBK, the first television station in Chicago. Paramount was granted an experimental license from the US Federal Communications Commission, the government body regulating television, in 1940 (and a commercial license in 1943). In 1941 Paramount created a subsidiary, Television Productions Inc. In 1943 it started W6XYZ in Los Angeles. (After the war the latter became Los Angeles' first television station, KTLA.) With DuMont's licenses for stations in New York and Washington, Paramount had established ownership of four of the first nine television stations in the United States. In 1945, Paramount-owned theater chains began to bid for additional television licenses. New England Theaters Inc., a wholly-owned subsidiary, applied for a license in Boston. Comerford-Publix sought a station in Scranton, Pennsylvania that same year. In 1946 came applications for Detroit and Dallas; in 1948, Des Moines and Tampa. DuMont also continued to expand. In addition to WABD in New York, DuMont activated WTTG in Washington and WDTV in Pittsburgh, and applied to begin stations in Cleveland and Cincinnati.

Such corporate activity did not go unnoticed by the Federal Communications Commission. To promote 'competition' the FCC passed a rule limiting ownership by one corporation to five stations, but the crushing blow came with decisions in the famous Paramount anti-trust case against the Big Five and Little Three. The 1934 Communications Act authorized the FCC to refuse licenses to any concern convicted of monopolistic practices (direct or indirect). The Commission of the late 1940s applied this covenant to television. The District Court's decision in the Paramount anti-trust motion picture case in 1946 led to a delay of all Paramount's television applications. (This initial court decision called for divestiture of theater chains. Since Paramount had applied through local theater chains, the Commission argued it was justified to terminate all decisions until it knew if Paramount would continue to own these chains.) Paramount could only wait, pending an appeal of the anti-trust case to the US Supreme Court. The negative Supreme Court decision put an end to Paramount's chances of directly acquiring valuable television licenses. A major secondary effect of the famous Paramount anti-trust case was thus to shut out all motion-picture companies, Paramount in particular, from direct ownership in the television business.

Paramount sought an alternative – theater television. In 1948, it held a series of demonstrations, and began to plan how to integrate television into its theater chain. Innovation took place in Barney Balaban's old haunt, Chicago's Balaban and Katz chain. To launch this theater television in June 1949, Balaban and Katz organized a spectacular show at the Flagship house, the Chicago theater. The television equipment would record the stage acts (of whom only Henny Youngman is still remembered) in a studio across the street, and then telecast them into the theater. A beauty pageant was also held in conjunction with opening day. All the publicity seemed to pay off. A capacity audience of 4000 people welcomed the mid-western premiere of theater television. A remote crew recorded the crowd entering. Then through the intermediate film process the audience saw themselves on the theater's television screen several minutes later. Chicago's mayor, Martin H. Kennelly, appeared on stage to congratulate Balaban and Katz.

Gradually, Balaban and Katz tried to fit theater televi-

37

sion into its regular movie house programming strategy, but with little success. Sports seemed, for a time, to work: the 1949 World Series, Big Ten football featuring the University of Illinois in the fall of 1950, and championship boxing matches. Occasionally there were news events, for example speeches by Generals Douglas MacArthur and Dwight Eisenhower. However, all operations ceased in mid-1951 because costs far exceeded extra revenues. For example, one house lost more than $3000 on the 1949 World Series, $18000 on Big Ten football and $2000 on the Saddler-Pep Fight of 26 September 1951. Barney Balaban cut Paramount's losses and turned to 3-D and widescreen production (in the company's own Vistavision) to revive sagging revenues. Paramount made a half-hearted thrust into pay-television later in the 1950s, but theater television in essence signalled the end of nearly thirteen years of innovation and investment into television.

Despite its unsuccessful ventures in television, Paramount surged ahead on motion-picture fronts during the 1940s. Indeed, Paramount once again took over the number one spot in film industry profits in 1946, when profits rose to an industry record, twice those of second-placed 20th Century-Fox. Furthermore, in the decade under Balaban's direction the corporation had rid itself of all debt. By 1946, neither Paramount nor any of its subsidiaries had any interest-bearing obligations outstanding. It owned the Paramount Building (and enclosed theater) free and clear. No other major motion-picture corporation approached Paramount's corporate health, nor was any as broadly based. During the boom in the Second World War Paramount's theaters, so much a burden during the 1930s, had turned into money machines. The boost in attendance helped Paramount most since it had the theaters to hold all the new patrons.

By the mid-1940s, Barney Balaban had formulated a corporate strategy which would regularly produce the popular fare to fill Paramount's theaters. It had not always been thus. In the early 1930s, unlike MGM (with Louis Mayer), Warners (with Jack L. Warner) or 20th Century-Fox (with Darryl F. Zanuck), Paramount did not have an executive continuously in charge of production. In the late 1920s Jesse L. Lasky and B.P. Schulberg presided in California. Like many others they left in 1932. Their replacement, Emmanuel Cohen, would last only two years. Cohen came aboard during the worst part of the Great Depression, and so faced an impossible job. His legacy to the studio was his signing of Mae West and Bing Crosby to long-term contracts. Cohen was succeeded by a team – director Ernst Lubitsch and lawyer Henry Herzbrun. On 4 February 1935 this duo took charge; a year later they were gone. This was certainly the only time in Hollywood studio history that such a noted director was given full creative control of a major studio's product. While in charge, Lubitsch adopted a 'retake and remake' procedure whereby a feature could be put back into production after principal photography had been completed if Lubitsch deemed there were ways to improve it. He centralized story purchases in his office, and took a very tough line *vis-à-vis* fellow directors.

At precisely the mid-point of the Lubitsch administration, the reorganization of the parent corporation took place, and John Otterson began his presidency. Otterson surely made Lubitsch's life miserable and for a time moved directly to California to supervise. But all Otterson's orders for efficiency and cost accounting did were to further demoralize Lubitsch.

6. William LeBaron

After an abortive attempt to lure Irving Thalberg away from MGM Otterson replaced Lubitsch with producer William LeBaron. Otterson's dismissal and the Kennedy reports re-emphasizing cost over-runs, disregarded shooting schedules and alienated stars required LeBaron to institute a great number of changes.

When Balaban moved in he wanted his own man in California, so he placed Y. Frank Freeman in charge of production. However, Freeman was not an experienced movie-maker, so he concentrated on finding an assistant to oversee actual production of films. LeBaron functioned as that assistant for a time, but in 1941 songwriter-producer B.G. DeSylva replaced him. Although DeSylva did a good job, developing the profitable Hope-Crosby 'Road . . .' series, ill-health forced him to resign in September 1944. In his day, DeSylva had presided over Paramount's movement from Lubitsch-like European products to far more profitable American material. He is also given credit for boosting the careers of Betty Hutton and Alan Ladd.

From 1944 until the end of the decade, Paramount's most profitable era, two men controlled its production destiny. Y. Frank Freeman took on more day-to-day responsibilities, especially handling difficult labor and contractual disputes. The executive in charge of production was the former Paramount studio manager, Henry Ginsberg. Ginsberg had accumulated a decade of experience with small studios such as Preferred, Sterling Pictures and Hal Roach before joining Selznick International Pictures in 1936 as general manager. He moved to Paramount in 1940. Freeman and Ginsberg put Paramount production on a business-like basis, co-ordinating some 3000 employees including 52 cameramen, 13 directors, 283 electricians, 103 musicians, 131 actors, 3 gardeners and 27 hairdressers. They built up a backlog of pictures so that at any point in time if there was a strike or other trouble Paramount's theaters would always still have films to show. After the Second World War the duo cut costs by 25 per cent and lowered the number of films made, hoping for selective long runs from a few hits, but Paramount always produced its share of 'B' films, first under Harold Hurley, later under William Pine and William Thomas. In part, Paramount produced its 'Bs' in order to train future stars and directors. A certain number of so-called 'Super-Bs' did much to fill Paramount theaters for 'in-between' weeks.

Throughout the studio era, Paramount minimized its risk in feature film production by relying on talent and properties with 'spill-over' fame from other entertainment sectors. The top-grossing Paramount films of the early 1930s featured European talent, singers Marlene Dietrich and Maurice Chevalier, and the vaudeville Broadway-trained Marx Brothers. All achieved considerable reputations before they ever stepped on the Paramount lot. All did well for the studio, but none lasted for more than three or four popular films. The Paramount star of the early

7. Mae West in **Belle of the Nineties** (courtesy MCA, Inc.)

1930s with the greatest drawing power was Mae West, yet another veteran of vaudeville. West helped considerably, since her most popular films came in 1933 and 1934, the years of the studio's reorganization. She had had a long career on the stage before making her first film in 1932. William LeBaron, who had written for West in the past, lured her to Paramount and produced **I'm No Angel** (1933) and **Belle of the Nineties** (1934). And she was paid accordingly, a reported $220,000 in 1933, $340,000 in 1934, and $480,000 in 1935; in the latter year she was the highest salaried woman in the United States. With the coming of a stricter Hays Code, and an apparent shift in public taste to child stars like Shirley Temple, the West craze died as quickly as it had begun. She made her last film for Paramount in 1938, and returned to the stage whence she had come.

In the mid-1930s Paramount had no immediate replacement for the star power of Mae West. Stars were on the lot, of course: Claudette Colbert, Fred MacMurray, Miriam Hopkins, Loretta Young, Charles Laughton and the now infamous Frances Farmer, but the studio could only claim one major star, Gary Cooper. Paramount-bred, Cooper first appeared in silent films as early as 1926. He stayed with Paramount until his contract lapsed and then moved to Goldwyn. Paramount seemed unable to take full advantage of him; his most popular mid-1930s effort was for Columbia, **Mr Deeds Goes To Town** (1936). Cooper would go on to more consistent popularity in the 1940s (3 in 1942, 2 in 1944, 4 in 1946, 1947 and 1948 in the annual polls of top-ten money-making stars) for Goldwyn, International Pictures and Warners.

In the confused era of the 1930s Paramount had no lack of powerful directors: Cecil B. De Mille, Leo McCarey, King Vidor, Rouben Mamoulian and temporary production chief Ernst Lubitsch. The latter may have been head of production, but in the long-run it was De Mille who made the studio far more money. De Mille had begun with Famous Players, left and returned in 1932.

8. Cecil B. De Mille'
Cleopatra (courtesy
Cecil B. De Mille
Trust)

From 1935 on he got into his stride, creating one of the studio's top grossing films every other year: **The Crusades** (1935), **The Plainsman** (1936), **The Buccaneer** (1937), **Union Pacific** (1938), **Northwest Mounted Police** (1940), **Reap the Wild Wind** (1940), **The Story of Dr Wassell** (1943), **The Unconquered** (1946) and **Samson and Delilah** (1949). De Mille would continue his streak of hits with his last two films, both the industry's top grossers of their respective year: **The Greatest Show On Earth** (1952) and **The Ten Commandments** (1957). From 1935 until 1957 none of De Mille's films failed to get into the industry list of top-grossers of the year. He worked with many of Paramount's stars of the 1930s (Loretta Young, Gary Cooper, Jean Arthur, Fredric March, Barbara Stanwyck, Joel McCrea and Paulette Goddard) and 1940s (Ray Milland, Gary Cooper, Laraine Day, Paulette Goddard, Hedy Lamarr and Betty Hutton). Critics of the day found little of value in his work, but corporate boss Barney Balaban knew a money-maker and kept funding larger and larger De Mille budgets. Indeed, all of De Mille's work in the 1940s was in Technicolor, requiring far greater than average production outlays.

However, Barney Balaban found his most significant successes of the 1940s on the radio in the form of crooner Bing Crosby and comic Bob Hope. Table 2.2 records their nearly continuous ranking in the top ten most effective box-office attractions. For the 1940s, certainly 1944-9, this duo functioned as the most popular combination in American films. Crosby's record of five consecutive years as the industry's number one star (1944-8) was rivalled only by Shirley Temple (1935-8), Mickey Rooney (1939-41) and in a later era Doris Day (1962-4). All Hope and Crosby's **Road** films of the 1940s finished among the top grossers of their respective years: **Road to Singapore** (1940), **Road to Zanzibar** (1940), **Road to Morocco** (1942), **Road to Utopia** (1945) and **Road to Rio** (1947). This series grossed more than any other during the studio era.

9. Bing Crosby, Bob Hope and Dorothy Lamour in **Road to Utopia** (courtesy MCA, Inc.)

In keeping with Paramount policy, both had achieved fame in radio and vaudeville before Paramount began to promote them. Crosby's career took off with **Holiday Inn** in 1942 (where he introduced his long-time hit *White Christmas*). With **Going My Way** (1944), which earned Crosby an Oscar for best actor, his popularity was unmatched; **Here Come the Waves** (1944), **Blue Skies** (1946), **Welcome Stranger** (1947), **The Emperor Waltz** (1948) and **A Connecticut Yankee in King Arthur's Court** (1949)

Table 2.2: Top Ten Star Ranking

	Bob Hope	Bing Crosby
1940	–	7
1941	4	–
1942	5	–
1943	2	4
1944	3	1
1945	7	1
1946	5	1
1947	6	1
1948	5	1
1949	1	2
1950	2	3

all finished among the top grossers of their respective seasons. Like many Paramount cross-over stars of the 1940s (including De Mille with his Lux Radio Theater) Crosby appeared continuously in other media. In his case, phonograph records (he would sell a total of 300 million) and radio were always near the top of some ranking.

Today Bob Hope is rarely thought of as a movie star. An experienced vaudevillian and radio performer, he came to Hollywood as part of Paramount's interest in radio tie-ins for **The Big Broadcast of 1938** and stayed with the studio until 1956, appearing in an average of two films per year except for an interruption for USO tours in the Second World War. His comedies, all among the top grossers of their respective years, included **Caught in the Draft** (1942 with Dorothy Lamour), **Louisiana Purchase** (1941 with Victor Moore), **My Favorite Blonde** (1942 with Madeleine Carroll), **Let's Face It** (1943 with Betty Hutton), **Monsieur Beaucaire** (1946 with Joan Caulfield), **My Favorite Brunette** (1947 with Dorothy Lamour and Peter Lorre), **Paleface** (1948 with Jane Russell), **Sorrowful Jones** (1949, with Lucille Ball), **The Great Lover** (1949 with Rhonda Fleming) and **Fancy Pants** (1950 with Lucille Ball). This extraordinary string of hits, coupled with those of Crosby and De Mille, accounted for more than two-thirds of all Paramount's top grossing films of its most profitable decade, the 1940s.

There were others at Paramount trying to reach the

box-office potential of Hope, Crosby and De Mille. A former De Mille protegé Mitchell Leisen directed **I Wanted Wings** in 1941. This Second World War film boosted the careers of William Holden, Ray Milland and Veronica Lake, all of whom stayed on with Paramount in the 1940s. Leisen's **Frenchman's Creek** (1944 with Joan Fontaine) and **Kitty** (1945 with Paulette Goddard and Ray Milland) also did quite well at the box office. But the director who drew critical fame as well as box-office receipts to Paramount was Preston Sturges. From **The Great McGinty** (1940) to **The Miracle of Morgan's Creek** (1944) Sturges created a string of seven comedies about America. Two, **The Lady Eve** (1941) and **The Miracle of Morgan's Creek,** did extremely well at the box-office.

The studio's forte lay with talent recruited from vaudeville, radio and the stage. In 1936, Paramount initiated the first of its three Big Broadcast films. Through the years this series included the talents of George Burns and Gracie Allen, Ethel Merman, Bill Robinson, Jack Benny, Martha Raye and Dorothy Lamour. These all-star extravanganzas resurfaced for audiences in the Second World War with **Star Spangled Rhythm** (1942) and **Duffy's Tavern** (1945), two of the studio's more popular features during the Second World War. In features, Paramount never produced the quantity of attractions of an MGM but managed with strong connections to other media, and a few very popular stars and directors, to force its way to the top of the American film industry during the 1940s. Barney Balaban and Y. Frank Freeman had created a trim profit-making machine, reaping the benefits from stars developed by others, principally the radio networks and phonograph record companies.

Like all other members of the Big Five, however, Paramount produced more than feature films. It offered theaters a 'complete service'. With one of two major production centers in New York (Warners had the other) Paramount lured stars from Broadway and vaudeville to appear in shorts. In this way Paramount could test the market for these potential stars in a cost-effective manner. If successful, Paramount would sign them on long-term contracts and send them to California for exploitation in feature films. During the late 1920s and early 1930s Paramount maintained a successful pipeline. Visual records of entire vaudeville sketches and musical numbers of Eddie Cantor, George Burns and Gracie Allen, Lillian Roth, Rudy Vallee, Ruth Etting, Joseph Smith and Charles Dale, and George Jessel were filmed. In the 1940s Paramount moved all its operations to Hollywood to take advantage of the talent shift that had occurred in the radio industry. The focus shifted to big bands: Louis Armstrong, Ben Bernie, Cab Calloway and Duke Ellington recorded for Paramount. Paramount even delved into the daily lives of songwriters as part of its 'Paramount Pictorial' series. The public could see Hoagy Carmichael, Harold Arlen and even Richard Rogers and Lorenz Hart 'at work' (though little work seemed to be involved, songs being apparently the product of happy-go-lucky tunesmiths).

Paramount constantly publicized its own features through its short subjects. Through 'Hollywood on Parade' and 'Hedda Hopper's Hollywood' Paramount stars, most notably its former vaudevillians and current radio performers, appeared in vignettes to promote upcoming Paramount features or simply to keep their names and images before the movie-going public. This prudent corporation used (and re-used) musical numbers. Even though 'Paramount Pictorial' was intended as a general interest screen magazine series covering such diverse topics as 'Artistry in Glass Making' and 'Ann Leaf at the Organ', invariably these shorts would include shots of Paramount stars or scenes from past Paramount productions. Paramount's 'Screen Souvenirs' even featured clips from the studio's silent features and silent news-reels. Frequently, there were one-shot short subjects promoting specific Paramount features, often the work of director Cecil B. De Mille.

Paramount also handled short subjects for independent producers. In 1932 and for part of 1933 it distributed the comedies of Mack Sennett. That arrangement ended in 1933 when Sennett went out of business. Through the 1930s and 1940s Paramount also handled the 'Sportslights' series developed by sportswriter Grantland Rice at Pathé. But Paramount's most original experiment in the shorts area came during 1930 and 1931 when it produced and distributed commercial advertisements. Often contracted at the local level, such shorts appeared off and on during the 1930s and 1940s. Paramount's theaters tried to innovate these money-making shorts on a regular basis in the early 1930s, but quickly retreated when rival exhibitors openly mocked the practice in newspaper advertisements.

Paramount offered a first-rate newsreel service. The company had begun making newsreels in 1915, about the same time as competitors Fox and Universal. But with the market flooded, Famous Players withdrew 'Newspictures' in 1916. Famous Players waited until its economic power was considerably greater before it ventured into newsreel production again in 1927. To fill its program for its expanding chain of Publix theaters,

Paramount lured away two veteran newsreel producers from Pathé as well as a handful of Pathé cameramen. First presented in silent form ('The Eyes of the World'), 'Paramount News' became 'The Eyes and Ears of the World' in 1928. With its considerable economic clout, Paramount this time was able to build one of the top newsreel organizations, one which secured its share of the scoops from which the wire services enlarged Paramount News frames to provide photos for newspapers. The studio continued production on a regular, twice-a-week basis for precisely thirty years. In 1957 Paramount recognized television, abandoned newsreels, and turned to concentrate on other activities.

In 1927 Paramount also formalized access to animated shorts by signing a contract with the Fleischer studios. This arrangement lasted for fifteen years. The two Fleischer brothers, Max and Dave, started as independent cartoon-producers after the First World War with the 'Out of the Inkwell' series featuring Koko the clown. They released through states-rights (regionally-based) distributors. Max Fleischer handled the business end; younger brother Dave supervised actual production of the cartoons. What gave this small operation a boost was its innovation of the 'Bouncing Ball' series in 1924. The Fleischers did not invent the sing-along, but simply brought to film what had been a static form using song slides. In addition the Fleischer studio often integrated animated and live-action figures to help along the bouncing ball. In 1924 the studio also formed its own distribution subsidiary, Red Seal Pictures. By 1926, Red Seal was deeply in debt, precisely when Adolph Zukor and Sam Katz were looking for a steady supply of cartoons for the rapidly growing Publix theater chain. Paramount signed up the Fleischer studio, took over distribution and paid off all debts,

In June 1929, Paramount announced a Fleischer-produced sound series – 'Talkartoons'. Out went Koko. Out went combinations of animation and live action. What gave the Fleischers a big advantage at this point was access to Paramount music, and the use of the voices of stars (Rudy Vallee, Ethel Merman, Lillian Roth and the Mills Brothers) in 'Bouncing Ball' cartoons. A new cartoon star in the sixth 'Talkartoon' of 1930 was Betty Boop. Modeled on popular singer Helen Kane, Betty Boop was quickly given her own series, which during the early 1930s dealt directly and openly with sexual matters. Betty Boop was the perfect flapper, a flirt and tease who never lost her innocence and purity. The Paramount music publishing subsidiaries kept her supplied with popular songs; the studio added the voices of its major stars: Maurice Chevalier, Fanny Brice and Cab Calloway participated in several very popular Betty Boop cartoons. Unfortunately for Paramount, it proved to be a short-lived fad. The new Hays Office Production Code of 1934 dictated a conservative approach toward sexual material. Numerous complaints about Betty Boop were filed. Immediately the character was covered up; gone were her garter and short skirt. She became a single woman with no interest in men. And her songs, previously as *risqué* as those of her Paramount counterpart, Mae West, became sanitized, extolling virtue and kindness to animals.

Thus in the mid-1930s in the midst of Paramount's corporate reorganization, the Fleischers had to develop a new star quickly. Fortunately their search was short-lived. The Fleischers found him in the funny papers – Popeye the Sailor. The newspaper strip had originated in 1919, and was a staple throughout the 1920s. In 1933 came the first official Popeye cartoon; in 1934 came the style and character which continued for forty years. Popeye quickly earned a place as one of Paramount's important stars, capturing newspaper attention and top billing on theater marquees. Just as Disney's Mickey Mouse had done several years earlier the Popeye figure took on a life of its own through clever marketing and merchandizing. The series was so popular that when conservative Barney Balaban took over, he went beyond monthly black and white offerings to sponsor Technicolor specials: **Popeye the Sailor Meets Sinbad the Sailor** (1936), two-reels long, followed by **Popeye Meets Ali Baba and His 40 Thieves** (1937) and **Popeye Meets Aladdin and His Wonderful Lamp** (1939).

Paramount under the Balaban administration sought to push the studio back to the top of the American film industry. In the animation area this meant matching the success of Disney's unexpected 1937 hit **Snow White and the Seven Dwarfs.** To produce a feature-length animated film, **Gulliver's Travels,** the Fleischer operations expanded three-fold. To avoid union problems and gain a significant tax break the Fleischer studio moved in 1938 from New York to Miami, Florida. In critical reviews **Gulliver's Travels** never matched Disney's **Snow White,** but it did well at the box office, partly because of Paramount's strength in distribution. But all was not well with the Fleischer operation. **Gulliver's Travels** had stretched the cartoon studio's resources too thin. A new series 'Raggedy Ann and Raggedy Andy' never went well. Nor did a second full-length animated feature, **Mr Bug Goes To Town** (1941). Even with the limited success of an animated 'Superman', Paramount executives figured the Paramount corporation should develop its own in-house production unit and so in 1942 Paramount severed contractual ties with the Fleischer studio, bid away three Fleischer animators and opened the Famous Studios animation shop. This operation was placed in New York, under the direct supervision of the main office.

To signal a new beginning, Paramount announced that from the 1943-4 season on, all Famous Studios cartoons including 'Popeye' would be in Technicolor. The 'Superman' series was dropped, and a new character, Little Lulu, introduced. Like Popeye, Little Lulu had had a long successful career in another medium, in this case the **Saturday Evening Post,** before Famous Studios converted her into a cartoon star. She ran for five years, but in 1948 to save money by avoiding copyright fees, Paramount dropped Little Lulu in favor of a studio-created (and owned) substitute, Little Audrey. Paramount would continue to produce cartoons well into the television era. Indeed, a very successful character, Casper the Friendly Ghost, was introduced as a regular series in 1950. Owned completely by the Famous Studios, Casper became a big hit, but in 1956, recognizing the end of cartoons in theaters, Famous Studios became Paramount Cartoon Studios, and Popeye was 'retired' and sold to television. Soon after this the whole Paramount operation turned to television production. New owner Gulf & Western closed up Paramount's cartoon shop in 1967.

The Paramount integrated empire came to an end in 1949. With the Supreme Court's final decision in the long-drawn-out anti-trust case, Barney Balaban, still looking forward to a significant place in the expanding television market, ordered the corporation to follow the court order, and divorce and divest its theater chain. To Paramount Pictures went the studio and its sales organization, about 380 theaters in foreign countries (mostly Canada), the residual value of old films, the stock in DuMont and the television station KTLA in Los Angeles. These last three assets were kept to help with Paramount's venture into television. To the new theater company, United Paramount Theaters, went just the theater chain and one television station, WBKB in Chicago. United Paramount, ironically, gained the far stronger position in the television market through its 1953 merger with American Broadcasting Corporation. Sales of old Paramount theaters supplied the cash to help ABC through its weak years in the 1950s and 1960s. Thus, although Paramount reached its peak in 1946, using stars from radio and the stage, and sought a major role in television, it was its theatrical spin-off, under former Balaban assistant, Leonard Goldenson, which by the 1970s became one of America's dominant television networks, ABC.

Paramount Pictures was sold to a conglomerate, Gulf & Western, in 1967 and eventually become a major supplier of television, fulfilling part of Barney Balaban's vision.

3:

Loew's and Metro-Goldwyn-Mayer

Metro-Goldwyn-Mayer, with its roaring lion symbol, may have been the most famous of the Hollywood studios, but from a business perspective MGM represented simply one successful subsidiary of a major motion picture corporation, Loew's Inc. Loew's earned steady profits throughout the 1930s, coming to represent the Tiffany of movie corporations to Wall Street analysts. The fully-integrated corporation never declared bankruptcy for any of its theaters, nor ever had to be reorganized. Under the direction of a management team headed by Nicholas Schenck, Loew's never lost money during the entire studio era (see Table 3.1) In the 1940s, the corporation continued to earn large profits, but competitors – mostly notably Paramount and 20th Century-Fox – had caught up and surpassed Loew's. Part of this relative decline came because Loew's owned a relatively small theater chain – the smallest of the Big Five. Having a few well-placed theaters in the depressed economic environment of the 1930s made good business sense. However, a small number in the boom 1940s – at least until 1948 when outside factors began to erode demand – was a decidedly negative factor. Loew's, of all the Big Five, tried to hold on to the past, playing it safe and seemingly trying to return the company to the 1930s. Warner Bros. is often thought of as the representative studio of the 1930s, but it was Loew's – with MGM providing popular features – which profited during that bleak decade, doing far better than Warners or any other member of the Big Five.

The origin of Loew's goes back to the era when the motion picture business was just forming. Founder Marcus Loew

Table 3.1: Loew's Balance Sheet

Year	Net Profit (millions of dollars)	Assets (millions of dollars)
1930	14.6	128.6
1931	11.8	129.4
1932	8.0	124.8
1933	4.3	123.7
1934	8.6	131.0
1935	7.5	129.3
1936	10.6	138.6
1937	14.3	142.5
1938	9.9	143.8
1939	9.5	157.3
1940	8.7	161.0
1941	11.0	164.2
1942	11.8	167.6
1943	13.4	192.5
1944	14.5	190.0
1945	12.9	206.9
1946	17.9	218.3
1947	10.5	229.9
1948	4.2	223.1
1949	6.0	219.6

was born on Manhattan's Lower East Side and went to work at the age of 6. He declared bankruptcy in 1889, when he was 19, through a failure in the fur business, but it was in that business that he met Adolph Zukor and invested in several of Zukor's early theater ventures. In 1904 Loew abandoned the fur trade, and plunged into show business. Backed by friends, he formed the People's Vaudeville Company to tender 'nickel vaudeville', a middle-range variety show which included both films and live entertainment. Loew offered a bargain to middle- and lower-middle-class patrons – people raised on high-class Keith-Albee and Orpheum vaudeville. Motion pictures were considered the twentieth century's latest marvel. By combining the two, Loew could compete with the entrenched East Coast giant, Keith-Albee. The use of movies helped to keep his costs low. The vaudeville/motion-picture mixture varied, depending on the characteristics of the potential audience and the availability of live versus filmed attractions. But in the beginning, Loew considered himself in vaudeville, not the fledgling motion picture industry.

By 1909, it was clear that Loew was in the entertainment business to stay, on his way to building a vast theatrical empire located in the New York City environs. That summer (1909) Loew leased the concessions at the Paradise Amusement park in Manhattan from brothers Joseph and Nicholas Schenck. Soon after, the two joined as managers. In February 1910 Loew's Consolidated Enterprises was incorporated, to bring together all the assets of the far-flung Loew empire. To facilitate further expansion, Loew's Consolidated issued $200,000 worth of new stock, most of which was subscribed by the Schubert organization, a power in the legitimate theater business. Loew assumed presidency of his new corporation and Nicholas Schenck became secretary-treasurer.

Loew's Consolidated quickly moved to expand, first to all five boroughs of New York City, then west into the state of Ohio, but the new corporation, worth an estimated $5 million, moved judiciously, from the beginning establishing a go-slow, conservative stance which was to become its trademark during the studio era. While others (in particular, Universal's founder, Carl Laemmle, and William Fox) battled the Motion Picture Patents Company trust, Loew's co-operated, ready to return to full-time vaudeville if necessary. Indeed, at this time Loew's expanded its position in the vaudeville, not the film, business by entering into an agreement with Sullivan and Considine, a large booking agency, for second-line (non-Keith-Albee) vaudeville acts, but Loew's focussed on the bricks-and-mortar end, slowly building and acquiring a substantial chain of theaters. In 1917, for example, the corporation invested more than $8 million to open theaters in eight major cities in the populous north-east. Even when the Patents trust was broken, Loew's continued to emphasize vaudeville over filmed entertainment.

That all changed after the First World War. The various Loew enterprises were doing so well that the corporation was recapitalized, now at $17.5 million, and renamed simply Loew's Incorporated (hereafter Loew's). Moving into the 1920s, management finally acknowledged its dependence on films and, long after its major competitors, moved into their production and distribution. With Famous Players-Lasky and First National already vertically integrated, Loew's was forced to pay higher and higher prices to rent top films. In addition, motion pictures were gradually forcing vaudeville from the top of the marquee. Patrons

10. MGM Studios

would come to see and hear first-line vaudeville talent, but not Loew's cheaper acts. To maintain profits, Loew's needed popular movies. In 1919, Loew's looked toward Metro Pictures. This company had been formed in 1915 to distribute the films of five small production companies, much in the same manner that Paramount handled the films of Famous Players and other producers. Utilizing stars Francis X. Bushman, Ethel and Lionel Barrymore and Mary Miles Minter, Metro earned substantial profits in the beginning. Indeed, for its first two years it was able to finance all activities from profits alone. In 1917 Metro incorporated with a $2.5 million capital base and took over all its production affiliates. However, all that the new corporation could produce was debt. In 1920 Loew's agreed to absorb the ailing producer–distributor and take over all its obligations.

The acquisition of Metro committed Loew's to motion-picture production. From 1920 on vaudeville took second place to movies in Loew's theaters. Now fully integrated, Loew's went on to expand in film production, distribution and exhibition. Its circuit of movie houses continued to grow. Loew's opened its flagship house in 1921, the 3500-seat Loew's State theater on Times Square. Loew's added fifty more theaters, bringing its total to more than 100 by mid-decade. Simultaneously, production and distribution capabilities were enlarged. In 1924 Goldwyn Pictures was losing a great deal of money. Goldwyn Pictures not only included a Hollywood studio but also a small chain of theaters, including the largest movie house in the United States at that time, the 5000 seat Capital located just north of Times Square.

Loew's was easily able to acquire this distressed corporation and add it to its empire. To manage this expanding production unit, centered in Culver City, California, Loew's hired former Metro executive Louis B. Mayer. The package was completed in 1924 and Loew's famous subsidiary, Metro-Goldwyn-Mayer, was formerly dedicated.

11. (l. to r.) Fred Niblo, Marcus Loew, Louis B. Mayer

The years prior to the coming of sound were prosperous ones for Loew's. The theater chain continued to expand, but much more slowly than rival Paramount. Loew's concentrated its theatrical chain in a few states, never seeking to blanket the entire country. MGM, under Louis B. Mayer, did remarkably well for a new organization. Within three years MGM would become one of Hollywood's major production units. Quickly Loew's had shed its image of a regional family vaudeville enterprise. By the mid-1920s, Loew's Inc. represented a fully-integrated, well-run major movie company. The coming of sound, initiated by Warner Bros. and Fox in 1926, was resisted for a time by Loew's along with Paramount and the rest of the industry, but on 11 May 1928 Loew's, Paramount, and United Artists signed with Western Electric for rights and equipment to use in production and exhibition. The three corporations had bargained as one, and on that Friday in May signed identical contracts with favorable terms for all. MGM took less than twelve months to switch over to the production of talkies. Loew's theaters were among the first to be wired. Loew's took advantage of its vaudeville connections, and recorded innumerable short subjects of a wide variety of popular acts. Loew's theaters quickly substituted these short films for more expensive live stage shows.

The coming of sound precipitated several of the biggest mergers in motion-picture history. The most spectacular, and most short-lived, was Fox's takeover of Loew's. As detailed in the next chapter, the Fox Film Company had grown in remarkable fashion as a result of its innovation of sound. By 1929 Fox ranked with Warner Bros., Loew's and Paramount at the top of the US film industry. Fox was able to move to takeover Loew's because, on the death of founder Marcus Loew in 1927, the widow and sons had inherited almost one-third of the outstanding stock – which they decided to sell. Meanwhile, Nicholas Schenck had assumed the presidency of the corporation and moved to negotiate on behalf of the Loew family. Schenck collected enough other shares to offer any buyer majority control. Fox officials entered secret negotiations with Schenck, bidding $125 per share, far above the prevailing market price of $80 per share. On 28 February 1928 the deal was struck. (The stockholders' pool split $41 million; Schenck and his lawyer pocketed $9 million for negotiation services.) The new Fox-Loew's now represented the largest corporation in the motion-picture industry, with assets of $200 million and an annual earnings potential of $20 million. It controlled over 750 theaters and purchased 115 more theaters in 1929 to bring its total to 865. This merger surpassed even RKO's formation, or Warner Bros. expansions which are described in Chapters 5 and 6. In a series of bold maneuvers Fox had created the largest entertainment complex in the world.

Two factors combined to undo this amalgamation. First, the US Justice Department, under recently-elected President Herbert Hoover, moved to undo the Fox takeover. In November 1929 the Justice Department formally filed suit to untie the merger. At the same time Fox's intricate set of $50 million worth of loans, taken out to pay for the Loew's stock, began to unravel in the face of the fall of the stock market. Fox had received the major portion of these loans through American Telephone and Telegraph, Fox Film's supplier of sound film equipment and then the world's largest corporation. Specifically, a $15 million note was due in March 1930. AT&T's collateral was a block of Fox stock. (AT&T had already benefitted from the deal because Fox had written contracts for the installation of sound equipment in its chain of theaters, the American film industry's second largest.) In 1930 Fox could not meet its obligations to AT&T. To ward off bankruptcy Fox took two dramatic steps. In one it signed a consent decree with the Justice Department whereby it agreed to divest itself of all Loew's stock. (In the other step, it eventually went to court to reorganize its theaters and settle with AT&T. For details on this proceeding see Chapter 4.) So although Fox formally 'owned' Loew's for more than eighteen months, it was never in the position to effect a great deal of control. Indeed, most observers argued that Fox lost all leverage some six months after its stock purchase in February 1929.

The Fox merger had little effect on Loew's corporate prosperity. The profits of $14.6 million in 1930 set a corporate record which would last until 1946, the industry's best year ever. In fact, Loew's continued to prosper throughout the Great Depression. All other members of the Big Five and Little Three (except Columbia) bathed in some red ink in the early 1930s, while Loew's never earned *less than* the $4.3 million it made in 1933. Loew's and Warner Bros. were the only members of the Big Five not to have to go to court to reorganize their theater divisions. During the 1930s, Loew's dominated the motion-picture industry, taking away the lead in profits from long-time champion Paramount, recent 'success story' Warner Bros. and radio-sponsored Radio-Keith-Orpheum.

By the mid-1930s the former vaudeville theater company had become a fully integrated, international motion-picture corporation with nearly 125 subsidiaries. Metro-Goldwyn-Mayer Pictures Corporation, a wholly owned subsidiary, created features and shorts at its Culver City, California, studio on forty acres with (in 1936) eighteen permanent buildings and twenty-two standing sets. MGM expanded to sixty-six acres in the late 1930s, adding five more stages plus laboratories for film processing, property rooms, a woodworking plant and administrative offices. Even more Culver City property was acquired after the Second World War, bringing the total to 168 acres. The total number of stages reached twenty-seven by 1949. MGM's support facilities were awesome. Its film laboratory could process 150,000 feet of film in 24 hours. The property room contained more than 15,000 separate pieces of potential *mise-en-scène*. Dubbing studios in Paris, Barcelona, and Rome enabled MGM to create sound tracks for versions of its films sent around the world.

To wholesale its products, Loew's maintained thirty-two branch offices (exchanges) throughout the United States. With the smallest theater chain of any member of the Big Five, Loew's had to take special care to sell MGM films to affiliated and independent theaters alike. Therefore, its distribution staff was one of the industry's largest. That staff maintained meticulous records, even to the point of generating a data bank on all possible clients. Overseas distribution was run from New York by the founder's son, Arthur M. Loew. Prior to the Second World War Loew's also had the industry's most efficient and widespread foreign sales network (in every country in the world except the USSR) extracting more than half an average feature's revenue from abroad. The Second World War took away part of Loew's comparative advantage, and helped in no small way to lessen the corporation's lead in profitability.

In the 1930s, Loew's owned, leased and/or operated some 150 theaters. Separate subsidiaries were maintained for theaters in Cleveland, Boston, Dayton, Ohio, Toronto, Pittsburgh, Jersey City, New Jersey and the states of Connecticut and Massachusetts, but fully half of Loew's theaters were in the New York metropolitan area. The rest were scattered in thirty-eight cities in seventeen states plus three in Canada, and seventeen in England and France. Loew's played the theater ownership game very conservatively, acquiring only first-run houses outside New York City. Therefore, the corporation held a strong position in a number of large US cities including (rank in population in 1940 in parentheses) New York (1), Los Angeles (5), Cleveland (6), Boston (7), Pittsburgh (10), Washington, DC (11), San Francisco (12), Buffalo (14), New Orleans (15), Newark (18), Kansas City (19), Rochester (23), Columbus (27), Atlanta (29), Jersey City, New Jersey (30), Memphis (32), Dayton (40), Syracuse (41), Worcester, Massachusetts, (44), Richmond (45), Hartford, Connecticut (51), New Haven, Connecticut (54), Springfield, Massachusetts (58), Bridgeport, Connecticut (59), Norfolk, Virginia (60), Yonkers, New York (61), Wilmington (76) and Reading, Pennsylvania (79). Unlike Paramount, Loew's purposely did not try to blanket the entire country, but rather sought to establish a stronghold in urban America east of the Mississippi River. Single theaters in Kansas City, Los Angeles and Houston provided exceptions.

Loew's had its corporate fingers in other pies. There was radio station WHN in New York City, which Loew's purchased to gain publicity for its films in the market in which it owned half of its theaters. Loew's added an FM station in the late 1940s and changed the name of its AM outlet to WMGM. The Robbins Music Publishing subsidiary gave Loew's control over the vast amount of popular music which contributed to MGM's musicals. Loew's entered the record industry in 1947 to reap further profits from this music publishing enterprise. Loew's, under an MGM label, sent out its first phonograph record in conjunction with the film biography of composer Jerome Kern, **Till the Clouds Roll By.**

Finally, Loew's functioned as a real estate company. Several of its wholly-owned theaters were situated in office and/or commercial buildings in the center of the busiest shopping areas of their respective cities. For example, Loew's owned the sixteen story Loew's State Building (the corporation's world headquarters) at 45th and Broadway in Times Square, a twelve-story building in downtown Los Angeles and an eight-story building in downtown Syracuse, New York.

In 1936, flush with profits, Loew's expanded into Europe by purchasing (with 20th Century-Fox) one-fifth of the Gaumont-British Corporation. This deal guaranteed Loew's access to 'British' films in order to circumvent British quota laws. In addition, the agreement gave Loew's the ability to distribute films in the UK at far lower costs, while gaining access to Gaumont's theaters. In 1937 Loew's actually took up production at the Denham studio outside London. Michael Balcon ran the operation. Loew's stayed only one year, despite two successful films (of a total of three) coming from the venture: **A Yank at Oxford** (1938) and **Goodbye Mr Chips** (1939). In 1943 it resumed operations under Alexander Korda, who merged his London Film Productions into the newly-titled MGM-British. This alliance produced only one film, **Perfect Strangers** (1945), even though Loew's had purchased the Amalgamated Studios at Elstree. Before Korda could even make full use of the studio, he resigned. He could not function under several bosses at Loew's; he demanded absolute freedom. Loew's in turn did not want to stick with a deal which had produced an estimated £1 million deficit in one year. Remarkably, Loew's did return to Britain once more before the end of the studio era, this time to set up shop at the Borehamwood studio in order to 'spend' blocked earnings. This operation collapsed in the mid-1950s, once again making no significant contribution to corporate earnings.

Loew's was much more successful with theaters, the operation with which the corporation had begun. Because of the death of Marcus Loew in 1927, the corporation expanded far less than Warners or Paramount during the late 1920s. Indeed, from March 1929 until the Fox matter was settled in April 1931, Loew's stood back as Paramount, Warners, and even RKO built and/or acquired hundreds of theaters, and millions more in debt. These obligations proved to be almost intolerable encumbrances during the Great Depresion. Loew's escaped the ravages of reorganization, and alone of the Big Five was able to operate at near 'normal' profit rates throughout the entire decade of the 1930s. Loew's in fact did not have to dip into its storehouse of reserves – in cash and government securities – to see it through this crisis. Profits reached record levels during the Second World War boom, peaking in 1946, but relatively speaking, the decade of the 1940s was a prosperous period for the film industry in general, and others – Paramount, 20th Century-Fox – passed Loew's in terms of profits. Paramount, Fox and Warners had more theaters than Loew's and thus were in a far better position to participate in a Second World War boom. In short, Loew's benefitted from the small size of its theater division during the 1930s, and suffered from that size in the 1940s. During the period 1946–8 Loew's fell to fourth place in the industry in profits, with 1948 being the worst year since 1924, when MGM was created. By 1948, Loew's had become an also-ran member of the Big Five, not the profit leader it had been throughout the 1930s.

Still, Loew's was the only member of the Big Five not to experience a loss through the 1930s, even paying a dividend in the worst part of the Great Depression. One reason for this was its management. All had been with Loew's for several decades. Nicholas Schenck joined Loew's in 1906, became president in 1927 and held that post until 1956. Other veterans, part of the Schenck management team, were corporate counsel Leopold Friedman (with Loew's 1911-54), accountant-treasurer David Bernstein (1905-45), theater manager Charles C. Moskowitz (1913-57), studio counsel J. Robert Rubin (1920-54), director of exhibition Joseph Vogel (1910-60), overseas manager Arthur M. Loew (1920-58) and distribution executive William Rogers (1924-52). All except Rogers began with Loew's in the vaudeville era. All stayed with Loew's (and mentor Nicholas Schenck) until well into the television era. When Schenck was eased up to the post of chairman of the board in 1956 it was the effective end of nearly thirty years of management continuity at Loew's. The theater division then split off – the last of the Big Five to do so – and the mighty Loew's empire, managed by this seven-member group, crumbled.

For thirty years the Schenck management team brought sizeable profits to Loew's Inc. For this they were well compensated, often ranking among the highest paid corporate executives in the USA. Indeed, in 1939 in a rare bit of corporate disruption, several of Loew's stockholders sued the corporation to halt what these dissidents considered were excessive 'personal service contracts'. What the stockholders objected to were the hundreds of thousands of dollars paid per year to Schenck and his associates plus studio boss Louis B. Mayer, dollars which could have been converted into dividends. Throughout the studio era Nicholas

Schenck, Arthur M. Loew, David Bernstein and J. Robert Rubin were paid a large salary *plus* a fixed percentage of the company's profits. As Loew's Inc. racked up profits, year after year after year, the money from these percentage deals mounted into millions of dollars. In 1941, for example, the four were paid the following:

Schenck	$2500 per week plus 2½ per cent of net corporate profits.
Rubin	$2000 per week plus 1¼ per cent of net corporate profits.
Bernstein	$2000 per week plus 1½ per cent of net corporate profits.
Loew	$3000 per week plus 5 per cent of certain foreign profits in excess of $3,640,000.

Although Arthur Loew's salary was greater than Schenck's (as was Louis B. Mayer's) his cut of profits entitled him to far less. Only Warners also provided its executives with salaries directly tied to the creation of corporate profits.

The Schenck management group supervised all essential corporate tasks. J. Robert Rubin was Schenck's liaison with the MGM studio on the west coast. Schenck never tried to be a movie producer, only an efficient theater executive. Rubin handled often blustery relations with studio bosses Louis B. Mayer (1924–48) and Dore Schary (1948–54). A lawyer by training, Rubin also represented MGM in the New York theatrical and literary world, bidding for the screen rights to numerous plays and musicals. Certainly he was one of the more important and influential money men on Broadway from 1930 to 1950. In a typical case Rubin obtained the movie rights to Vicki Baum's novel, **Grand Hotel,** by arranging first for its production as a play on Broadway. Rubin came to Loew's as the counsel for Metro Pictures and through his association with Louis B. Mayer engineered the merger which became Metro-Goldwyn-Mayer.

Arthur M. Loew and David Bernstein operated behind the scenes. Loew, son of the company's founder, joined his father after graduation from New York University. He began with overseas distribution, a subsidiary set up after Loew's takeover of Metro Pictures in 1920, and assumed full charge of all foreign distribution in 1927. David Bernstein supervised the corporation's books and helped to steer Loew's through the Great Depression with no financial complications. Earlier, when Loew's issued debentures (bonds) for the $15 million to take over and form MGM, it became the first movie corporation to go directly to the money markets; before that movie companies had to work through banks. Bernstein's coup saved Loew's several million dollars in agent fees and signalled, as much as any single event, the coming of age of the motion-picture business.

12. Nicholas M. Schenck (l.) and Arthur M. Loew

But the czar of this management team, the person in charge for nearly thirty years, was Nicholas Schenck. Known in industry circles as 'The General', by choice and design he remained out of the public's eye, shunning publicity in direct proportion to the growing level of his enormous power. Schenck sought high profits and for thirty years successfully placed them in the Loew's corporate cash-register. For a long time Marcus Loew's chief assistant, Nicholas Schenck succeeded to the presidency in 1927. But loyalty never exceeded a drive for riches. It was Schenck, seizing the moment, who engineered the deal to sell to Fox. Schenck took his commission and remained on as president, never missing a step. Age, new technologies and government decrees finally dethroned him. Even though he passed the usual retirement age of 65 in 1946, Schenck did not retire for another decade. He probably should have. Although interested in television, Schenck did not maneuver Loew's into a favorable position to take advantage of that new technology with the same skill he had employed to deal with the coming of sound, color and radio broadcasting. Schenck also failed to recognize the inevitability of the Paramount decrees. Loew's did not begin with its divorcement and divestiture until 1954, the final member of the Big Five to do so. Schenck resisted, in part because Loew's theaters continued to generate sizeable profits through the mid-1950s. Finally, with profits falling (Loew's first lost money in 1957) a new management group took over on 14 December 1955. Schenck tried for a comeback in 1956, but failed.

Film production at Loew's subsidiary, MGM, reflected Schenck's conservative philosophy. At first, MGM handled only features, letting others produce the necessary shorts, newsreels and cartoons. Loew's engineered distribution deals with Roach (short subjects), Hearst (newsreels) and several studios for cartoons. MGM remained the least diversified Big Five studio until the end of the Great Depression. Furthermore, with Loew's relatively small theater chain, MGM had to create features which were attractive to others. They could not simply play in Loew's houses and even come close to turning a profit. Of course, all studios tried to produce popular feature films, but during the 1930s it was a more pressing necessity for MGM. To meet this goal, the studio accumulated the greatest number of stars, and with these stars produced more top-grossing films than any other studio. Even in the 1940s when Loew's lost its position as the most profitable of the Big Five, MGM continued to lead the industry in top-grossing feature films. Only during 1942–3 and 1946–7 did it have poor seasons. In fact during the 1930s MGM ruled supreme, gathering in nearly one-third of all top-grossers each year. Only the Second World War boom era enabled the other majors, especially Paramount and 20th Century-Fox, to catch up.

MGM is often referred to as the Tiffany of studios – high-class and elegant. Film critics point to the sophisticated image created through stars like Greta Garbo, Norma Shearer and Joan Crawford, but if one looks closely at MGM's top-grossing feature films and ranking box-office stars for the studio era one gets a different picture. Certainly Norma Shearer (**Strangers May Kiss, Riptide**), Joan Crawford (**Grand Hotel, Chained**) and Greta Garbo (**Mata Hari, Queen Christina**), were reigning stars of the early 1930s. But MGM's number one box-office attraction during those years was none other than Marie Dressler, who ranked as Hollywood's number one star in both 1932 and 1933. Her **Min and Bill, Politics, Reducing, Emma** and **Tugboat Annie** generated vast amounts of dollars for Loew's during the Great Depression. Marie Dressler was hardly an elegant young movie star. A veteran of the legitimate and vaudeville stage as well as silent films, she came to MGM in 1927, and in 1930, when she had already turned 61, became the studio's

13. Wallace Beery and
Marie Dressler in
Tugboat Annie (©
1933 Loew's Inc.)

top star. Her homely appearance and full figure hardly matched
the classic beauty of Garbo or the young Joan Crawford, but Nick
Schenck did not care. All that mattered to the 'The General' were
the returns at the box-office. Marie Dressler's roles both as
Tugboat Annie and in comedies with Polly Moran provided
enormous, consistent revenues during the first half of the 1930s.
She even won an Academy Award for her performance in **Min
and Bill.** Marie Dressler pushes us to reconsider the 'Tiffany'
image, for she surely represented MGM to the movie-going public
of America in the Depression.

Vaudeville is a French term for variety show. Loew's
began as a corporation providing vaudeville. A move toward
diversity also seems the best way to characterize MGM's strategy
for feature-film production. In the early 1930s along with the
earthy comedies of Marie Dressler (and Wallace Beery) other
popular MGM genres included jungle adventures (**Trader Horn,
Tarzan the Ape Man**), slapstick comedy (Laurel and Hardy in
Sons of the Desert) and drama with assorted members of the
Barrymore family (**Grand Hotel, Rasputin and the Princess**).
Variety continued through the late 1930s as well. There were
versions of classic literature (**David Copperfield, Anna Karenina**),
more comedy (**Ninotchka, The Philadelphia Story, A Night at the
Opera**), musicals (**Broadway Melody of 1936, The Girl of the
Golden West, Sweethearts**) and detective and family series (**The
Thin Man, Judge Hardy** and his family). If a strategy of diversity

14. Spencer Tracy and Clark Gable in **Boom Town** (© 1940 Loew's Inc.)

continued throughout the 1930s, what did change were the major stars. Leading ladies (of whatever image) dominated during the early 1930s, while the late 1930s and early 1940s saw MGM's men rise into the top ten box-office attractions. Year-in, year-out MGM's three biggest stars were a set of quite different male types: Clark Gable, Spencer Tracy and Mickey Rooney.

At first rejected by MGM brass, Clark Gable became a leading MGM player in 1931 and gradually rose in polls ranking stars from number 8 in 1932 to 7 in 1933 to 2 in 1934. Gable's consistent popularity was remarkable: 3 in 1935, 2 in 1936, 2 in 1937, 2 in 1939, 3 in 1940, 2 in 1941 and 2 in 1942. During the studio era the only period when he failed to be among the top-ten-ranking stars was when he was in the army. His rugged masculine persona seemed to be just right in 1930s (and 1940s) America. Spencer Tracy ranked second to Gable in long-running star power at MGM. Tracy did not come to MGM until 1935 but from then on he was rarely out of the list of top-ten stars. Never quite as popular or as highly ranked as Gable, Tracy did bring the studio added prestige with his Academy Awards for **Captains Courageous** (1937) and **Boys' Town** (1938). Tracy represented a more sensitive male, straightforward and unpretentious in his screen image, always seeming to underplay his role. He was rarely thought of as a leading man, more a character actor. MGM needed diversity and Tracy gave it to the studio for nearly the length of the studio era.

If Gable and Tracy represented long-run popular screen

65

images, they never topped Mickey Rooney as a short-lived money machine. Rooney ranked as Hollywood's number one star at the box office for three successive years, something Gable and Tracy never achieved. Only Marie Dressler, Shirley Temple and Bing Crosby ever came close. Rooney could not play either a strong, rugged masculine role like Gable, nor a quiet underplayed hero like Tracy. Instead, he stood out as a pint-sized, red-headed ball-of-fire who came to project an image of the American male growing up. Rooney was only 19 when he became the number one star. The Hardy family series, **Boys' Town** and **Babes in Arms** made enormous amounts of money for Loew's, but as soon as

15. Mickey Rooney and Judy Garland in **Babes in Arms** (© 1939 Loew's Inc.)

Rooney's popularity began to fade (with the coming of the Second World War), his career was over. Rooney's films after the war made little money. No one seemed to be able to accept him as a grown-up male. He was released by MGM in 1948 at the age of 28, and soon declared personal bankruptcy. (Meanwhile, Gable and Tracy remained top attractions: Gable was 7, Tracy 9 in the top-ten star-poll in 1948, the year Rooney's contract was terminated.)

The 1940s saw MGM develop fewer stars and hit films. After Rooney in 1941 no MGM star ever again reached number one at the box office in the studio era. Gable and Tracy with career interruptions for the Second World War continued but others seemed to shoot up for a year or two and then quickly fade: Van Johnson, Margaret O'Brien and Esther Williams provide but three examples. The only new MGM star with any degree of

16. Greer Garson and
Lionel Barrymore in
The Valley of Decision
(© 1945 Loew's Inc.)

long-running power was Greer Garson. She was MGM's most popular female star since Marie Dressler in the early 1930s. **Mrs Miniver** (1942), **Random Harvest** (1942), **Madame Curie** (1943), **Mrs Parkington** (1944), **The Valley of Decision** (1945) and **Adventure** (1945) all ranked among the top grossers for their respective movie-seasons. Greer Garson did not become a star until she was in her mid-30s. She did not project the image of a glamorous younger woman; a veteran of the stage, she was typecast as 'Mrs Miniver' – the courageous, moral wife and mother. When she finally escaped from this image, her popularity declined and she quietly retired.

At the tail-end of the studio era MGM took up a new strategy – Technicolor spectacles. Maintaining its conservative posture, Loew's had not taken the lead with color, but in 1938, with **The Wizard of Oz,** it began regularly to produce two or three films per year in Technicolor. The trouble was that these expensive films did not seem to do any better at the box-office than MGM's black-and-white features. **The Wizard of Oz,** for example, lost nearly $1 million upon its initial release. (It went into profit only with re-releases and constant television screenings.) But in 1948 MGM stepped up color production to fully one-fourth of all its features, twelve to fifteen per year, and in the later 1940s MGM accounted for one-third of all feature films in color. The genres for which MGM utilized color were mainly

17. Esther Williams in
On An Island With You
(© 1948 Loew's Inc.)

musicals (**Easter Parade, A Date With Judy**) and Esther Williams spectacles (**On an Island With You**). Films in color came to represent the bulk of the studio's top grossing films. MGM did well with this strategy and deserves some credit for pushing the Hollywood studios into routine production of color films. Indeed, after an extremely poor year in 1948, Loew's increased its profits to an average of more than $6 million per year until 1954, when it spun off its theaters.

The MGM which was producing hit after hit in the early 1930s was continuously presided over by one man, Louis B. Mayer. Mayer, the highest paid American executive in the 1930s, was a central part of the merger which had created MGM. Nicholas Schenck ran Loew's but for the 1930s Mayer was one of the corporation's more valuable employees. He had a great deal of help. The MGM studio was not managed by one man but by a team of specialists, all paid weekly salaries of several thousand dollars. These men, like their counterparts in New York, all stayed on board for very long periods of time, and in most cases their names were unknown to the public. Mayer's most powerful assistants were 'above the credits', for they selected those who could make the films, allocated budgets and resources and approved the final form for release. Directly below Mayer four men constituted the core decision makers: general manager Edgar (Eddie) Mannix, labor relations specialist Benjamin Thau, production specialist Sam Katz and distribution expert Al Lichtman. Mannix joined Mayer in 1925 and kept the organization of the studio going for thirty years. Thau handled labor problems, negotiating contracts with stars and crafts people. He came to MGM from the Loew's front office in 1929 and remained in power until 1956. Katz and Lichtman were former executives with other firms (Paramount and United Artists respectively) who came to Loew's in the mid-1930s and remained until Dore Schary replaced Mayer in 1948. Both were directly responsible to Schenck. Lichtman, in fact, was often critical of Mannix and Mayer's organizational set-up. MGM may have the reputation of being Louis B. Mayer's fiefdom, but in fact Mayer and his assistants made few major moves without first clearing them with Nicholas Schenck.

Below Mayer and his four assistants came the producers in charge of specific units. Each producer could secure individual projects and stars only with Mayer's approval. (Mayer then kept 'hands off' until a print was assembled.) These were the producers who received credit on the film. All producers noted below participated in the profit-sharing plan of the company; less important producers did not:

Harry Rapf (1924–48)	specialist in sentimental films (**The Champ; Lassie** series)
Hunt Stromberg (1924–42)	specialist in dramas and musicals, especially those of Jeanette MacDonald and Nelson Eddy.
Bernard Hyman (1924–42)	supervised jungle films (**Tarzan**) in early 1930s, and later more literary properties (**The Good Earth**)
Lawrence Weingarten (1927–68)	began with comedies (Buster Keaton, Marie Dressler and Polly Moran), and moved to Hepburn–Tracy vehicles.
Mervyn LeRoy (1938–56)	was more noted as a Warners' director. Moved to MGM as producer-director of prestige films. A consistent 'money' producer for the 1940s (**Waterloo Bridge, Madame Curie**).

Two important additions must be made to the above list. The first, David O. Selznick, had put in an apprenticeship with the new MGM in 1926 and 1927. He returned in 1933 as Mayer's son-in-law to substitute for an ailing Irving Thalberg. When Thalberg recovered, Selznick, wanting his own empire, moved on. Thalberg, probably MGM's most famous producer ('the boy wonder') must be considered a special case. Before MGM instituted the unit producer system in 1933, Thalberg and Mayer approved everything. After his illness and return, he became a special-projects producer, more the equal of those noted above. It was Thalberg and his special projects with which MGM gained its reputation for polished elegant craftsmanship: **The Barretts of Wimpole Street** (1934), **Mutiny on the Bounty** (1935) and **Romeo and Juliet** (1936). With his passing in 1936 came the end of the short-lived super-producer position.

The unit producer system took advantage of specialization of labor. The resources from which producers could draw were enormous. The production staff exceeded 6000, with a weekly payroll of half-a-million dollars. The average budget was $500,000. (The **Dr Kildare** and **Hardy** family series cost half the normal amount.) Nothing disrupted the workings of the MGM production system in the late 1930s. Child stars, inspired by Fox's Shirley Temple, were developed: Mickey Rooney, Judy Garland, Freddie Bartholomew and Elizabeth Taylor. In trade for Gable MGM distributed **Gone With the Wind** and made millions. During the Second World War came **Mrs Miniver, Lassie** and Arthur Freed and Joseph Pasternak musicals. MGM fully participated in the Second World War boom, helping push Loew's to record profits in 1946.

But after the boom came problems. A 40 per cent decline in profits during 1947 gave Nicholas Schenck pause. He pushed Mayer to do something extra at MGM. In September 1947 Mayer responded. He fired a quarter of the studio's staff and scrapped the 14-year old unit producer system. Mayer, assisted by Benjamin Thau and Eddie Mannix, would make all decisions. In other words, MGM took on an extremely centralized producing system. But Mayer had little skill as a strong organization man, and in addition he was going through a bitter divorce at the age of 60. Schenck determined the studio needed a new foreman to return MGM to its former glory. Overtures were made to David O. Selznick, Joseph E. Mankiewicz and Walter Wanger; all refused, preferring to pursue careers as independent producers with other studios. The next choice accepted, and so in July 1948 Dore Schary assumed the post of head of production at MGM, replacing Mayer who 'moved upstairs'. Schary had come to Hollywood in 1932 as a contract writer at Columbia and moved to MGM in the mid-1930s. After helping **Boys' Town** win an Academy Award, he turned producer, putting together 'quality-B' films for MGM: **Joe Smith, American** and **Lassie Come Home.**

In 1947 Schary moved to RKO as head of production in the new Howard Hughes regime. (For more on this see Chapter 6.) Schary had intellectual tastes, (Democratic Party) liberal leanings and promised a new and different MGM.

Schary helped to turn MGM around. Realizing where corporate power lay, he never cultivated Louis Mayer's favor. A power struggle ensued, and finally Schenck was forced to act. In July 1951 Mayer 'resigned', but his assistants, Mannix and Thau, stayed. The compromise seemed to work, at least in the short run. Schary's job remained secure for as long as Schenck remained in power, but a system of feature film production controlled by one studio boss – however liberal – was doomed in the 1950s. On the corporate level Schenck clung to the past, endorsing methods which had worked for nearly thirty years. A bitter stockholders' rebellion broke out in 1955, and Schary was gone within the year. No single, powerful executive would replace him. MGM's feature film output gradually declined to the point at which the studio ceased production altogether in 1973. Loew's, through MGM, had tried to force the studio era past 1950 to 1956, and so in the long run was never able fully to adjust to a television world.

However, Loew's always offered exhibitors more than profitable, popular feature films. In the early 1930s Loew's was the distributor of the shorts of the Hal Roach studio. Roach had begun in the 1910s, and by the 1920s was an established producer of comedy. The Roach operation prospered during the coming of sound, partly because of the studio's alliance with Loew's. Roach's comedy stars were tops in their day: Laurel and Hardy, Charley Chase, Thelma Todd, ZaSu Pitts and the children in the **Our Gang** comedies. During the early 1930s Roach did well with monthly series from the aforementioned stars. Such a production schedule guaranteed that Loew's could distribute a new comic short each week, but suddenly Roach seemed unable to develop new stars. By 1935, Hal Roach felt shorts were on their way out (because of double features), and decided to move into feature film production. Some stars stayed with him for features (for example Laurel and Hardy) while others went to work directly for MGM. In 1938 Roach sold the **Our Gang** series to Loew's and set up a formal alliance for feature film-making with United Artists. Loew's continued the 'Our Gang' series until 1944.

In the mid-1930s, Loew's established its own shorts department. As Roach was phased out, this unit, under producer Jack Chertok, phased in more and more indigenous series. MGM, more than the other major corporations, used its shorts unit to train and test talent for features. Robert Taylor, James Stewart and Judy Garland all began in short films. Directors Fred Zinnemann, John Farrow, Joseph Losey and Jules Dassin all learned from their experience in the short film unit. The longest running in-house shorts series was 'Pete Smith Specialties'. Smith, a former studio press agent, established a style which integrated stop-printing, running footage backwards or upside down and narrating with puns and verbal twists. After first doing two sports series, he satirized his own industry with 'Goofy Movies'. In 1935 Smith regularized his output, producing one short per month from 1935 through 1955 – with no interruptions. 'Pete Smith Specialties' earned twenty Academy Award nominations and two Oscars. In 1935, 1938 and 1941 he created 3-D short films. But the typical Smith short film dealt with everything from ordinary experiences (make-up application, bounced checks, amateur radio) and 'how-to' instruction (bowling, archery, cooking) to interviews with famous athletes. The series remained popular well into the 1950s and was only terminated with the coming of television and the retirement of Smith.

Loew's developed numerous other series. Probably second in popularity to 'Pete Smith Specialties' was 'Crime Does Not Pay' (1935–47). Releasing one short every other month, this series earned two Academy Awards. The narrative of each centered on the exposure of how a racket was 'duping' the public. This type of exposé is more usually associated with Warner Bros., but in the long run MGM gathered publicity mileage from this crime series. (FBI chief, J. Edgar Hoover, often testified to its positive value.) During the Second World War the series turned its attention to uncovering fifth columnists and Nazi spies. 'Crime Does Not Pay' ended in 1947 as the studio cut back on more expensive short series.

No other series lasted as long as either 'Pete Smith Specialties' or 'Crime Does Not Pay'. Robert Benchley surfaced at MGM twice for shorts: 1935–4, and 1943–4. Gossip flowed from 'Jimmy Fidler's Personality Parade' during the 1930s. There were numerous travelogues as well. Loew's took particular care regularly to present musical reels with MGM's new musical vocal talent plus noted big bands of the day. With the studio's direct connection with music publishing and phonograph records, Loew's pushed hard to develop popular songs and new musical talent. The short subject was an efficient, cheap way to test the market and exploit fads and trends.

During the early 1930s Loew's contracted with others for animated shorts. MGM developed no cartoon unit during the silent era, and seemed to ignore animation until the success of the

Disney studio in 1929. Then Loew's tried to work out an agreement to distribute for Disney, but never succeeded. So Loew's went after the next best alternative, Disney's head animator, and the rumored 'genius' behind the Disney magic, Ub Iwerks. Iwerks designed Flip the Frog, which Loew's hoped would become as famous as Mickey Mouse. Such success never came. Flip lasted into 1933 before Iwerks tried Willie Whopper, a human figure distinguished by his ability to tell outrageous lies, but after a year and fourteen cartoons, Loew's abandoned the character.

In 1934 Loew's signed as his replacement Hugh Harman and Rudolph Ising. Like Iwerks, Harman and Ising had started with Disney. From 1930 to 1933 they co-produced 'Looney Tunes' and 'Merrie Melodies' for Leon Schlesinger and distributed through Warner Bros. Loew's agreed to double their Warners budgets and the two agreed to produce eight to twelve color cartoons per year under the title (which aped Disney's 'Silly Symphonies') of 'Happy Harmonies'. These had to be done in two-strip Technicolor since Disney owned exclusive rights to three-strip Technicolor until 1935. But 'Happy Harmonies' also did not go over very well. There were other sporadic attempts to create a star to match Mickey Mouse. None ever worked out. Other studios, especially Paramount with Popeye, seemed to be making greater progress. So in 1937, admitting failure for a second time, Loew's terminated the Harman and Ising agreement.

For the third attempt, Loew's created an in-house animation unit. To shore-up relations with exhibitors, Loew's placed Fred Quimby, a man with a background in exhibition, not animation, in charge. Quimby, in turn, hired away a good portion of the Harman and Ising staff, as well as others from the Terrytowns studio in New York. From this latter group came two men who eventually turned MGM into a power in the cartoon field: William Hanna and Joseph Barbera. Success, however, did not come until 1940, when Hanna and Barbera introduced Tom (the cat) and Jerry (the mouse). This duo became cartoon stars who could rival Mickey Mouse, Donald Duck, Popeye (Paramount), and Bugs Bunny (Warners). Their 'Puss Gets the Boot', released in February 1940, was held over in several theaters and was nominated for an Academy Award. With this success, Hanna and Barbera produced nothing but Tom and Jerry cartoons for the next fifteen years. In a ten-year period, 1943 to 1952, 'Tom and Jerry' earned seven Oscars. No other continuing series ever won as many within one decade except Disney's 'Silly Symphonies'. At last MGM had achieved profits in the field of animation to rival its achievements in feature films. Even the critics applauded 'Tom and Jerry' especially those shorts created by Tex Avery, and 'appearances' by the duo highlighted several MGM features: **Anchors Away, Holiday in Mexico** and **Dangerous When Wet.**

MGM's animation unit roared into the 1950s on the continuing strength of 'Tom and Jerry', but with the decline of the studio system Quimby began to seek ways to trim costs. Running times were cut from eight to six minutes, but since demand was going down as theaters closed, it was only a matter of time before Loew's shut down its cartoon unit. Quimby retired in 1955, the same year that all MGM cartoons went to wide-screen. Hanna and Barbera took charge – temporarily. In the spring of 1957, Loew's closed the unit. This timing may have been the luckiest thing ever for Hanna and Barbera. They used their management experience to open their own studio, probably the most successful (from a business point of view) in US television history. Ironically, later when the new MGM (separated from Loew's) tried to return to cartoons – this time for television – it was unable to compete successfully with former employees Hanna and Barbera.

As with its other shorts series, at first Loew's also looked outside the corporation to find the newsreels necessary to round out the package of entertainment which it offered to exhibitors. In 1927 Loew's agreed to distribute the Hearst newsreel, one of the oldest in the business; during the early 1920s Hearst had distributed through Universal with little success. (The boss, William Randolph Hearst, had transferred his Cosmopolitan Pictures organization to the newly-formed MGM in 1925 so the newsreel alliance, coming two years later, was not unexpected.) With the coming of sound, Hearst produced two versions exclusively for MGM: the silent 'MGM International Newsreel' and its sound counterpart, 'Hearst Metrotone News'. The silent version passed out in 1931 and Hearst retitled its service 'News of the Day'. Thereafter this newsreel was solely identified as an MGM product, even though the Hearst organization continued to produce it. The newsreel did a serviceable job throughout the 1930s, 1940s and 1950s. In the television era 'News of the Day' tried to form an alliance with television (it supplied footage to Edward R. Murrow's 'See It Now'). But the onrush of network news operations signaled the end of the newsreel. 'News of the Day' continued until November 1967 (January 1968 overseas).

In 1954 Loew's became the last of the Big Five to set up an exhibition subsidiary and transfer all domestic theaters to it. Loew's, with a $30 million debt to divide between production-distribution (the new MGM) and exhibition (the new Loew's), did not complete divorcement until March 1959, nearly ten years after the Supreme Court decision. This recalcitrant behavior turned out to be a mistake. While Paramount, Fox and Warners, as producer-distributors, quickly rebounded from the divorcement of their theaters, the still-integrated Loew's profitability continued to slide. With Schenck's retirement the situation did improve, but the new MGM moved on to a profit roller-coaster. Management changed constantly. Meanwhile Loew's diversified and became a conglomerate. In 1969, MGM under new owner Kirk Kerkorian, developed MGM Grand Hotels. MGM stopped distribution in 1973; resumed again in 1979 when the hotels were spun off; absorbed United Artists in 1981; and now faces a rocky road toward a future with cable- and pay-television in the 1980s. The years since 1954 can be seen as the direct antithesis of the stable, consistently profitable world of Loew's Inc. during the studio era.

4:

20th Century-Fox

The third most successful motion picture corporation of the studio era, in terms of profits, was the Fox Film Corporation. In 1935 Fox merged with 20th Century to become the now famous 20th Century-Fox. (To avoid confusion, hereafter the corporation will be referred to as Fox. This means Fox Film before 1935 and 20th Century-Fox thereafter.) Fox nearly failed in the early 1930s, but with the revitalization provided by Joseph Schenck and Darryl F. Zanuck's Twentieth Century Pictures profits increased steadily, peaking in 1946. By the mid-1940s Fox had climbed to a place in the industry competitive with Loew's and Paramount, returning the corporation to the glory and profits Fox had first experienced with its successful innovation of sound. Fox achieved this renaissance not under the leadership of William Fox, who was forced to retire in the early 1930s, but with Sidney Kent (1932–42), Joseph Schenck (1935–41) and Spyros Skouras (1942–52) handling the distribution and exhibition end in New York and Darryl F. Zanuck (1935–56) handling production at the Westwood studios in Los Angeles. This degree of management continuity paralleled Paramount (under Balaban and Freeman), Loew's (Schenck and Mayer), Warners (brothers Harry, Abe, and Jack) and Columbia (brothers Jack and Harry Cohn). Fox's experience was closest to that of Paramount – revitalization under strong management after a disastrous journey through the Great Depression.

Also like Paramount, the origins of the Fox corporation began with the founding of the American film industry at the turn of the century. William Fox was born in Tulchva, Hungary in 1879

Table 4.1: Fox's Balance Sheet

Year	Net Profit (millions of dollars)	Assets (millions of dollars)
1930	6.5	173.2
1931	(2.3)	138.5
1932	(9.2)	81.9
1933	1.7	45.9*
1934	1.4	46.8*
1935	3.5	54.2*
1936	7.7	56.8*
1937	8.6	60.4*
1938	7.3	60.7*
1939	4.2	58.8*
1940	(0.5)	58.9*
1941	4.9	66.3*
1942	10.6	76.3*
1943	14.4	132.4
1944	15.1	145.3
1945	15.7	149.0
1946	25.3	163.4
1947	15.9	164.1
1948	13.8	168.7
1949	13.5	172.7

*Theaters held by separate corporation National Theaters Inc.

and came to the United States with his family shortly thereafter. After a brief tenure in the New York City public schools, Fox tried the garment trade, but with little success. Like contemporaries Marcus Loew and Adolph Zukor, Fox found better opportunities in the new motion picture business. His first theater was opened in New York City in 1904. Buoyed by new-found riches, Fox began to build a chain of theaters. At this point, his career path diverges from those of Loew (who went into vaudeville) and Zukor (who almost took over the movie industry). Fox Metropolitan Theaters grew rather slowly, so that by 1920 it consisted of only twenty-five houses, all located within the New York City environs. During these early years of slow growth, Fox gained its greatest fame for its challenge of the Motion Pictures Patents Trust. Fox thereby expended a great deal of its resources, finally suing and winning several court battles. Gradually, of course, the stranglehold of the Patents Trust was broken.

18. William Fox (l.) and F.W. Murnau in April 1928 as Murnau leaves for Germany after completing *Sunrise*

His experience with the Motion Picture Patents Company convinced William Fox that he had to push his fledgling exhibition company into film production and distribution. For a time in the early 1910s Fox rented a studio in Fort Lee, New Jersey, and produced half a dozen films. The Fox Film Corporation, set up to produce and distribute films, officially opened for business in 1915. That same year Fox Film developed its first star, Theda Bara. Now fully participating in the industry's expansion during the late 1910s, Fox Film grew more quickly. In 1917 it opened its first studio in Hollywood, at Sunset and Western. In 1919 a combined studio and headquarters building in New York City was acquired. Net earnings increased from $500,000 in 1915 to over $2,500,000 in 1924. Fox became a public corporation, but despite consistent growth lagged far behind giants Famous Players and Loew's. Like Warner Bros. and Universal (discussed in later chapters) Fox occupied a slot amongst mid-sized competitors in an industry increasingly becoming a duopoly controlled by Famous Players and Loew's.

Fox, along with Warners, innovated motion pictures with sound and the two rapidly grew in size and profit potential to match Paramount (the former Famous Players) and Loew's. Fox formulated a plan for expansion in 1925. By marketing $6 million worth of common stock, the corporation was able to increase budgets for feature films and enlarge its successful newsreel division. Fox was a leader in newsreel production and distribution at a time when Paramount and Loew's did not offer such a product to exhibitors. But Fox's major corporate thrust came through a newly-titled subsidiary, Fox Theaters. Fox set out to acquire and build a national chain of first-run motion picture theaters; at that time Fox still controlled only twenty-five houses in the New York City environs. In July 1925 a one-third interest in West Coast Theaters was acquired, guaranteeing access to the best theaters in the state of California. By 1927 the Fox chain included grand picture palaces in Philadelphia, Washington DC, Brooklyn, New York City, St Louis, Detroit, Milwaukee and a score of cities west of the Rockies. Its flagship was the Roxy – in the heart of Manhattan's Times Square. Fox had moved very quickly to develop a chain of theaters which could challenge, although not yet match, the collections of Paramount and Loew's. What was needed were special attractions to fill these theaters.

Fox has not been given much credit for its pioneering efforts in the innovation of sound, but its introduction of sound-on-film helped the corporation to expand to become a member of the Big Five. Fox initially took on the new technology because executives reasoned it might help to sell newsreels. Innovation began in July 1926 with the formation of the Fox-Case corporation. Inventor Theodore Case tendered several crucial patents. Fox-Case added more by acquiring the rights to the German Tri-Ergon system and by contracting for amplification equipment from the Western Electric subsidiary of American Telephone and Telegraph. Sound newsreels provided a way in which Fox could gradually perfect necessary new techniques of camerawork and editing and test consumer interest at minimal risk. Fox's strong newsreel division continued to produce and distribute silent newsreels, so even if revenues from alternatives with sound did not exceed costs, the corporation would lose little. Warners was utilizing the same sort of business strategy, quite successfully, with its sound recording of vaudeville and musical acts.

On 30 April 1927, Fox premiered its first sound newsreel. At the corporation's flagship house, the Roxy in New York, Fox presented a four-minute reel of cadets marching at West Point. This first Movietone newsreel drew an enthusiastic response from the trade press and New York-based motion-picture reviewers. Soon after, Fox Movietone was able to seize upon one of the more important symbolic news events of this century. At 8 a.m. on 20 May 1927, Charles Lindbergh departed for Paris. That evening Fox Movietone News presented footage of the take-off – with sound – to a packed house (6200 persons) at the Roxy theater. The throng stood and cheered for nearly ten minutes. The press saluted this new motion-picture marvel and noted how it had brought alive the heroics of the 'Lone Eagle'. In June Lindbergh returned to tumultuous welcomes in New York City and Washington DC. Fox Movietone News cameramen recorded portions of those celebrations on film and Fox Film distributed a ten-minute Movietone newsfilm to the few theaters equipped for sound. Again, press response proved overwhelming. Fox had launched onto a propitious path of technological innovation.

That summer, Fox sent cameramen to all parts of the globe. They recorded the further heroics of aviators, harmonica contests, beauty pageants and sporting events, as well as the earliest sound-film statements of public figures such as Benito Mussolini, Al Smith and Admiral Richard Byrd. Newspaper columnists, educators and other opinion leaders hailed these latter short subjects for their didactic value and wide appeal. Fox Film's principal constraint now was the paucity of exhibition outlets. During the fall of 1927 Fox Film made Movietone newsreels the standard in all Fox-owned theaters, but that represented only a tiny portion of the market. (To be able to reap more extensive profits, Fox further accelerated its push to create a larger and larger chain of first-run theaters.) By 1928, Fox had established a regular release of Movietone newsreels – one ten-minute reel per week. It also increased the permanent staff of cameramen and laboratory employees and developed a world-wide reticulation of stringers.

Fox was now in a position to round out its innovation of sound. It began to produce vaudeville shorts and feature films with synchronized musical accompaniment. Before 1928, only one feature with a musical sound track had been released – **Sunrise.** Fox moved quickly, and by 1 January 1928 it had signed up a dozen major vaudeville artists (including Eddie Cantor), filmed ten vaudeville shorts, and even announced a part-talkie feature, **Blossom Time.** During the spring of 1928 these efforts, Fox's newsreels and Warners' shorts and feature films (one of which was **The Jazz Singer**), proved to be the hits of the movie season. Thus in March 1928, William Fox declared that fully 25 per cent of the forthcoming production schedule would be 'Movietoned'. By May 1928 he was confident enough to raise that figure to 100 per cent. Simultaneously Fox continued to wire for sound all the houses in its rapidly expanding chain as quickly as possible and drew up plans for an all-sound Hollywood-based studio.

Throughout the crucial year of 1928, Fox continued to

exploit its comparative advantage in newsreels with sound. As Paramount and Loew's braved the conversion to talkies, Fox Movietone News increased its weekly output to two 'issues' per week. In June it had twenty-seven Movietone units in the field; by October the number reached forty. In January 1929, there were fifty, with thirty-five for US news, and fifteen for the rest of the world. During the fall of 1929 output reached its apex with the release of four separate newsreel editions per week, produced by seventy crews stationed round the world. The theater division even opened America's first all-newsreel theater, the Embassy, in the heart of New York's Time Square, and most important for company profits, Movietone was able to sign hundreds of theaters to five-year exclusive agreements for Fox newsreels – at rates double those for silent newsreel competitors. The dominant US theater chains quickly acceded to these stiff terms. Only Paramount and Loew's possessed the economic muscle to be able to resist and wait for their own recently-formed newsreel divisions to catch up with Movietone News and create newsreels with sound.

Fox wisely pressed its advantage in newsreels, because in the other motion-picture forms – all-talking features, and vaudeville shorts – Fox had little leverage. Warner Bros. switched completely to all-sound features by September 1928; Fox did not release its first all-talkie feature film until four months later. By then, even Paramount and MGM were producing all-talking features. (The rest of the motion picture industry trailed Warners, Fox, Paramount and MGM by six months.) In particular, for vaudeville shorts Fox was for a time the only firm with the facilities and technical staff to compete effectively with Warners. Yet Fox quickly learned that in fact this segment of the market for all-sound motion picture entertainment offered little real profit potential. Wisely Warner Bros. had early signed the most popular vaudeville musical performers to exclusive long-term contracts. Fox Film, not wanting to go with second-rate talent, quickly phased out the production of vaudeville shorts, releasing its last one in May 1930. Again, only Paramount and Loew's commanded the resources necessary to challenge Warner Bros. and these three controlled the market for vaudeville shorts well into the 1930s.

Building on all phases of its expansionary strategy, the popularity of sound films rapidly thrust Fox Film toward the acme of the US motion-picture industry. The corporation aggressively reinvested all profits and borrowed the maximum available during the economic distension of the 'Roaring Twenties'. On 28 October 1928 Movietone City opened. This all-sound facility, located in the then distant Los Angeles suburb of Westwood, California, included a $10 million plant which had taken 1500 workers in three shifts (24 hours a day, seven days a week) only four months to build. Fox's largest commitment of resources was to theaters. Fox took over theater chains in New England, New York, New Jersey, California, Wisconsin, and the Pacific North-West. Funds came from the Halsey Stuart banking house and Western Electric. The latter knew that for every theater Fox acquired, Western Electric sound equipment, cross-licensed with Fox-Case patents, would be installed. Western Electric and Fox Film worked closely together during 1928 and 1929. At the pinnacle of its power in 1930, Fox controlled 532 theaters in the United States and 450 overseas – second in size only to the Paramount-Publix chain.

The independent, egocentric William Fox now neared the top of an industry he had helped to found. In fact, events momentarily pushed his enterprise past even Paramount to become the world's largest and potentially most profitable film company. In 1927 the founder of Loew's, Marcus Loew, died. Soon thereafter, as noted in Chapter 3, the Loew family indicated that its one-third interest in Loew's Inc. was for sale at the current stock market price – $28 million. That proved to be too large an investment for any entrepreneur in the US film industry – except William Fox. Intoxicated by recent successes, Fox maneuvered to purchase a controlling interest in Loew's by securing the shares of the Loew family plus shares from Loew's top officers (collected and tendered by president Nicholas Schenck) and shares bought on the open market. On 3 March 1929, William Fox held a press conference and announced the Fox-Loew's amalgamation. Fox-Loew's controlled the largest motion-picture production-distribution enterprise in the world, owned more than 1000 theaters and foresaw nearly unlimited profit potential. In five years, Fox had pioneered a sound-on-film process and parlayed that into the creation of the world's largest motion picture corporation.

But the stock market crash of 1929 and the subsequent economic depression hit Fox very hard. Problems first arose when President Herbert Hoover installed his new administration in the summer of 1929. The new Justice Department did not approve of the Fox takeover of Loew's, and so on 27 November 1929 filed suit against Fox under section seven of the Clayton anti-trust act. As noted in chapter 3, Fox signed a consent decree in 1931 agreeing to divest itself of all Loew's stock. Part of the reason the Justice Department had singled out Fox was the enormous amount of unfavorable publicity generated by its financial problems. After taking over Loew's, Fox added the Gaumont British Pictures Corporation to its empire, bringing some 300 theaters located in all parts of the United Kingdom into the Fox chain. The cost, $14 million in cash and $6 million in notes due in six months, made Fox's short-term debt position untenable. Moreover, a serious automobile accident on 17 July 1929 removed William Fox from direct personal supervision of this vast new enterprise. The company's debt position gradually worsened and the corporation reached a critical financial juncture immediately after the stock market crash in October 1929.

Fox took action in November 1929, selling its share in First National to Warners for $10 million in cash, but Fox's financial obligations required the corporation to generate even more cash. Accordingly, William Fox approached the two men who had helped so often in the past – John Otterson of AT&T and Harold Stuart of the investment banking firm of Halsey Stuart. William Fox proposed to place the corporation's affairs in the hands of a board of trustees consisting of himself, Otterson and Stuart. Otterson and Stuart only consented because William Fox reluctantly agreed to turn over complete control of Fox-Loew's to the trustees. Immediately, AT&T and Halsey Stuart endorsed $4 million in short-term notes to enable Fox to repay debts for three more months. Otterson and Stuart planned to work – and vote – as one, relegating William Fox to minority status in the company he had founded more than twenty-five years before. Fox quickly hustled to acquire more co-operative allies. He seemed to find them in the Bancamerica-Blair group, which included bankers Elisha Walker, Clarence Dillon and A P Giannini. In January and February of 1930 he negotiated a plan to refinance Fox Film for $65 million through this syndicate. Otterson and Stuart, of course, would not agree to the plan. (Further complicating the situation, three Fox stockholders sued to force Fox Film into bankruptcy.) The whole matter went into court. In the meantime, Stuart and Otterson filed an alternative proposal for refinancing the Fox companies. On 5 March 1930, the day the Fox stockholders were to decide between the two refinancing plans, the court ruled that Stuart and Otterson held majority ownership. However, the Fox stockholders meeting chose to ignore the decision and let William Fox vote his own shares, and the Bancamerica-Blair financing plan was approved. Otterson and Stuart filed suit. Meanwhile, complex informal negotiations were begun among all parties.

On 8 April 1930, the matter was finally settled. Otterson and Stuart triumphed. William Fox sold his share (a controlling interest) to Harley C. Clarke, President of General Theaters Equipment, a close friend of Harold Stuart. (William Fox bowed out with $18 million plus a contract as special advisor at $500,000 per year for five years.) AT&T chipped in with a $5 million loan to help refinance the company's debts. It would take one more year to work out all the refinancing details, but, for the corporation, the damage was already done. Fox staggered into the Great Depression in the worst shape of any of the Big Five. Valiantly, Harley Clarke tried to put all the financial and corporate pieces together, but during 1931 and 1932 Fox's losses rose to nearly $11.5 million. Mortgages were called due, and so in 1933 Wesco, the holding company for the theaters, went into receivership. Reorganized a year later as the National Theaters Corporation, the former Fox theaters were finally cleared of debts. The court awarded the new Fox Film a 42 per cent interest in National Theaters. In 1943, Fox formally re-absorbed its former chain, although from 1934 it had operated National Theaters for the chain's other stockholders.

Fox's theaters had almost, but not quite, bankrupted the company. Fox Film, a shell of its former self, was still a vast multinational operation. In 1936 it controlled forty-two different subsidiaries, two of which represented real estate holdings in Los Angeles and New York City studios. The studio in Los Angeles comprised some 100 acres with stages, power plants, developing and printing facilities and an administration building. In New York, a separate facility housed production and editing of newsreels as well as corporate world headquarters. Fox operated thirty-one film exchanges in the United States (two wholly-owned their buildings) and 116 exchanges overseas. These foreign subsidiaries, incorporated in more than thirty countries in the world, served all countries except the USSR. Throughout the 1930s and 1940s the corporation also maintained an active interest in overseas production and exhibition. As already noted, Fox owned a share of the Gaumont organization in England, with its complete production unit and some 300 theaters. In addition, Fox controlled the Hoyts Circuit, dominant in Australia throughout the studio era. Fox also maintained theaters in New Zealand and South Africa.

Through National Theaters, Fox controlled more than 500 US movie houses. Because of its take-over of the West Coast circuit in the 1920s, most were located west of Denver, except for concentrations in Kansas, western Nebraska, Missouri and Wisconsin. Thus, among America's largest cities Fox held dominion in Los Angeles (5th largest US city in 1940), San Francisco (12th),

Milwaukee (13th), Kansas City (19th), Seattle (22nd), Denver (25th) and Portland, Oregon (26th). Because Fox came so late to theater acquisition, it was not able to establish control in as many major cities as Paramount. Fox did establish a presence in a number of cities by constructing a major first-run movie palace downtown and trying to take away a significant market share from another member of the Big Five. That corporate strategy never worked very well, and was brought to a halt by the corporation's financial woes of the early 1930s. Still, throughout the studio era Fox did maintain a limited presence in the following cities: Philadelphia (3rd largest US city in 1940 census), Detroit (4th), Oakland (28th), San Diego (43rd), Long Beach, California (53rd), Spokane, Washington (68th), Wichita, Kansas (74th) and Sacramento, California (85th). In 1927 Fox had acquired one of America's most famous theaters, the Roxy. The Roxy went into bankruptcy in 1932 and was reorganized and sold in 1937. That year Fox signed a twenty-year rental franchise to guarantee that all Fox films would play at the Roxy, usually receiving their world premiere there.

Fox had other motion-picture and non-motion-picture interests. Fox Movietone News maintained offices in New York, London, Paris and Sydney, Australia and from there dispatched numerous stringers around the world. These offices also dubbed 'Movietone News' narration into nineteen different languages. Like Paramount, Loew's and Warner Bros., Fox maintained a strong position in music publishing through four subsidiaries. For a time in the late 1930s Fox underwrote Broadway plays through its New Art Plays Inc. subsidiary. Fox invested in the Scophony Corporation of America in 1943, a manufacturer of large screen television equipment. On a much more limited scale than Paramount, Fox unsuccessfully tried to gain a foothold in the emerging television business after the Second World War. It applied for television licenses in New York and Los Angeles, but failed to secure either. Once the Federal Communications Commission decided the Big Five should not be granted licenses until the Paramount anti-trust case was decided, Fox quickly withdrew and, except for a half-hearted bid in 1948 to buy the American Broadcasting Company, did not explore other opportunities.

Despite this formidable set of assets, Fox traversed a rough road through the 1930s. Management, which had turned over several times, constantly struggled with the difficulties of financial underpinnings, of theaters and a seeming inability to produce popular films. William Fox's replacement as president and chief operating officer, Harley Clarke, was a former mid-western utilities mogul, protégé of noted Chicago utilities czar Samuel Insull. Clarke had first come to the attention of Fox's owners through his interest in Grandeur, a widescreen process which Fox tried in 1930. Clarke agreed to try to straighten out Fox's financial problems in part to protect his investment in Grandeur. He felt he could 'clean up' the mess by applying techniques of scientific business management which had worked so well in the utilities industry. But as Otterson discovered five years later at Paramount, standard business practices did not always work in the motion picture business. During the Great Depression they produced only debt. Clarke resigned in 1931, after only one year on the job.

In 1931 Fox was floundering in a financial morass. Logically enough, the board of directors turned to a man with financial experience and appointed as president Edward R. Tinker, former board chairman of the Chase National Bank. Tinker turned in an even worse performance than his predecessor. Losses continued to climb and the theater division had to file for bankruptcy. Within a year, Tinker was gone. Neither a former utility executive nor a bank chairman had been able to save the ailing corporation; possibly a veteran of the movie business might. Sidney Kent was available, having recently resigned his position as head of distribution at Paramount in 1932. Throughout the 1920s Kent had been one of the driving forces behind Paramount's rise to power. In that decade he had reorganized its world film distribution. Kent resigned early in 1932 during Paramount's own reorganization. The Fox presidency offered him the power he had never been able to secure at Paramount. Kent's considerable managerial skills enabled Fox acually to turn a profit in 1933; he helped to reorganize the theater division and put distribution back on the right track. What Kent needed were popular films to sell. Toward this goal he repeatedly clashed with long-time studio boss and survivor from the William Fox days, Winfield Sheehan. In 1935, Kent began actively to seek new management for Fox's West Coast studio.

Kent did not have to work very hard at this task, easily luring Darryl Zanuck and Joseph Schenck away from United Artists. Zanuck, who had joined Warners in 1924 as a screenwriter, rapidly moved up the ladder at that expanding studio, but had resigned his post as production executive in 1933. He had developed a reputation as a producer of gangster films and fast-paced musicals. **Little Caesar** (1930) and **Public Enemy** (1931) started the gangster cycle and **42nd Street** (1932) proved to be the

19. Darryl Zanuck
(second from r.) being
presented with an
illuminated address by
Sidney Kent

musical hit of that Depression year. Zanuck knew when he left
Warners that he would be able to solicit offers from other studios.
The most tempting came from Joseph Schenck, head of United
Artists. Schenck proposed that they should team up to produce
films for UA. Such a deal seemed to guarantee Zanuck an outlet
with the maximum creative freedom allowable in the studio
system – nearly the opposite of the situation under which he had
worked at Warners. With financial support from Schenck's
brother Nicholas (then president of Loew's) Twentieth Century
Pictures was formed in April 1933 in the depths of the Great
Depression.

Twentieth Century Pictures started off with some real
successes. Of the twelve features produced and released in its first
season, spanning the years 1933 and 1934, nine did extremely well
at the box-office. United Artists had expedited the necessary
financing and studio space. Nicholas Schenck lent the new
competitor two of MGM's leading players, Spencer Tracy and
Wallace Beery. As discussed in more detail in Chapter 9,
Twentieth Century helped United Artists to achieve near-record
profits in the otherwise dismal year of 1934. But one thing UA's
directors would not do was to admit Twentieth Century to full
partnership status. Mary Pickford, Sam Goldwyn, Douglas
Fairbanks and Charlie Chaplin, the full UA partners, all agreed
that Twentieth Century's contributions should be encouraged,

but not to the point of sharing dividends and control. Frustrated, Joseph Schenck resigned and he and Zanuck sought to merge their successful production operation into a Big Five company. Kent approached Schenck and in May 1935 a merger, through an exchange of stock, was effected. Joseph Schenck became Fox's chairman of the board at $130,000 per year; Kent remained president at $180,000 per year; Zanuck was elevated to vice-president in charge of production at $260,000 per year. (The new company paid Winfield Sheehan $360,000 to resign.) 20th Century-Fox was off and running as a viable corporate entity.

The management triad of Schenck, Kent and Zanuck boosted Fox's profits and the company began to grow again. Unfortunately, this management trio lost two members within six years. In 1941, Joseph Schenck went to jail. This extraordinary situation was precipitated by a union, the International Alliance of Theatrical Stage Employees and Moving Picture Operators (IA). IA possessed enormous power because all US projectionists belonged to it. This union could, in one gesture, shut off the source of revenues for the entire motion-picture industry. In the 1930s George Browne and Willie Bioff from Chicago assumed command of IA. Theatening to disrupt (or close) theaters of the Big Five, Browne and Bioff began to extort bribes. Joseph Schenck, representing the Big Five, dealt directly with Browne and Bioff. The exchange was straightforward. IA would keep its wage demands low and 'provide safety' in the theaters for $50,000 per year from each of the Big Five. More than $1 million passed hands during the late 1930s. The racket was eventually exposed and Bioff, Browne and five others were sent to jail. In complex court proceedings, Joseph Schenck was convicted of tax evasion and served four months and five days in a federal prison in Danbury, Connecticut. Schenck returned to Fox in 1944 and was immediately reappointed to the board of directors, but from then on he stayed out of the limelight, operating from behind the scenes as producer and industry gadfly.

In 1941, Sidney Kent died suddenly of a heart attack aged 56. With Schenck unavailable, a power vacuum was created at the top of 20th Century-Fox. A person with experience in distribution and exhibition was needed. The board of directors promoted Spyros Skouras, then head of Fox Metropolitan Theaters. Skouras, a Greek immigrant, with his brothers Charles and George had built a chain of theaters in the St Louis metropolitan area. By 1926, they controlled thirty-seven houses in St Louis and, in collaboration with Paramount Publix, addition- al theaters in Kansas City and Indianapolis. In 1929, the

). Spyros Skouras
:entre) with Eddie
isher (l.) and
lizabeth Taylor

Skourases cashed in, selling their theaters to Warner Bros. During the Great Depression Spyros Skouras became an expert in salvaging heavily mortgaged theaters, first for Paramount, then for Fox Metropolitan theaters in New York. In 1932, the three brothers teamed up once again to try to save the Fox-controlled Wesco chain, the bulk of Fox's theater holdings. Wesco was reorganized in 1934 into the National Theater Corporation. Skouras then stayed on with National Theaters. In fact, one of his first actions as Fox's president was to reacquire the chain, giving Fox complete control until 1951, when the theaters were spun off as part of the Paramount case decision.

Skouras operated best behind the scenes, squeezing maximum profits from distribution and exhibition. A more well-known figure was needed to represent the company for intercorporate and public matters. In April 1942 Wendell L. Wilkie, the Republican candidate for president in 1940, became chairman of the board of 20th Century-Fox. During the 1930s, lawyer Wilkie had done legal work for the Motion Picture Producers and Distributors Association as well as for 20th Century-Fox. Wilkie served as more than a figurehead in his two years as chairman. (He died at age 52 in 1944.) In 1943 he sold the rights in his best-selling book, **One World,** to Fox. Lamar Trotti completed a script, but the film was never made. (In 1945 with Wilkie dead, it did not seem right or proper.) Immediately upon Wilkie's death, Spyros Skouras ascended to the position of chief operating officer with no chairman – not even a figurehead – listed above him. Throughout the remainder of the studio era Skouras supervised from New York while his brother Charles handled the day-to-day theater operations. All the while Darryl F. Zanuck ran 20th Century-Fox production in California. From 1935 until well past the end of the studio era, Zanuck, unchallenged, controlled Fox's film-making. Zanuck deserves his reputation as a ruthless studio boss; he was as powerful as anyone in Hollywood, maintaining this position through all the changes in management above him.

Analyzing the film-making strategy at Fox during the studio era is a straight-forward process since there were only two production bosses, Winfield Sheehan and Darryl Zanuck.

21. Winfield Sheehan receiving an award

Sheehan, a former newspaper man and New York City politician, joined up with William Fox in 1914. He organized the original Fox Hollywood studio and during the late 1920s he alone represented Fox on the west coast. Sheehan certainly must be given part of the credit for the corporation's meteoric rise during the late 1920s. He did not fare as well during the doldrums of the 1930s. His solution to the downturn in attendance was to step up the production of genre films of an epic scale. Early on, he seemed brilliant. **The Big Trail** grossed $1.5 million in 1930. (Unfortunately, it cost $2 million.) But as the Great Depression deepened, even larger losses became commonplace. Moreover, the studio began to lose valuable talent to more stable, prosperous studios. Apart from **Cavalcade** (1932), few popular feature films were produced.

Such success as Fox enjoyed in the early 1930s came with features starring either Will Rogers or Shirley Temple. Rogers was Fox's first important star of the talkie era. From 1929 until his untimely death in 1935 Rogers turned out an extraordinary string of popular films, especially surprising considering the state of the Fox corporation. The star popularity polls reflected his steady rise. In 1932 he finished 9th (of ten). Then came a 2nd in 1933, 1st in 1934, and 2nd (to Shirley Temple) in 1935. It had not always been thus. Rogers' career began as a star of Wild West shows and then moved to vaudeville and the Ziegfeld Follies. The cornerstone of his success was his ability to tell droll anecdotes in what today would be labelled a comic monologue. It seems, in retrospect, understandable that Rogers would fail in silent films. A two-year cycle (1919–20) for Sam Goldwyn went nowhere as did efforts for Paramount and Hal Roach. The coming of sound (and Winfield Sheehan) enabled Rogers to become a movie star. Rogers gradually developed the role of 'Uncle Will', the down home, country hero, until a plane crash in Alaska cut short an altogether remarkable movie career. Rogers never worked for Zanuck, the plane crash taking place even before his final film, **Steamboat Round the Bend** (1935), was released.

22. Will Rogers (l.) in **Steamboat Round The Bend** (courtesy 20th Century-Fox)

Shirley Temple spanned the Sheehan–Zanuck epochs. She stood as the number one star in the United States in 1935 and maintained that lofty rank in 1936, 1937 and 1938. Unfortunately for Fox, Shirley Temple grew up and fell to 5th place in 1939 (when aged 11), and out of the top ten the next year, never to return. Her mother had pushed little Shirley. By the time she was four she was appearing in short films for Educational Studios,

distributed exclusively by Fox. Shirley Temple followed the trail
blazed by successful child-stars of the 1920s – Jackie Coogan,
Jackie Cooper and the children in Hal Roach's 'Our Gang'. At
first, Educational put Shirley in its version of 'Our Gang', 'Baby
Burlesks', where children parodied adult movie stars. Shirley
Temple moved up to features in 1934 (when she was 6) with **Stand
Up and Cheer.** Then the hits came, as if off an assembly-line,
despite Fox's corporate reorganization, the Twentieth Century
merger, the exit of Winfield Sheehan and the entrance of Darryl
F. Zanuck. **The Littlest Rebel** (1935) and **Wee Willie Winkie**

23. Shirley Temple in
Wee Willie Winkie
(courtesy 20th
Century-Fox)

(1937) made millions. Shirley Temple's prime flew by all too
quickly. Always profit-conscious, the studio dropped her when
she reached puberty. She continued with her career, however,
working for other studios until she reached her 21st birthday in
1949.

Zanuck took over as production chief during the summer of 1935 and ran Fox's film-making operations for the rest of
the studio era – and beyond. When Zanuck stepped on to the Fox
lot, his problems were different from those as head of independent Twentieth Century. He had a budget of approximately
$400,000 per feature, better than before, but now had to ensure
that one new feature appeared each week. Since plans called for
B-films to count for half, Zanuck needed to worry about
producing twenty-four A films that first year. He inherited two
important stars, Shirley Temple and Janet Gaynor, and brought
along to Fox Fredric March, Ronald Colman and Loretta Young.

He was able to borrow stars, principally from MGM through Loew's president Nicholas Schenck, but Zanuck knew he could not count on such assistance forever. Loew's would help Fox only so long as it remained a poor cousin. Zanuck needed to build his own stable of stars plus producers, writers, directors and other crafts-persons so Fox could legitimately challenge MGM. In the meantime Zanuck borrowed (doing best with Dick Powell in **Thanks a Million**) and played up his inherited prize, Shirley Temple (**The Littlest Rebel** was Fox's biggest moneymaker for the 1935–6 motion-picture season).

Zanuck moved quickly. In **The Littlest Rebel** he utilized the services of Nunnally Johnson as a producer. Johnson went on to become Zanuck's most important assistant. This Georgia-born former newspaperman turned full-time to Hollywood during the Great Depression. In 1933 he joined Zanuck and Schenck at Twentieth Century, helping to write such hits as **The House of Rothschild, Bulldog Drummond Strikes Back** and **Kid Millions.** Zanuck promoted Johnson to producer in 1935. Producer Johnson then supervised an extraordinary string of hits including **Country Doctor, Slave Ship, The Grapes of Wrath, Chad Hanna, Wife, Husband and Friend, Rose of Washington Square** and **Tobacco Road.** Furthermore, **The Grapes of Wrath** brought needed prestige to a studio which had gathered precious little during the 1930s. However, Johnson chafed under Zanuck's total and complete control and moved – with another Zanuck assistant, William Goetz – to form International Pictures in 1943. (That move is analyzed in Chapter 7 since Universal merged with International in 1946.)

Producers like Johnson and Goetz helped Zanuck to give his organizational stamp to the new 20th Century-Fox. Zanuck still needed stars. Remarkably, he developed three within the space of two years. The first, Sonja Henie, had achieved world fame as an ice-skating champion. After the 1936 Olympics she turned professional and began to tour with her own ice show. Fox signed her in 1936. When her first film, **One in a Million,** proved to be a smash hit, finishing among the industry's top earners for the 1936–7 season, Henie vaulted to seventh position on the top ten star list behind Fox's duo of child stars, Shirley Temple in first place and Jane Withers in sixth. Henie moved up to third place in 1938, but dropped to tenth in 1939, and then fell permanently off the list. She continued to make films for Fox until 1943, but her salad days (1937–9) proved to be the shot of star power which Zanuck needed. (Sonja Henie retired from films in 1943 and returned to touring full-time with her ice show.)

24. Sonja Henie (centre) in **One in a Million** (courtesy 20th Century-Fox)

Zanuck drew his other two stars from the stage. It was band leader Rudy Vallee who spotted Alice Faye in the chorus line of Broadway's **George White's Scandals.** In 1931 he signed her to sing and tour with his band. Zanuck lured her to Fox in 1935, first projecting her in a Jean Harlow-blonde bombshell type image. But when she was cast as the 'girl-next-door' in the musical **King of Burlesque** (1936) she seemed to click. Like Sonja Henie, her career was short-lived. **In Old Chicago** (1938) thrust her onto the list of top ten movie stars for a short stay (9th in 1938 and 7th in 1939). Her decline began in 1940; she retired from films in 1945. Starring with Faye in **In Old Chicago** was Zanuck's third new star, Tyrone Power. Heir-apparent in a talented acting family, Power arrived at Fox in 1936. For one of his first big budget productions, Zanuck substituted Power for Don Ameche in **Lloyds of London.** That film went on to become the studio's top grosser of the year. In the absence of other male stars, Zanuck cast Power in all genres – westerns, comedies, historical melodrama and musicals. The strategy paid off. In 1938, Power jumped into tenth place on the top ten list of stars, giving Fox in that one remarkable year fully one-half of the top ten (Temple 1st, Henie 2nd, Withers 8th and Faye 9th). Power vaulted to 2nd place in 1939, but fell to 5th in 1940. The Second World War interrupted his career, and he never achieved the top ten again, although he remained with Fox until 1955.

Unfortunately for Zanuck, all his new (and inherited) stars seemed to lose their drawing power in 1940 or 1941. Adjusting, he took up two strategies: one to save money, the other to differentiate Fox's products in a way which would determine that they would not rely on the star system so much. To cut costs Zanuck began to rely more and more on sequels and remakes. This was a conservative strategy which worked well during the years of the Second World War when nearly everything, regardless of cost, made money; purposely or not, Zanuck took up conservative cost-cutting measures precisely at the correct time. Zanuck used several plots over and over again. One of Zanuck's more durable remake 'series' began in 1935 with **Folies Bergère,** in which the show's star (Maurice Chevalier) was mistaken for a Parisian financier. In 1942 Zanuck moved **Folies** to Rio de Janeiro for **That Night in Rio** and in 1951 he sent it **On the Riviera.** Zanuck also closely studied rival hits, and soon after MGM's **Meet Me in St Louis** came Fox's **Centennial Summer,** and there were innumerable other such 'sequels'.

Fox differentiated its products with Technicolor. RKO had released the first Technicolor feature (with the modern three-strip process) in 1935. The newly-formed 20th Century-Fox plunged in that very year, adding Technicolor sequences to Shirley Temple's **The Little Colonel.** From this beginning, Fox made more than seventy-five Technicolor films (full or with sequences) through 1949, the year when other processes became available. In that same period MGM did sixty-two, Paramount filmed only thirty-nine, RKO thirty-five and Warners thirty-three. From 1940 until 1947 Fox consistently released more Technicolor films, year in and year out, than any other studio. It created an average of six to eight per year, one-sixth of all Fox feature films produced.

Zanuck found a profitable formula for Fox's Technicolor spectacles in the Betty Grable musical. To say this was a successful strategy is to underplay how valuable Betty Grable became to Fox during the 1940s. The evidence is imposing. For *ten* consecutive years (1941–51) she was among the top ten money–making stars. She was paid accordingly. By 1945, Grable ranked among the highest of all salaried persons in the United States, and she reportedly received more than 10,000 fan letters per week through the Second World War. Surprisingly, she had had one unsuccessful turn in Hollywood in the mid–1930s. It turned out so badly that Grable was forced to return to the stage, appearing in 1939 in **DuBarry Was a Lady.** Zanuck signed her and when Alice Faye became ill placed her in the 1941 Technicolor musical, **Down Argentine Way.** One year later she was a fixture in lavish formulaic Technicolor musicals. In all she made twenty-two Technicolor films for Fox, with **Coney Island** (1943), **Sweet Rosie**

95

25. Betty Grable in
Down Argentine Way
(courtesy 20th
Century-Fox)

O'Grady (1943), **Diamond Horseshoe** (1945), **The Dolly Sisters** (1945), **Mother Wore Tights** (1947) and **When My Baby Smiles at Me** (1948) all finishing near the top revenue generators for their respective years. Except for Tyrone Power (1940) and Gregory Peck (1947), no other Fox star of the 1940s made it into the annual top ten ranking of stars. As Fox's economic fortunes improved in the 1940s, it was surely due in no small part to the continual popularity of Grable musicals in Technicolor.

After the Second World War (in which he served for a time) Zanuck seemed to lose his gift and was able to develop very few stars to go along with Grable. Gene Tierney, who had been on the lot since 1940, did shine for a time in **Leave It to Heaven** (1945), **Dragonwyck** (1945) and **The Razor's Edge** (1946). Near the end of the decade, Zanuck discovered Clifton Webb. Webb had first appeared on stage before the turn of the century, but did not achieve movie fame until he was 55 when, in 1948, he portrayed the stuffy middle-aged Mr Belvedere in **Sitting Pretty.** A sequel, **Mr Belvedere Goes to College,** thrust him into the top ten stars of 1950. Webb continued as a Fox staple into the mid-1950s.

But Zanuck's boldest move came in attempting further to differentiate Fox's features. He tried to better a post-war trend and produced a score of films with significant social themes. Apart from **Gentlemen's Agreement,** the eighth highest grossing film of 1947, none did very well at the box office. Zauck tackled legal corruption with **Boomerang** (1947), anti-semitism with **Gentlemen's Agreement** (1947), racial prejudice with **Pinky** (1949) and mental health with **The Snake Pit** (1948). To add realism, Fox began to send crews on location. In this way the studio added a distinctive touch to its *films noirs:* **Call Northside 777, Cry of the City** and **The Street With No Name,** all in 1947. But serious and realistic films, however entertaining, were not enough to stave off a decline in attendance. By 1951, Fox's earnings had fallen by 50 per cent. Across-the-board pay cuts were instituted. Budgets were halved. The studio era was over for Darryl F. Zanuck and 20th Century-Fox.

Throughout the studio era, 20th Century-Fox produced far more than Zanuck's A films. Until the corporation became flush in the mid-1940s, Fox maintained a strong B-production unit, under producer Sol Wurtzel. (At one point he had been William Fox's personal assistant.) Wurtzel's B unit turned out from ten to twenty-five films per season – at half the cost of Zanuck's A features. Fox sought to develop long-running series. **Charlie Chan** began in 1931 and lasted a full decade. This 'oriental' detective constantly changed locales in order to solve his mysteries, so in 1936 he went to the **Circus,** visited the **Race Track,** and attended the **Opera.** Fox initiated other series as best it could. MGM had the Hardy family. Fox followed with the Evans, then the Jones for a total of seventeen films. In 1937, to follow on its own success with Charlie Chan, Fox acquired the rights to the character of Mr Moto, a 'Japanese' detective played by Peter Lorre. This series lasted only two years. The Jane Withers films, sometimes four a year, were a budget-wise answer to Shirley Temple A-features. Withers, ironically, went on in her part well past the point at which Temple exited Fox for another studio. The Ritz Brothers were Fox's B-film answer to MGM's Marx Brothers. It took the Second World War boom to bring a halt to this frenetic activity. By then the corporation had become so prosperous, it chose to continue solely with its A features, short subjects, and newsreels.

Fox's short subject operations can be neatly divided by decade. In the 1930s Fox distributed the shorts made by Educational Pictures Inc. Established in 1919 to make films for schools, Educational soon turned to more profitable work – silent film comedies. During the 1920s it prospered; in the 1930s, it did not. The Depression and the reorganization of Fox's theaters crippled Educational badly. Production values fell consistently throughout the decade. More and more, Educational turned to stars on their way down. Such 1920s favorites as Harry Langdon and Buster Keaton, as well as producer Mack Sennett, spent a good portion of their declining years at Educational. New talent did appear in

Educational shorts (Bert Lahr, Danny Kaye and Imogene Coca) but all eventually moved on to achieve fame and fortune elsewhere. Unable to develop a consistently popular star or series, Educational went out of business in 1939.

Needing shorts to package to its own theaters (and perhaps to others also), Fox retained Educational's cartoon series, the Terrytoons. This was certainly a cut-rate operation. Its output of twenty-six cartoons per year equalled Disney's, but was done at one–fifth the budget. Disney developed its stories over the course of two months; the Terrytoons schedule permitted two weeks. Founder Paul Terry, a former newspaperman, had started an animation studio well before the First World War. In the 1920s, Terry produced **Aesop's Fables** for Pathe. In the 1930s, the studio seemed unable to find suitable new characters. Puddy the Pup, Kiko the Kangaroo and Farmer Al Falfa all failed. Fox nearly abandoned Terrytoons in 1935, but budgets were increased just enough to satisfy irate theater owners. In 1938, Terrytoons produced its first color short, with a new character Gandy the Goose (modeled on comic Ed Wynn's voice and mannerisms). When Spyros Skouras became president in 1942, he pushed Terry to seek additional new characters. Finally, success, albeit modest, did come about with Mighty Mouse, a Superman imitator. This super hero never spoke, only rescued. Terrytoons also developed a popular Bugs Bunny alternative, Heckle and Jeckle, in 1946, but even with Terrytoons, Fox could do no better than fifth among the Big Five in cartoons (RKO was handling Disney). It was with other short subject forms that Fox eventually gained a degree of comparative advantage.

During the 1940s Fox helped to popularize a new type of short with its 'March of Time' quasi-documentary series. 'March of Time' began on radio in 1931. Instead of reporting the news, it 'recreated' events using actors and a heavy-handed narrator. The motion picture 'March of Time' served as an advertisement for Time–Life magazines. It premiered in 509 independent (non-Big Five) theaters in January 1935. Wrapped up in controversy as it was from the beginning, no one could quite figure out how to program this strange hybrid, which was issued only once a month, ran twenty minutes, dealt with only a limited set of topics, and employed actors. In 1942 when Spyros Skouras began as Fox's president he took on 'March of Time' and sold it as a short subject, not a newsreel. He toned down its controversial stance and turned it into probably the most famous and popular documentary short-subject series of the 1940s. 'March of Time' ran successfully until 1951, when Time–Life abandoned production.

But Fox's real advantage in the shorts field rested with its legitimate newsreels. Fox News started up in the fall of 1919 with an initial investment of $5 million. To keep costs low, Fox affiliated with the United Press syndicate. Issues were released twice a week to an estimated audience of 30 million and cameramen were sent to all parts of the globe. By 1922, there were more than 1000 free-lance cameramen serving Fox on a regular basis. Fox prided itself on scoops. In the early 1920s, it recorded the first pictures of Mexican revolutionary Pancho Villa and the first 'offical' pictures of the Ku Klux Klan. As already analyzed, Fox adroitly used its strength in newsreels to innovate sound. The new Fox Movietone News prospered. Through special contracts, revenues rose to $100,000 a week. Although the Great Depression abruptly cut off growth, independent theaters turning to cheaper services, usually Universal, Fox still maintained its leadership. Movietone had the largest organization and the longest list of stringers. Fox's four competitors typically purchased footage from foreign newsreels sources; Fox could provide its own. Fifty-one countries were served through nine editing centers located throughout the world. Announcer Lowell Thomas became a household name through his commentary on Fox newsreels in the turbulent 1930s and war-torn 1940s. Fox held on until 1963, with overseas operations open for several years longer, but by 1964, Americans had begun regularly to view half-hour evening newcasts provided by the three television networks.

In 1951 20th Century-Fox signed its court-ordered consent decree and began to spin off its theaters. For a time, the new National Theaters chain worked closely with Fox since Spyros Skouras's brother Charles had assumed its presidency. The studio did well in the 1950s with CinemaScope films (Fox introduced the first with **The Robe** in 1953) and a new star, Marilyn Monroe. It accumulated $60 million in profits during the decade, vying with Paramount for industry leadership. In 1956, the corporation began its transition into the era of television. That year, after more than twenty-one years, Darryl Zanuck left to go into independent production. Of course, Fox would distribute his films. Spyros Skouras tried a number of new studio bosses; none worked out. After the disaster of **Cleopatra,** Zanuck returned as president and Skouras moved upstairs to a figurehead position. But the techniques he had used so well during the 1930s and 1940s did not work well for Zanuck in 1960s Hollywood. **The Sound of Music** (1965) only temporarily interrupted a downward spiral which resulted in Zanuck's final departure from the studio in 1970. His resignation symbolized the close of an era. With some

$77 million in red ink in 1970 – an industry record – the corporation nearly went under. As it goes into the 1980s, Fox has become a private corporation (owned by Denver oil-man Marvin Davis) which turns out popular theatrical films (**Star Wars, Return of the Jedi**) and television series (**M*A*S*H**).

5:

Warner Bros.

Warner Bros. (never Brothers) was the only family-run member of the Big Five. Harry Warner (1881–1958), the oldest brother, supervised all operations as president. Albert Warner (1884–1967), also working from New York, ran Warners' worldwide distribution network. The most publicly-known brother, Jack Warner (1892–1981), functioned as production chief at the California studios. (Another brother, Samuel (1888–1927), died before Warners grew into a vertically-integrated motion picture giant.) Warners is best known for its bold social and genre films of the early 1930s. But, from a business point-of-view, those films did not do well at the box-office, helping the company to lose more then $30 million in four years (see Table 5.1). In fact in terms of profits, Warners trailed far behind Loew's in the 1930s, and Paramount and 20th Century-Fox during the 1940s. It was only during the last years of the studio era that Warners moved from fourth place in the industry (always ahead of RKO) to second place in 1947 and 1948, third in 1949 and first in 1950, 1951 and 1952. That is, although Warners is famous for its 1930s films, its later 1940s and early 1950s operations (including films) made far more money, in an absolute and relative sense. It took this family business another twenty years to reach the corporate profit and power it had momentarily held in 1929 and 1930. Warners did well at the beginning and end of the studio era, but faltered otherwise.

The Warner family came to the US in two waves. First, father Benjamin emigrated from Poland. His wife Pearl, son Harry and daughter Anna came later. The other brothers were

Table 5.1: Warner Bros.' Balance Sheet

Year	Net Profits (millions of dollars)	Assets (millions of dollars)
1930	7.0	230.2
1931	(7.9)	213.9
1932	(14.1)	182.7
1933	(6.3)	169.8
1934	(2.5)	168.3
1935	0.7	168.5
1936	3.2	173.0
1937	5.9	177.5
1938	1.9	174.4
1939	1.7	168.6
1940	2.7	166.7
1941	5.5	169.6
1942	8.6	182.9
1943	8.3	181.7
1944	6.9	183.8
1945	9.9	179.3
1946	19.4	188.1
1947	22.0	184.6
1948	11.8	176.3
1949	10.5	161.2

born in Baltimore. In 1893, the family moved to Youngstown, Ohio. The brothers tried many business ventures before 1904, when Harry and Albert brought a film projector and began presenting travelling movie shows. From 1905 to 1907 the brothers operated the Cascades cinema in Newcastle, Pennsylvania, and a small states-rights distribution company. These enterprises ran smack into the General Film Company, and went out of business in 1910. Through the 1910s, the Warners dabbled in production and distribution, on the fringes of an industry dominated by Famous Players. Limited success finally came with the production of **My Four Years in Germany** in 1917. Profits enabled them to open up a small studio on Sunset Boulevard in Hollywood. At first, production stabilized at about five features a year. Gradually, the company grew. Ernst Lubitsch signed on; the dog Rin-Tin-Tin starred in several profitable films; the company was incorporated in 1923. Still Warners paled next to Loew's or

26. The Warner brothers: (l. to r.) Jack, Albert, Harry and, in the picture on the wall, Sam

Famous Players, for it had neither a permanent distribution network nor any theaters.

Prior to 1925, Warners raised money for production using what was known as the franchise technique. Dividing the US into twenty-eight zones, Warner secured from each 'franchise holder' – usually a major exhibitor – backing for five to ten films. Warners then guaranteed each 'franchise holder' first rights to a fixed percentage of the profits. Dissatisfied with this unstable, costly system, Harry Warner began to seek an alternative method of financing. In December 1924 he met Waddill Catchings, head of the investment division of Wall Street's Goldman Sachs. Catchings was famous for his willingness to back small firms which he thought could grow into giants; in 1924 he was in the process of helping Woolworths and Sears-Roebuck to grow from small, regional businesses into large, national chains. Catchings thought that the motion picture industry was ripe for expansion, and so, after carefully scrutinizing Warner Bros.' operations, he agreed to help.

In 1925 Warners began its expansion by taking over Vitagraph, a pioneer motion picture concern. For $1 million Warners acquired twenty-six distribution offices in the US, twenty-four abroad, a studio in Brooklyn and another in Hollywood. This initial takeover broke Warners' dependency on the franchise system. Catchings then obtained permanent financing for production in the form of a revolving line of credit of $3 million. Finally, Warners completed the year by opening two more exchanges in the US and twenty-nine more in foreign countries. In six months Warners had created a distribution system equal to those of Famous-Players and Loew's (MGM). At the same time, it purchased ten first-run houses – including Broadway's Piccadilly theater (renamed the Warners) as the flagship – and leased half a dozen first-run theaters in key locations, beginning with the Orpheum in Chicago's Loop.

In its year of expansion, Warners acquired a Los Angeles radio station. Through this deal, Samuel Warner learned of the new Western Electric system for recording and reproducing sound motion pictures. Fascinated, he and Harry conceived of a plan to make profits from this new technology. Warners would record popular musical acts and offer them as substitutes for stage show presentations. So, on 25 June 1925, Warner Bros. and Western Electric signed a letter of agreement calling for a year of experimentation. Throughout the remainder of 1925 Sam Warner and a small staff attempted to integrate the Western Electric inventions into a workable system of motion picture production.

During this phase of experimentation with sound, Warners continued its expansionary activities, some of which even began to pay off. Ernst Lubitsch's **Lady Windermere's Fan** established box office records on its debut in January 1926 at the Warners' theater in New York City; **The Sea Beast** with John Barrymore opened the following month to the same reception. To extract the maximum revenue from these hits, Warners rented a number of theaters to 'road-show' these films at a 2-dollar admission price. Still, because of expansion, Warner Bros.' yearly statement issued in March 1926 stood in the red at $1,337,000. The company did not face bankruptcy because this loss was self-imposed. Warner's new investments included an international distribution network and a growing chain of theaters. Moreover, it could now produce higher-priced films. Warners had begun its climb toward the top of the motion picture industry.

By December 1925 experiments with sound were going so well that Western Electric proposed that negotiations be opened for a permanent agreement, and on 20 April 1926 Western Electric granted an exclusive license to Warners' newly-created subsidiary for sound-film production and distribution – the Vitaphone Corporation. As the trade papers announced the first news of the alliance, Vitaphone organized its assault on the market-place. Warners signed a great number of popular musical artists, and secured the New York Philharmonic to record orchestral accompaniments for feature films. By June 1926, Vitaphone had begun to produce musical shorts and orchestral accompaniments. That month Vitaphone moved its studio to the vacant Manhattan Opera House on 34th Street in New York City. Warners rewired the theater, added lights and even built a deck over the seats in the orchestra section.

Vitaphone's première on 6th August 1926 was the climax of more than a year's effort. A seven-number 'Vitaphone Prelude' replaced the overture and stage show. The first vaudeville short presented Will Hays congratulating Warners and Western Electric. Next came the overture from **Tannhauser** played by the New York Philharmonic. Six 'acts' in a colossal 'head-liner stage show' followed. Five performed serious music. Only Roy Smeck provided an alternative with his harmonica and banjo act. Tenor Giovanni Martinelli's aria from **I Pagliacci** was the hit of the evening. Warners' strategy of providing the most popular musical stars had begun very conservatively. No one could object to new technology that could bring classical music to the masses. The feature film which followed was **Don Juan** starring John Barry-

27. John Barrymore in **Don Juan** (courtesy MGM/UA)

more. Most applauded it as one of Warner's better films to date. Few even noticed that the usual live orchestra had been replaced by a Vitaphone recording of the New York Philharmonic.

Following its long-run strategy, on 6 September 1926 Warner Bros. opened the **Don Juan** package at the Globe Theater in Atlantic City. The show drew a packed house, an especially good sign since Atlantic City was a popular summer resort. Next, Warners rented the McVicker's theater in Chicago's Loop and presented the **Don Juan** package to overflow crowds. In October the **Don Juan** show was offered in half a dozen major American cities. A second Vitaphone package, with the feature **The Better 'Ole,** had its première at Moss's Colony Theater in New York on 7 October 1926. This not only gave Vitaphone two 'shows' on Broadway, but, more importantly, represented a major shift in programming strategy. The program's shorts all featured vaudeville artists whom (according to *Variety* estimates) only the four largest motion picture theaters could have afforded to present live. The 'headliner' was Al Jolson, who did three songs while standing before a set of a Southern plantation. *Variety* could see only a bright future for an invention that could place so much high-priced vaudeville talent on one stage at one time.

Warner Bros. continued to improve financially despite considerable investments in Vitaphone. Foreign operations had grown extremely profitable. Rentals in Great Britain alone rose by $2 million for the American fiscal year ending 31 August 1927. Catchings was always able to generate the necessary financing for all Warners' new investments. In 1927, for example, he secured a $1 million loan to construct a new Hollywood studio and renegotiated extensions of all outstanding obligations. But such extraordinary financial support did not satisfy Western Electric. This AT&T subsidiary wanted to purchase Vitaphone and then let Warner Bros. produce shorts and scores while it controlled all the technical activities and licensing power. Only then could Western Electric seize a desired monopoly position and, hence, not be out-maneuvered and out-distanced by RCA, which had started later in the field.

In December 1926, Western Electric took the offensive. First, it organized Electrical Research Products Inc. (ERPI) as a wholly-owned subsidiary to market sound equipment. From this new base it pressured Famous-Players, Loew's and Fox to take out direct licenses for sound, even though this activity was legally reserved for Vitaphone. Fox signed up on 31 December 1926, but Western Electric could not persuade Famous-Players or Loew's. An alternative bid from RCA and Western Electric's stiff terms provided major stumbling blocks. Moreover, legally, Warners through Vitaphone would have to grant the license to Famous-Players or Loew's, and neither wished to become the licensee of another movie corporation. Thus, in February 1927 Famous-Players and Loew's formally postponed any decision concerning sound for one year. In reaction, Western Electric forced Warners to sign two new agreements. The first terminated the earlier contract as of 2 April 1927 and transferred to ERPI Vitaphone's contracts with exhibitors, and its sub-license with Fox-Case. The second granted Vitaphone a *non-exclusive* license to employ Western Electric sound-recording equipment and patents at the usual royalty fee.

After its settlement with ERPI, Warner Bros. was free to continue expansion. In May 1927 it announced that during the 1927–8 season it would release twenty-six features and four road-show specials – all with Vitaphone musical accompaniments. In addition, Vitaphone would add talking sequences to some of its feature films. Vitaphone continued to produce shorts at the rate of five per week and release them to the growing number of theaters with installations. By October 1927, at least 150 of these shorts had been recorded and released. Two new Vitaphone shows opened in June 1927: **Old San Francisco** at the New York Warners and **The First Auto Race** at New York Colony theater. The three original shows were playing now at popular prices in New York, Chicago, Minneapolis, Dayton, Denver, Philadelphia, Detroit, Buffalo and Portland, Oregon. Vitaphone opened on Labor Day 1927 in theaters in Newark and Milwaukee.

To meet its new schedule of 'talkers' and shorts, Warner Bros. instituted an intensive building programme. In October 1927 it completed four new Hollywood stages devoted to the production of Vitaphone shorts and features and shifted all its production to Hollywood. The new stages were 90 by 150 feet; all walls were felt-lined and specially sealed. Fifteen feet above the floor was a glass-enclosed booth to monitor the recording. The camera was enclosed in a soundproof, moveable booth. To maintain absolute quiet, Warners installed incandescent lamps to replace the usual motor-driven arc lights and carbon lamps. One

28. Al Jolson in **The Jazz Singer** (courtesy MGM/UA)

of the first films finished in these new studios was **The Jazz Singer.**
Completed in August 1927, **The Jazz Singer** cost an estimated
$500,000, making it the most expensive feature in Warner Bros.
history.

As the 1927–8 season opened, Vitaphone began to
develop new forms of sound films for its program. Although **The
Jazz Singer** had its première on 6 October 1927 to lukewarm
reviews, its four Vitaphoned segments of Jolson songs proved a
success. Vitaphone contracted with Jolson immediately to make
three more talkies for $100,000. The shorts unit took on new
programming strategies. On 4 December 1928 Vitaphone released the short, **My Wife's Gone Away** – a ten minute, *all-talking*
comedy based on a vaudeville playlet developed by William
Demarest. Critics loved this short; so did audiences. Under Jack
Warner's supervision the unit began to borrow even more from
available vaudeville acts and 'playlets' to create all-talking shorts.
During Christmas week, 1927, Vitaphone released a twenty-
minute, all-talking drama, **Solomon's Children.** Again, revenues
were high and in January 1928 Warner initiated a production
schedule of two all-talking shorts per week.

Warner Bros had begun to experiment with alternative
types of shorts as a cheap way to maintain the novelty value of
Vitaphone entertainment. Moreover, with such shorts it could
develop talent, innovate necessary production techniques and
thus create an audience for feature-length, all-sound films. In the
spring of 1928, with the increased popularity of its shorts, Warner
Bros. began to change its feature film offerings. On 14 March
1928, it released **Tenderloin** – an ordinary mystery that contained
five segments in which the actors spoke all their lines (for twelve
of the film's eight-five minutes). More part-talkies followed that
spring. Warners knew its investment in sound was a success, by
April 1928, when it became clear that **The Jazz Singer** show was
more than a mild success; it was the most poular entertainment
offering of the 1927–8 season. In cities that rarely held films for
more than one week **The Jazz Singer** package set records. It took
Warner Bros. only until the fall of 1928 to convert to the complete
production of talkies – both features and shorts. With distribution
and theaters in place, Warner had laid the foundation for rapid
growth, and hence could extract maximum profit from
Vitaphone. In 1928, Paramount and Loew's moved to imitate
Warners' behavior, and soon the American film industry's rapid
switch to sound was on in full force.

Warners' successful innovation of sound facilitated
further expansion. In May 1928 – as Paramount and Loew's were

29. The Warner Bros. lot in 1937

signing with Western Electric – Warners began its push to the very top of the US motion picture industry. The corporation needed a viable theater circuit to match Publix and Loew's and so moved to take over the Stanley Company, which controlled nearly all first-run houses in the mid-Atlantic states. Since Waddill Catchings was on the board of directors of both corporations, negotiations proved simple and straightforward. By the end of 1928, Warners owned Stanley and was the equal of the other vertically-integrated giants of the movie business. A bonus in the Stanley deal was the acquisition of a one-third share of First National. To secure control of that studio and its exchanges, Warners purchased additional shares from exhibitor members. Quietly and quickly Warners took controlling interest of an operation which included a California production center and an international distribution network. To complete its vertically-integrated empire, Warners added more theaters, the most significant of which came with the take-over of the Skouras chain of St Louis. Warners hired former owner Spyros Skouras – later president of 20th Century–Fox – to run the new Warners' chain of some 500 houses.

Warners then moved to expand into non-filmic areas. In January 1929, it purchased its first music publishing company, M. Witmark and Sons. This paralleled earlier actions by Paramount and Loew's. The Witmark catalog included works by Victor Herbert, Sigmund Romberg and George M. Cohan. Warners then hired the Witmark family to run the new operation. In May 1929, Warners closed negotiations with Max Dreyfuss, head of

Harms Music Publishing Company, not only for the purchase of Harms but for 50 per cent of Remick Music Corporation and a minority interest in DeSylvia, Brown and Henderson. This latter firm had written most of Jolson's songs for **The Singing Fool,** for which Warners had paid dearly. To consolidate these musical operations, Warners formed Music Publishers Holding Corporation. For a short time Warners even began to establish a chain of music stores to co-ordinate sales with premières of Warner films, but this venture, as well as the proposed Paramount–Warners merger described in Chapter 3, was cut short by the effects of the Great Depression.

By 1930 Warners had risen with Fox and RKO to rank with Loew's and Paramount, constituting the 'Big Five' of the US motion picture industry. Like the others, the Great Depression hit Warners hard. Corporate revenues fell from $130 million for the fiscal year ending in August 1930 to $72 million for the year ending in August 1933. As seen in table 5.1 losses piled up, but although Paramount, RKO and Fox filed for complete reorganization, the brothers Warner refused. Assets were sold; expenses, including wages, were cut. Budgets for film production were pared to the lowest figure for any major studio. The number of theaters was reduced from 700 to 400 through both outright closure and voluntary termination of leases. Warners pressed to meet all the debts it had accumulated during the expansionary 1920s. In this project Harry Warner succeeded beyond all expectations. In 1930, total debt stood at $113 million; by 1938 it had been reduced to $29 million. This remaining obligation was rolled over and fully retired by 1943.

By the late 1930s, Warners was a lean enterprise pushing toward the high profits available from the boom era of the Second World War. At that point Warner Bros. Pictures Inc. consisted of nearly 100 subsidiaries. Production of films was handled under three labels: Warner Bros. and First National for features, and Vitaphone for shorts. The central studio was located at the former First National lot in Burbank, California. Others were in Hollywood and Teddington (England). Up to 1941 Vitaphone produced shorts in Brooklyn, New York. Distribution operated throughout the entire world through twenty-seven separate foreign corporations. The theater chain consisted of some 425 houses, concentrated in Pennsylvania, Maryland, New Jersey, and Washington, DC. In addition, Warners acquired or built theaters in other large cities to gain entry to markets controlled by others. Thus, the corporation was represented in New York (population rank in 1940: 1), Chicago (2), Philadelphia (3), Los

Angeles (5), Cleveland (6), Pittsburgh (10), Washington, DC (11), Milwaukee (13), Newark, New Jersey (18), Jersey City (30), Memphis (32), San Antonio (37), Syracuse (41), Oklahoma City (42), Worcester, Massachusetts (44), Youngstown (49), Hartford, Connecticut (51), New Haven, Connecticut (54), Springfield, Massachusetts (58), Bridgeport, Connecticut (59), Patterson, New Jersey (64), Albany, New York (65), Camden, New Jersey (71), Erie, Pennsylvania (72), Wilmington, Delaware (76), Reading, Pennsylvania (79) and Utica, New York (90).

Warners gradually revived outside interests during the 1940s. It had a Hollywood-based radio station, KFWB, music publishing operations, a plant to print sheet music and film-developing laboratories. In the late 1930s it acquired an interest in Associated Music Publishers Inc. which, in turn, controlled Muzac, Inc., forerunner of today's piped-in music for restaurants and shopping malls. In 1947, with profits again high, Warner purchased the RKO–Pathe newsreel. Warners also looked overseas. In 1941, through a wholly-owned subsidiary, it purchased one-quarter of the stock of the Associated British Picture Corporation. This investment helped Warners to 'unfreeze' British revenues and to gain access to one of the three most powerful theater chains (400 houses) in the United Kingdom. Warners purchased more shares in 1946, though it never acquired a working majority. For a long time, Warners had produced films in England. In 1931, to create films to circumvent the British quota, it had leased the Teddington Studios. In 1934 it purchased the studio outright. More than 100 films for the British market were made there, generating a small profit until the end of the studio era.

Warners had the most stable management of any major US movie corporation of the studio era. The three Warner brothers ran the company through the 1930s, 1940s and into the 1950s. Only in 1951 when Warners began to sell its theaters did Harry Warner, then 69 years old, and Albert, 66 decide to retire. They announced that their shares of Warner Bros. stock – a controlling interest – were for sale. Since television and suburban living had caused movie attendance to decline significantly after the Second World War, the duo found it difficult to locate acceptable buyers, but finally in July 1956, they did sell their stock (for $16.5 million) to a syndicate headed by Serge Semenenko, a Boston banker. This transaction caused a major split between Harry and Albert and brother Jack. Jack refused to give up his shares, and in fact replaced Harry as president. Jack Warner stayed on until the company was taken over by a Canadian firm,

Seven Arts Ltd., in 1967, but by that time Warner Bros. was more valued for its land, old films and television production than for its feature film-making potential.

Jack L. Warner is the famous Warner brother. He helped to created the stereotype of the crude, rough, all-powerful movie mogul. Like Louis B. Mayer at MGM, Warner ruled feature film-making with an iron hand. Yet his management style only mirrored his older brother Harry's wishes. The brothers Warner sought a cut-rate movie factory, which would produce the required number of features and shorts for Warners' theaters each year. Warner Bros. operated on a volume basis, trying to make a small profit on every film. Jack Warner supplied the films; Abe Warner routed them to appropriate theaters, but there was no question who mapped overall corporate strategy and had the last word in all decisions – Harry M. Warner. Not only was he president from 1924 to 1956, he was the eldest brother in a first generation immigrant family. Harry Warner was very tight with a dollar, trying to save money wherever possible. Though he demanded full control of the finances, he was content to let his younger brother play the role of the flamboyant studio spokesperson. Indeed, Harry Warner went out of his way to shun publicity, working quietly behind the scenes, knowing that all information and final authority flowed into and out of his office.

But Harry Warner was not a classic Republican breed of conservative. He was one of the first executives of any major US corporation to make a definitive stand on the Second World War, arguing that the US should intervene. He strongly supported President Franklin Roosevelt in 1932, arguing that a revolution might take place otherwise. But this movie executive was no radical, often speaking out publicly against socialism; he personally instituted a series of patriotic shorts which Warners released prior to and during the Second World War. His extreme fiscal conservatism led to an extremely paternalistic attitude toward labor. Warner Bros. took on protracted court battles against James Cagney and Bette Davis rather than give them more artistic freedom. And the company opposed unions. For example, in October 1945 Warners turned the hoses on hundreds of strikers picketing outside the Burbank studio. Since those unions were, in part, controlled by communists Harry Warner felt justified. In his view the corporation was like one big happy family, with Harry Warner as the resident patriarch.

The strategy of Warners' corporate machine was to produce films cheaply and efficiently. This cost-effectiveness led the studio to initiate various genre cycles, beginning in 1930 with

30. Hal B. Wallis (l.)
with Harry Warner

gangster films under producer Darryl F. Zanuck. At that time, the studio also turned out 'topicals' – films based on news events of the day – and musicals. Indeed **42nd Street** and **Gold Diggers of 1933** were the studio's sole significant hits in 1933. Warners never made money in the early 1930s. So when the Great Depression began to ease in 1935, Warners turned to other genre forms under producer Hal B. Wallis. From best-selling novels, the studio created **Oil for the Lamps of China** and **Anthony Adverse**. A romantic cycle – with Errol Flynn usually in the title role – included **The Charge of the Light Brigade, The Adventures of Robin Hood** and **The Private Lives of Elizabeth and Essex**. Biographical tales gained the studio a measure of prestige and Oscars: **The Story of Louis Pasteur, The Life of Emile Zola** and **Juarez**. Profits began to grow and Warners started to prosper.

Under Harry Warner's direction, Warner Bros. reacted strongly to the coming of the Second World War. **Confessions of a Nazi Spy,** released in May 1939, caused an immediate furor. Warners capitalized on the war boom to produce genre combat films (**Destination Tokyo, Objective Burma**) as well as lighter fare (**The Desert Song, Yankee Doodle Dandy**), but they took on controversy even during a popular war. **Mission to Moscow,** released early in 1943, supported American intercession on behalf of the USSR. Based on a best-selling novel, the request for filming came directly from President Franklin Roosevelt to his biggest supporters in the film industry, the brothers Warner. (After the war the brothers were embarrassed by this effort.) In 1946 Warner initiated its *films noir*. Pioneered by producer Jerry Wald with

31. Walter Huston (l.) as US Ambassador Joseph E. Davies meets Stalin (Manart Kippen) in **Mission to Moscow** (courtesy MGM/UA)

Mildred Pierce, the studio did not start this particular cycle, but profited from continuing it. In **Flamingo Road** (1947), **The Damned Don't Cry** (1950), **Nora Prentiss** (1946) and even musicals such as **Young Man With A Horn** (1950), the studio offered a bleak portrait of America. At the end of the 1940s Warners momentarily returned to the gangster genre it had pioneered nearly two decades before, with **White Heat** (1949), which many consider James Cagney's finest gangster portrait, **Kiss Tomorrow Goodbye** (1950) and **Caged** (1950).

Today, Warners seems to have been the most interesting of the Big Five Hollywood studios, dealing with topical public concerns and developing fascinating genre products. It was not, however, as great an economic success. The studio produced relatively few stars, never once placing a star at the top of the annual poll. While MGM produced nearly a dozen ranking stars during the studio era, Warners could count only three: James Cagney (later 1930s to early 1940s), Bette Davis (same period as Cagney), and Humphrey Bogart (mid-1940s). Only three others, Joe E. Brown, Errol Flynn, and Dick Powell, ever reached the industry's annual list of top ten stars. Indeed in 1933, 1934, 1937, 1938 and 1950 – fully one quarter of the studio era – Warners registered no-one in the annual top-ten poll of stars.

Warners also lagged in the production of feature films in color. MGM, Paramount and Fox annually produced twice as many color films. Perhaps it was because Warners had unsuccess-fully tried two-part Technicolor from 1929 to 1933. Warners did make a few Technicolor products, **The Adventures of Robin Hood**

114

(1938) being the most famous (and popular). Yet from 1939 to 1948, Warners produced fewer color films than *any* other major, at times even lagging behind Columbia and United Artists. Warners' conservative financial stance in the 1930s dictated little innovation. Only after profitable years in 1946 and 1947 did Warners step up production of Technicolor films to match other members of the Big Five as they entered the television era.

The lack of stars and films in color helps to explain Warners' paucity of top-grossing feature films. During the 1930s this major company should have accounted for about 15–20 per cent of top grossers. Instead, Warners achieved only half that proportion. Starting in 1938 the studio did better, but still finished behind MGM, Paramount and Fox more often than not. Warners' poor showng in top-grossing features correlated with its low rank in profits. The corporation consistently finished behind Paramount, Fox and Loew's. During the post-Second World War era, Warners made great strides, doing best in 1950 – its only first place finish in the profits race during the studio era. At another studio, Jack Warner might have lost his job. Instead, he achieved the longest tenure of any Big Five production boss.

Warners did not purposely try to produce top-grossing films. It operated on the smallest budgets of any Big Five members. Stories were used over and over again during the studio era. Studio staff were overworked and underpaid. Jack Warner did not even like to give his producers credit, preferring to refer to them as supervisors. Therefore, the turnover in supervisory staff below Warner was rapid and continuous. Only producer Henry Blanke stayed on as long as many of his counterparts at MGM. Some creative talent stayed on longer, but (except for a handful of stars) never became identified with certain films or even genres. Warners, not MGM with its unit production, best represented the studio as assembly-line, turning out movies as Ford did automobiles.

As a consequence, any film can illustrate how the Warner system worked. **High Sierra** (1941), a successful gangster film, will be used as a case study. To initiate this or any project, Jack Warner and his advisors of the time selected a potential story. In 1940, Warner had important reasons for choosing W R Burnett's forthcoming novel **High Sierra.** Burnett had a good track record. In 1931 Warner Bros. had turned his first novel, **Little Caesar,** into a very successful gangster film. Subsequently, Burnett had provided Warners with two more narratives for motion pictures: **Dark Hazard** (1934) plus a 1937 Warners remake **Wine, Women and Horses;** and **Doctor Socrates** (1935) with a

32. Humphrey Bogart
(l.) in **High Sierra**
(courtesy MGM/UA)

remake four years later, **King of the Underworld.** Warners purchased the exclusive movie rights to **High Sierra** on 27 March 1940 for $25,000.

Warner assigned experienced staff to help to shoot **High Sierra,** thus guaranteeing trouble-free production. Director of photography Tony Gaudio, whose career stretched back to movie-making's earliest days, came to Warners in the early 1930s. He was the consummate studio cameraman; he had no specialty. Just prior to filming **High Sierra,** he worked on a spectacle, **Juarez;** a war film, **Dawn Patrol;** and the 'B-film' **Torchy Blane** series. **High Sierra's** director, Raoul Walsh, also had a long, varied carer. He began as an actor in films in 1909, moved behind the camera in 1914 and went on to direct several of the most popular films of the 1920s: **The Thief of Bagdad** (1924), **What Price Glory** (1926) and **Sadie Thompson** (1927). He made his debut at Warners in 1939 with **The Roaring Twenties** and remained with the studio until 1951 as one of its most reliable and prolific directors.

Not all those behind the cameras had two decades of movie-making experience. For example, associate producer Mark Hellinger had worked at Warners for only a short time and went on to fashion the important part of his career at another studio, Universal. Only one newcomer, co-scriptwriter John Huston, helped the studio in the long run. After **High Sierra** and the extremely profitable **Sergeant York** (1941), Jack Warner permitted Huston to direct as well as write. He went on to win an Oscar for the studio for **The Treasure of Sierra Madre** (1946).

With the production of **High Sierra,** Jack Warner attempted to rework the image of two supporting players. **High Sierra** helped Humphrey Bogart to break out of supporting roles and define a star persona – the only long-running star of the 1940s for the studio. In 1941, Ida Lupino received top billing for **High Sierra.** Only later with the creation of the 'Bogie' myth did the star rankings seem reversed. Lupino was brought to Hollywood by Paramount in 1933 (when she was 15) to become another Clara Bow. She played minor *ingénue* roles for several studios until she landed a part in Warner's **They Drive By Night** (1940). Jack Warner then signed her to a standard seven-year contract and re-teamed her with Bogart (who also had a supporting role in **They Drive By Night**) for her next film, **High Sierra.** The minor figures in **High Sierra** – Henry Hull, Henry Travers, Jerome Cowan, Minna Gombell, Barton MacLane, Donald MacBride and Willie Best – all portrayed their usual 'character-types'.

Shooting took the scheduled three months at the Burbank studio. Immediately after, Warners assembly units took over. The music department under Leo F. Forbstein and a crew under editor Jack Kallifer began to prepare for a scheduled release three months later. **High Sierra** opened in New York on 25 January 1941. Warner Bros. sold the film quite predictably. Advertisements hailed **High Sierra**'s stars: 'Lupino and Bogart, the stars whose startling performances in **They Drive By Night** made them Top Box Office Names' and quoted author Burnett: 'My story to top **Little Caesar** is **High Sierra**' and director Walsh: '**High Sierra** is the most thrilling and unusual picture I have directed since **What Price Glory**'. The advertisements further reminded potential filmgoers that Warner Bros. had produced earlier gangster hits, **Little Caesar** and **Angels With Dirty Faces** (1938). Warners' publicists even provided exhibitors with a six-day serial story, rewritten from the movie, reviews for insertion in local newspapers and ideas for contests and promotions. **High Sierra's** production illustrates numerous traits common to the Warners' assembly line of the 1930s and 1940s. The studio liked to rely on popular fiction, pre-tested in the market-place if possible. Jack L. Warner and his top assistants approved all projects. (Warner had three assistants: Zanuck 1931-3; Hal Wallis 1933-44; Steve Trilling 1944-51.) Warner was constantly trying to develop new stars. Bogart had been with the studio for a long time, but only relatively late in his career was he elevated to star status. In contrast, there was a sense of stability in the support staff. Warners functioned as a trim, lean operation, looking for (and gaining) a tiny profit on each film, rather than a great return from a few big hits. The corporation's strong theater holdings guaranteed steady corporate profits after 1935. Warners 'A' features were steady, unspectacular performers.

Through the 1930s – until 1943 – Warners also produced a great number of 'B' (programmer) films, first under producer Bryan Foy and later under William Jacobs. The 'B' unit produced no less than half the Warner output, about twenty-six features per year on a total budget of $5 million. Production costs had to be kept low, so the films contained lots of inserts of newspaper headlines and close-up shots. Story-lines more often than not were drawn from already-successful films, including many silent productions with only the location or period changed. In comparison with other 'B' units, there were few series – principally John Wayne westerns (early 1930s) and films featuring detectives Torchy Blaine and Nancy Drew (late 1930s). Throughout the 1930s, Warner trained talent with 'B' films, graduating its most famous persona in Humphrey Bogart. Warners' 'B' films, largely undistinguished, serve to demonstrate how minor a 'major' Warner Bros. was. It took the boom of the Second World War to push Warners out of 'B' films into the arena of serious competition against MGM, Paramount and 20th Century-Fox, but during the 1930s Warners' powerful well-run theater circuit had guaranteed that even 'B' films would make small but steady profits.

Fortunately, Warners produced superior short subjects. As has been noted already, Warners innovated sound through recordings of popular vaudeville acts. By 1930 hundreds of vaudeville shorts were in the can and used as substitutes for stage shows. In 1931, once the novelty had worn off, Warners appointed veteran producer Sam Sax to take charge of production of all live (as opposed to animated) shorts. At that time, all production was done in the New York studio. The problem was how to maintain popularity. There seemed to be two strategies. Under the first, Warners continued to sign up popular musical stars, place them in front of a camera and let them go through an already prepared routine. Few performers escaped a Warners session, but increasingly, big name musical stars went directly to Hollywood (far from Warners' New York studios) and appeared in features, including Warners' own musicals. Thus, the 'Vitaphone Vanities' musical series had to resort to a second strategy: development of original material. A separate unit was instituted, at first in New York and later moved to Hollywood, to create short musicals. Principals included musical director David Mendoza and songwriters Sammy Cahn and Saul Chaplin.

Productions took three days, limited to normal business hours, enabling performers to work in clubs and/or on the stage at night. For example, in 1934, with **Fifty Million Frenchmen,** Sax took Cole Porter music – for which Warners already owned the rights – and created a mini-musical, staring newcomer Bob Hope. During the 1930s Warners produced numerous versions of musicals and operettas using Warner-owned music, thereby more fully amortizing some of the biggest musical hits of the day.

Warners produced more than musical shorts in its New York studio. In the early 1930s, there were miniature dramas ('playlets') which featured talent from the legitimate theater. Warners tried (and dropped) mystery series after little success with trial runs in 1931 and 1932. With comedy shorts, Warners never achieved the popularity of its rivals. The stars were there. Joe Penner, Jack Haley (the Tin Man in MGM's **The Wizard of Oz**), Ben Blue, Shemp Howard (later to join the Three Stooges at Columbia), William Demarest and Lionel Stander all appeared at one time or another. In 1932 and 1933 'Fatty' Arbuckle created six Vitaphone shorts as part of his career 'outside the mainstream'. Future stars Bob Hope and Edgar Bergen (with Charlie McCarthy) made comic shorts for Warners in the mid-1930s. For a variety of reasons, all these performers achieved fame elsewhere, or were at the end of their careers. Warners had achieved success with musical shorts and so never pushed its comic shorts unit too hard.

Finally recognizing the movement of popular musical talent to Hollywood (for radio and film production), in the late 1930s Warners closed up the New York studio and shifted Sam Sax and company to Burbank. The only new short productions to come from New York in the late 1930s were recordings of big bands, including reels of the Artie Shaw, Eddy Duchin, Woody Herman, Glen Gray and Vincent Lopez ensembles. This series, 'Symphony in Swing', also moved west in 1940. Like MGM, Warners moved west to consolidate the training of creative and production talent in one location. In the early 1940s, Warners established yet another shorts unit, headed by veteran producer Gordon Hollingshead. This unit did 'miniatures' of what the studio did best – musicals, dramas, and gangster films – with the added advantage of being in Technicolor. Sponsored directly by boss Harry Warner, a number of these shorts took on the complete sweep of American history. **Sons of Liberty** (1939), starring Claude Rains and directed by Michael Curtiz in color, won an Academy Award, but the major function of all shorts units was to turn out talent for feature film-making. Future stars

Dorothy Malone, Dane Clark, Nina Foch, Dennis Morgan and Jane Wyman moved up, as did directors Jean Negulesco and Don Siegel. (In 1945, Siegel won an Academy Award for **Hitler Lives,** a documentary short subject.)

A long-running comedy series was finally initiated in 1945. The 'Joe McDoakes' series lasted until 1956, when only Columbia, with **The Three Stooges,** was still putting out comic shorts. Directed by Richard L. Bare, they starred George O'Hanlan as 'Mr Average American' struggling with the neighbors, going to a lodge convention or trying out a new television set (**So You Want a Television Set,** released 23 May 1953). In the 1940s these shorts only cost an average of $12,000. The fourth entry, **So You Want to Play the Horses,** won an Academy Award in 1946. Warners often referred to features in this series; **So You Want to Play the Horses** contains a short spoof of **The Lost Weekend,** a popular Paramount attraction of the time. In **So You Want to be a Detective,** the McDoakes character interrupts the narrator and announces he's Philip Snarlowe, private eye. The short then takes up the camera as first-person, aping an effort tried several years earlier in Robert Montgomery's **The Lady in the Lake** (MGM, 1946). In 1956 director Bare turned to television, as Warners ventured into the new medium. He directed the studio's first television series, **Cheyenne.** In its ten years the Joe McDoakes series appeared seven times in the **Motion Picture Herald** poll of top-grossing shorts; it took television to bring it to a halt.

Surprisingly, Warner Bros. was the only major studio not to produce and/or distribute newsreels during the bulk of the studio era. During the coming of sound, Warners pressed to buy theaters and expand production and distribution capacity, leaving innovation with sound newsreels to Fox. Only Paramount had the resources to start a newsreel operation from scratch in this period. During the late 1940s, on the crest of corporate profitability, Warners picked up distribution of Pathé's newsreel. Howard Hughes had just purchased the former distributor of the Pathé product, RKO, and was looking for an instant return on his investment. Warners paid him $4 million – in cash. Unfortunately, Warners had chosen the wrong period to try to expand. Less than a decade later Warners' new management closed up that shop, becoming the first of the five major newsreels to call it quits. Warners was in the newsreel business only eight years, at the tail end of the studio era.

Warners did release other short subjects in the 1950s. Its travelogues, many in CinemaScope, were extremely popular.

One, in 1951, **Cruise of the Zaca,** was directed and narrated by Errol Flynn. This entry examined a scientific expedition supervised by the California Institute for Oceanography aboard Flynn's schooner, the Zaca. Producer Robert Youngson gave Warners yet another form of the documentary. While on the staff of the recently-acquired Pathé newsreel, Youngson produced a series of historical compilation films utilizing Pathé footage which went as far back as the mid-1890s and won two Academy Awards. Shorts production was dropped when Warners entered television production in 1956, one of the last studios to abandon them.

But Warners' best remembered shorts were its animated cartoons. Although Disney stood as a dominant force in the 1930s, by the Second World War Warners had risen to its equal. The Warners' cartoons of the 1940s have come to represent the corporation as much as its 'proletariat films' of the early 1930s and pro-war films of the Second World War. Warners commenced animation production in 1930. In that year of merger and acquisition it agreed to distribute the animated shorts of the Hugh Harmon and Rudolf Ising operation. Harmon and Ising had worked for Disney and, like many others in the studio era, left to work on their own. In 1929 they joined with entrepreneur Leon Schlesinger to work out a contract with Warners. In turn, Warners insisted that each cartoon should include music from a current Warners' feature film. In that way Warners not only reaped free publicity, but also stood to gain from the royalties paid to its music publishing division. To emphasize this musical connection, as well as to trade off Disney's success with 'Silly Symphonies', the series of Harmon and Ising cartoons was titled 'Looney Tunes'. The first, **Sinking in the Bathtub,** featured a reference to the title song from a Warners' feature, **The Show of Shows,** a Technicolor spectacle starring Monte Blue. The feature was released in December 1929, the cartoon in May 1930.

Harmon and Ising first tried out Foxy (Mickey Mouse with pointed ears and a bushy tail). Warners was pleased and contracted for a second series of monthly releases from Schlesinger. These 'Merrie Melodies' were one-of-a-kind cartoons, not a series. They also took titles from Warners' songs. But as Disney's work grew in popularity during the early 1930s, Harmon and Ising's products seemed to stagnate. The pair never seemed to recognize this, grew increasingly greedy, split from Schlesinger, and moved their cartoon operation to MGM. Schlesinger, not himself an artist, still had a contract to fulfill with Warners. Therefore, he raided several cartoon operations and in 1934 put together a new Warners unit.

Schlesinger attempted to match Disney. First, he contracted with Cinecolor and produced some 'Merrie Melodies' in color. He was forced to go to the two-color Cinecolor process because Disney had an exclusive contract for the new three-strip Technicolor. The reaction to even this poor use of color was so favorable at the box office that from 1935 on all 'Merrie Melodies' were made in color. ('Looney Tunes' remained in black and white until 1943.) Schlesinger's central problem was a lack of 'stars'. In 1936, this situation began to change with the introduction, among others, of Porky Pig. New 'Merrie Melodies' relied on caricatures of Warners' stars, for example, Bette Davis, James Cagney, Edward G. Robinson and even Al Jolson in blackface. During this period Schlesinger assembled a group of artists, directors and other creative people who would carry the studio to its glory years in the 1940s. Tex Avery, Chuck Jones, Bob Clampett and Frank Tashlin invented a new visual style; Carl W. Stalling developed the music and sound effects, and Mel Blanc did the voices. Warners finally began to achieve success in 1938. In that year, Porky Pig teamed with a new character, Daffy Duck, to form a popular cartoon duo. In 1940, came Elmer Fudd and Bugs Bunny. By the beginning of the Second World War the Warners animation factory was in full gear, turning out shorts now considered classics.

A significant change occurred in 1944 when Schlesinger sold all rights to Warners and retired. Edward Selzer, a former director of studio publicity, replaced him. After the war, Selzer cut production from forty to twenty-six: thirteen 'Looney Tunes' and thirteen 'Merrie Melodies'. All distinctions between the two series disappeared, except for title and theme music. Selzer presided over the development of several new stars. Tweety Pie (*sic*) appeared first in **Tweetie Pie** (with Sylvester the Cat) and this short won the Academy Award in 1947. Chuck Jones pioneered Pepe LePew and Robert McKimson introduced Foghorn Leghorn. Then came Wile E. Coyote, the Road Runner and Speedy Gonzales. Production rolled along through the 1950s, through ownership changes, into the television era. The first attempt to close the animation shop came in 1963, but the end did not come until 1969. Warners characters live on in television specials, compilation films and in theme parks. But it was the 1940s which were the Golden Age for the Warners animated films, so much so that they surpassed Disney and helped the parent corporation to its greatest profits.

The 1950s saw the Warner empire collapse. The theaters were spun off in 1951. Harry and Abe Warner left in 1956 when the first of a series of new owners took charge. Jack became an independent producer. The corporation's sole success in the 1950s came in the production of television series (**Cheyenne, 77 Sunset Strip, Maverick**). During the 1960s, feature releases were, by and large, independent deals, which ranged from the spectacular (Jack Warner's own **My Fair Lady, Camelot, The Great Race**) to more risky ventures (**Who's Afraid of Virginia Woolf?, Bonnie and Clyde**). The conglomerate Kinney National Service took over Warners in 1969. The new corporation became Warner Communications. Kinney sold Warners' pre-1948 features to United Artists and began to share the Burbank lot with Columbia. In the 1970s and early 1980s Warner Communications made (and lost) most of its money with its pioneering video game subsidiary, Atari. Film production was reduced to the role of just one subsidiary. The original movie corporation had made its name and profits by innovating a new technology. The new Warner Communications seemed to be trying a similar strategy some fifty years later with video games and cable television.

6:

Radio-Keith-Orpheum

Radio-Keith-Orpheum (RKO) had the shortest corporate life and was the least profitable of the Big Five. In 1928, Radio Corporation of America willingly bankrolled the creation of this vertically-integrated movie corporation; Western Electric had shut it out in the race for sound. RCA's stepchild expired twenty-eight years later, the only member of the Big Five not to survive into the 1980s. RKO struggled throughout the 1930s, registering losses more often than profits (see Table 6.1). The war boom probably saved RKO, pushing profits to a record $12 million in 1946, but its fall was rapid, and with the sale to billionaire Howard Hughes, fatal. All the other members of the Big Five had stable management after 1935; not RKO. This corporation rarely had the same managers for more than three years at a time. The studio produced many interesting films (**King Kong,** the Astaire–Rogers musicals, **Citizen Kane,** the Val Lewton horror films), but never consistent profits. RKO, from a business perspective, was the marginal major studio – closer in many ways to Columbia and Universal than Loew's or Paramount. Its solid theater chain, distribution of shorts by Disney (1937–54), features by Samuel Goldwyn (1941–54) and successful Pathé newsreel kept the enterprise going, and probably accounted for most of the profits the corporation was able to produce.

RKO's history can be traced to the origin of its parts: (i) the Radio Corporation of America sought an outlet for its sound equipment; (ii) the Film Booking Office (FBO), a low budget Hollywood studio, provided a base for film production and a network for distribution; and (iii) the Keith-Albee-Orpheum vaudeville circuit brought the new company a national chain of more than 100 theaters. In the joining of the three parts, RKO instantly became the fifth ranking motion-picture organization in the United States. The genesis of RKO came early in 1928 when officials at RCA realized they had failed to convince Loew's and Paramount to sign up for Photophone sound equipment. RCA president David Sarnoff began to look for a film studio, however small, which RCA could purchase. Joseph P. Kennedy (father of

Table 6.1: RKO's Balance Sheet

Year	Net Profit (millions of dollars)	Assets (millions of dollars)
1930	3.4	117.8
1931	(5.7)	132.3
1932	(11.2)	97.2
1933	(4.4)	67.7
1934	(0.3)	65.5
1935	0.7	66.1
1936	2.5	67.1
1937	1.8	71.0
1938	0.0	70.9
1939	(0.2)	71.5
1940	(1.0)	68.0
1941	1.0	70.1
1942	0.6	68.7
1943	6.9	79.3
1944	5.2	80.8
1945	6.1	82.9
1946	12.2	106.4
1947	5.1	113.6
1948	0.5	108.3
1949	–	–

President John F. Kennedy) was then in control at Film Booking Office (FBO), a marginal producer of cheap westerns. Sarnoff and Kennedy joined forces when RCA purchased a controlling interest in FBO for half a million dollars.

Now Sarnoff needed theaters in which to show sound films, using, of course, RCA Phonofilm equipment. The Keith-Albee vaudeville circuit, once the dominant power in the popular culture business, was fading fast. Even before the advent of talkies, in order to hedge its bets Keith-Albee had secured interests in two motion picture producer–distributors, Producers Distributing Corporation (with Cecil B. De Mille) and Pathé, a specialist in shorts and newsreels. (For a time, Keith-Albee sought to merge with Warners, but at the last minute the deal fell through.) By mid-1928 it was clear that Keith-Albee, now merged with the west coast theaters of the Orpheum vaudeville chain, would ally itself with FBO and RCA. Joseph P. Kennedy was the conduit of the amalgamation. At first, RCA simply provided Keith-Albee-Orpheum theaters and De Mille and Pathé producers with Photophone equipment. Studio head Joseph Kane then added musical scores to three new productions, **King of Kings, The Godless Girl** and **The Perfect Crime.** Keith-Albee-Orpheum's Pathé subsidiary began to create vaudeville shorts and newsreels with sound. From these dealings, it seemed logical to form one fully-integrated film company, closely connected to RCA, in order to maximize profits for all parties involved.

The new corporation, Radio-Keith-Orpheum (from *Radio* Corporation of America, and *Keith*-Albee-*Orpheum* theaters) was formed in October 1928. Technically RKO functioned as

33. (l. to r.) Joseph P. Kennedy, David Sarnoff and C. W. Stone in June 1928

a holding company for the interests involved, with only stock changing hands. David Sarnoff became the president of the new corporation. Assets totaled more than $100 million. Instantly, RCA had the broadest-based popular entertainment empire in the United States, with both radio (National Broadcasting Company) and motion pictures. Sarnoff moved quickly in 1929 to make sure RKO would prosper. Once production was on firm footing with Radio Pictures Inc., RKO began to add more theaters to the chain. In a major stroke, Sarnoff helped to broaden RKO's market by negotiating a deal with 1000 independent exhibitors. RCA would supply the sound equipment (at better terms than Western Electric) and RKO would supply the films. To match the productive capabilities of Paramount, Loew's, Warners and Fox, RCA created a subsidiary to publish popular music. Thus, by the end of 1929 RKO stood as 'nearly-the-equal' of the other major movie corporations, becoming the final member of the Big Five. RKO's comparative advantage lay with its ties to RCA. Together, they touched all spheres of popular entertainment technology: radio, motion pictures, phonograph records (RCA Victor) and music publishing.

After a rapid ascent into fifth place in the industry, RKO entered the 1930s with high hopes, but, unable to handle all the necessary mortgage payments for its theaters, RKO went into equity receivership in January 1933 – several months before Fox and Paramount. RKO was tied up in court for more than six years, emerging as a reorganized concern in January 1940. During the boom of the Second World War the corporation prospered, but in 1948 billionaire Howard Hughes purchased RKO. Quickly he agreed to sell its theaters, the first of the Big Five to do so. On remand from the Supreme Court, and even before a final decision in the case, RKO consented to divorce exhibition from the production–distribution units of the corporation. RKO, under Hughes, signed its consent decree on 8 November 1948; the final Supreme Court decision did not come until 25 July 1949. Hughes, with previous experience as a motion picture producer, took control of Radio Pictures. This sale signaled the end of the studio era.

In the 1930s, RKO was formally a holding company organized to control production and distribution (RKO Radio Pictures Inc.), and the theaters of the old Keith-Albee-Orpheum chain. In 1930, flush with enthusiasm, RKO had completely equipped the old FBO lot and acquired an additional 500 acres in the San Fernando Valley for outdoor shooting. Expansion continued into 1931 when RKO took over the assets of Pathé Exchange Inc., which included the Pathé studios in Culver City, California, the Pathé News and Pathé Review subsidiaries, creators of newsreels and shorts, a film-printing laboratory in Jersey City, New Jersey and a world-wide organization for film distribution. Properties of Pathé were folded into five wholly owned RKO subsidiaries: Pathé News Inc., RKO Pathé Pictures, RKO Pathé Export Corporation, RKO Pathé Studios Ltd. and RKO Pathé Distributing Corporation. This acquisition simply added to already existing Hollywood studios and a world-wide distribution network. The Pathé merger made RKO the equal of the rest of the Big Five in one respect – distribution. Its world-wide network matched even that of Loew's and Paramount.

But the majority of RKO's subsidiaries (and assets) were held in the form of theater buildings and properties. At the end of 1932 RKO, either directly or through subsidiaries, fully owned 180 theaters and held a half-interest in seventy more. To monitor this chain, RKO created five divisions: Radio-Keith-Orpheum Corporation, Keith-Albee-Orpheum Corporation, Orpheum Circuit Inc., B. F. Keith Corporation and Greater New York Vaudeville Theaters Corporation. RKO's circuit ranked with Loew's at the tail end of the Big Five. (These smaller circuits controlled one-third as many houses as Warners and Fox, one-sixth of Paramount.) The bulk of RKO's houses were concentrated in the New York City environs, splitting that market with Loew's. The remainder were scattered throughout the United States, representing the one or two former vaudeville houses in nearly every large American city. In 1939 RKO maintained a strong presence in these major US cities (with their relative rankings in the 1940 census): New York (1), Chicago (2), Los Angeles (5), Cleveland (6), Boston (9), Washington, DC (11), San Francisco (12), New Orleans (15), Minneapolis (16), Cincinnati (17), Newark (18), Rochester (23), Denver (25), Columbus (27), Jersey City (30), St Paul (33), Omaha (39), Dayton (40), Syracuse (41), Grand Rapids (52), Des Moines (55), Yonkers (61), Albany (65), Trenton (67) and Lowell, Massachusetts (89). Undoubtedly RKO's most famous theater was Radio City Music Hall, leased from Rockefeller Center Inc. Radio City provided a grand opening for all RKO productions throughout most of the studio era.

The 1940 reorganization streamlined RKO's holdings. RKO Pathé Pictures, RKO Pathé Distributing Corporation, RKO Pathé Export Corporation, RKO Pathé Studios Ltd.,

RKO Distributing Corporation, RKO Studios Inc, and RKO Export Corporation all disappeared into RKO Radio Pictures Inc. The theater circuits were consolidated under seven headings, with the Keith-Albee-Orpheum Corporation taking the bulk. (In 1946 came further consolidation, placing nearly all theaters under the banner of RKO Theaters Inc.) The 1940 reorganization forced the sale (or termination of the lease) of more than 100 theaters. Going into the Second World War, RKO controlled just over 100 houses, the smallest circuit of the Big Five, but it held on to its first-run houses in New York, New Jersey and Ohio and, despite its size, RKO's circuit retained enormous economic power through its holdings in America's largest city, New York. Because of its original relationship with RCA, RKO never diversified outside the motion picture business.

In 1944 RKO ventured into television, applying for several station licenses, but the FCC delayed decisions until the Paramount anti-trust case was settled by the US Supreme Court, and before that Hughes withdrew the applications. In 1955 he sold RKO's features to the General Tire Company for presentation on television. These were the first features from the Big Five to receive wide exposure on American television.

RKO, like the other members of the Big Five, participated in film production in Europe in order to circumvent quota and tariff restrictions. In 1931, RKO executed a pact to co-produce films in Britain with Associated Talking Pictures. From 1932 to 1939 (inclusive) one film per month was released under this arrangement. Only a handful ever made their way to the United States. The Second World War put an end to this arrangement. After the war, RKO announced an ambitious project of co-productions with J. Arthur Rank. Like many of Rank's projects of this period (a similar one was announced with Universal) little, save promises, ever came of this arrangement.

The management of RKO was in constant flux throughout the studio era. As soon as David Sarnoff put RKO together he returned to his first love, radio broadcasting. He appointed Hiram Brown, a former public utilities executive, as RKO's first true president. Sarnoff wanted Brown to squeeze maximum profits from an efficient business, not institute new policies or innovations. To handle film production, Brown settled on Joseph I. Schnitzer, an experienced movie executive and former vice-president of FBO, and producer William LeBaron. Brown and Schnitzer heralded RKO's beginning in grand style: RKO would be the modern movie company, linked to the new age of radio. Images of thunderbolts, skyscrapers and radio towers filled the

34. The RKO
management team in
June 1931: (l. to r.)
Joseph I. Schnitzer,
Charles Rogers, Hiram
Brown, Samuel
Rothefel, David
Sarnoff and William
LeBaron

corporation's advertisements and logos. Then the Depression struck. RKO, like Fox and Paramount, could not cover its mortgages. Special loans were taken out; debts were recapitalized, but nothing seemed to work. Inexorably, RKO began to sink toward bankruptcy.

Hiram Brown resigned in 1931. Sarnoff tapped one of his own to help turn RKO around. Merlin Hall Aylesworth, president of the National Broadcasting Company radio network, replaced Brown. Aylesworth was yet another former public utilities expert, who had become president (and organizer *extraordinaire*) of NBC. He continued as NBC president, spending mornings on motion-picture business and afternoons on radio business. Aylesworth turned to Benjamin B. Kahane, long-time Keith-Albee-Orpheum theater executive, to co-ordinate film production, and to Harold B. Franklin, former Fox theater executive, to try to lead the RKO theaters to profits. The new management team immediately cut costs on all fronts, including a 10 per cent salary reduction for all employees. RKO opened its Pathé studio in Culver City to independent producers, thereby generating needed revenues. Writers were laid off; the studio's prop department was reorganized; production crews were reduced. At the theater end, stage shows – a carry-over from RKO's glory days of the 1920s – were eliminated. But late in 1932 one set of expenses rose. Radio City Music Hall opened. This 6,200 seat theater, with its Roxyettes (later Rockettes), only served to drain off needed resources. In addition, as part of the lease, RKO was obligated to move its corporate offices into Rockefeller Center.

Unable to pay the required rent on either facility, RKO tendered stock. The Rockefeller family, owners and creaters of Rockefeller Center, soon became part-owners of the ailing movie company.

In 1933 RKO's condition worsened. In January the corporation formally defaulted on more than $3.5 million loans and went into the receivership from which it did not emerge until the end of the decade. From 1933 to 1939 a United States District Court administered its affairs. Going to court seemed to settle corporate turmoil for a time; indeed, RKO began to make progress toward profits in 1934. (In 1935 the corporation actually made money for the first time since 1930.) The Radio City Music Hall lease was transferred back to the Rockefellers; the Gower Street studio was so busy that three new sound stages (in addition to the existing ten), a film vault and a three-storey office building were added. But the corporation lacked strong leadership. Aylesworth was spending most of his time on radio business. In October 1935, a new party entered the RKO matrix. Floyd Odlum's Atlas Corporation, in conjunction with the Wall Street banking house Lehman Brothers paid $5 million for a large block (although not a controlling interest) of RKO stock.

Atlas Corporation's purchase precipitated yet another shake-up of corporate management. Leo Spitz became president, while Aylesworth temporarily moved up to chairman, finally leaving in 1937. Spitz, a Chicago lawyer, was a specialist in theater reorganization, having honed his act on Paramount's problems during the preceding two years. He prepared the corporation for settlement of reorganization and took an active interest in production, unwilling to leave that to assistants, but corporate profits began to sag, again hitting red ink in 1938. After some conflict, Spitz resigned in that same year.

Spitz had been Atlas' choice. Dissatisfied, the Rockefellers stepped in with a replacement, a former Paramount executive, George Schaefer. He needed all his acquired skills to push RKO's profits in a positive direction once again. Help came from the US District Court. On 26 January 1940 – seven years less one day from filing – RKO came out of receivership. During this longest of movie reorganization cases, RKO was able to reduce its outstanding obligations by more than $10 million. The 'new' RKO could begin afresh, with adequate working capital and no significant indebtedness. RKO did not have to pay dividends for one year; in fact, none had been paid since the company had been created some twelve years earlier. Schaefer involved himself in all aspects of RKO's operation, completely revamping the company

131

– once again – within the space of one year, but even with the beginning of the boom of the Second World War, Schaefer never seemed to push profits very far above zero. With profits falling – quite remarkably – even below a level maintained by Universal, Schaefer resigned in 1942.

In 1942, Atlas president Floyd Odlum moved in to supervise RKO directly. Atlas now owned a controlling interest. In June 1942, Odlum named his representative Peter Rathvon to be president and chairman of the board. Long-time assistant in distribution Ned Depinet became president of RKO Radio Pictures; Charles Koerner took direct charge of production. Yet another management team was in place, but this one, buoyed by easy profits in the Second World War economy, remained in place for an unprecedented four years. Profits soared to record levels in 1943. The years 1943 to 1947 were a golden age for RKO. The other four members of the Big Five did far better, but RKO was firmly in fifth place in terms of profitability, back ahead of Universal. The Rathvon management team continued in place until 1946 when Charles Koerner, unheralded studio boss, died at the age of 50 of leukemia. Dore Schary, a former writer, fresh from his success as a producer at MGM, became head of production. Schary, inheriting Koerner's production schedule, helped RKO to its best year in history in terms of profits, $12 million in 1946. This war-inflated amount was double that of any other year in the corporation's history.

Sometime in 1947, Odlum, always the speculator, reasoned that the studio era was almost over. The time had come to take one's earnings and move elsewhere. On the surface, surely, RKO seemed to have finally achieved corporate health. Odlum noticed his management team had increased the book value of the corporation by some $30 million in three years. At first, no one would meet Odlum's asking price of $9 million. Finally, billionaire Howard Hughes stepped forward. Hughes' record of eccentric behavior is well documented. His bizarre actions at the helm of RKO from 1948 until 1954 added to this legend. During the summer of 1948 Peter Rathvon, RKO's successful president, was fired, as were 700 other employees. Hughes' *alter ego,* Noah Dietrich, assumed the presidency of RKO. This signaled the end of RKO as a serious movie concern. Hughes dismantled RKO in the mid-1950s: the studio lot went to Desilu, the films to General Tire. RKO formally went out of the movie business in 1957, retaining only a skeleton staff to handle further film rentals. (The name lives on through General Tire which has labeled its various media enterprises – radio and television stations, distribution of films for television and others – the RKO division.)

With all the corporate ownership and executive changes at RKO, no strategy for feature film production existed very long. Continuity of production was a trademark for the other members of the Big Five, but not RKO. Production executives at other studios measured their tenure in decades. An RKO production chief was counted a success if he survived more than three years. As soon as new executives were installed in New York, they fired whomever was in charge in Hollywood. A new strategy for feature film production was established, and a new mogul was sent to run the studio accordingly. Remarkably, the short subject, animation and newsreel divisions were less affected, retaining a significant amount of continuity amidst all the change.

The initial production team, Joseph I. Schnitzer and William LeBaron, concentrated on musicals based on proven Broadway attractions: Florenz Ziegfeld's **Rio Rita** and Vincent

35. Bebe Daniels and John Boles in **Rio Rita**

Youman's **Hit the Deck.** A tie-in with RCA, **Radio Revels,** with original book, lyrics and music by Harry Ruby and Bert Kalmer, proved an exception. With writers Ben Hecht and Charles MacArthur and stars Bebe Daniels and Richard Dix RKO seemed to get off to a fast start. Unfortunately, the only big hit of those early days was **Rio Rita,** which contributed more than $1 million in profits to the new enterprise. Lacking a collection of stars and experienced production staff, RKO went outside the industry for performers and sought out narratives with already established market value. So, for example, in 1930 RKO signed Freeman Gosden and Charles Correll to create 'Amos 'n Andy', a sensation on RCA's National Broadcasting Company. Soon, the production bubble burst. Outsiders stayed for only one film. The studio seemed unable to develop replacements with long-run attractive star power. New musicals, **Hit the Deck** and **Dixiana,** failed at the box office. Success at the box office came with **Cimarron,** released early in 1931. Unfortunately this blockbuster, although winning the 1931 Oscar for best picture, could not cover its $1.5 million production cost. (RKO never again earned a best picture Oscar for an indigenous production although it distributed Samuel Goldwyn's **The Best Years of Our Lives,** best picture in 1946.)

Film production bosses Schnitzer and LeBaron helped to propel RKO into 1932 with a $5 million production deficit. Early in that year, they were replaced in Hollywood by David O. Selznick. Selznick took on two assistants, both of whom went on to play important roles in RKO. The first, Merian C. Cooper,

36. Pandro S. Berman

produced **King Kong** in 1933. Selznick's other assistant, Pandro
Berman, supervised the Astaire-Rogers musicals and, for a time,
was even in charge of production during the late 1930s. Selznick's
first move was to cut costs. Contract players were only guaranteed
six months of work. Radio Pictures and Pathé productions were
merged, thereby eliminating staff duplication. In Selznick's first
year, he saved an estimated $5 million and was still able to sign up
major talents including George Cukor, William Wellman and
Dudley Nichols. Popular films came with **The Animal Kingdom**
(based on a Philip Barry play, starring Leslie Howard and Myrna

37. Merian C. Cooper

Loy), Selznick's **What Price Hollywood** and **Bill of Divorcement**
and Cooper's **King Kong.** Selznick kept costs low and attracted
major talent to the studio through a system of unit production by
which he lured independent producers to RKO to create a
contracted number of films, with little direct studio supervision.
　　Selznick tried to build up RKO's shrinking stable of stars
by signing John Barrymore, Leslie Howard and Billie Burke. His
most important find was Katharine Hepburn. She first starred in
Selznick's own **Bill of Divorcement** and, with **Morning Glory,**
earned the Oscar for best actress for 1932–3. But November 1932
saw the release of two features, **Rockabye** and **The Conquerors,**

both of which lost a great deal of money. The New York office became concerned about Selznick's handling of the studio, and when Merlin Aylesworth became president he forced Selznick to resign in February 1933.

Aylesworth appointed a Selznick assistant, Merian C. Cooper, to take charge of the studio. Again costs were cut and a variety of players, writers and production workers let go. Cooper was able to slash negative costs of features by some 75 per cent. A form of unit production continued (John Ford came in to do **The Lost Patrol,** the top RKO grosser of the 1934 season), but Cooper relied on a group of his assistants to supervise production closely. Just as his system was beginning to get started, Merian Cooper suffered a heart attack. Pandro Berman substituted for a time. Films starring Constance Bennett, Ann Harding, Irene Dunne, Richard Dix and newcomer Joel McCrea delivered improved box office returns. Four films, **Melody Cruise** (directed by Mark Sandrich, promoted from the shorts unit), **Little Women** (with Hepburn), **Flying Down to Rio** (Sandrich directing, with Astaire and Rogers in minor roles) and the Kong sequel **Son of Kong,** did very well at the box-office, but Cooper never recovered his health to feel strong enough to continue as production chief, so he resigned in 1934 after only sixteen months on the job.

An operative sent from the New York office, J. R. McDonough, replaced Cooper. Berman, not selected for the position, stayed at the studio as a producer. McDonough had no production experience, and had only been with RKO for a year, but he was willing to follow Aylesworth's orders. B. B. Kahane, an old RKO theater hand, handled the day-to-day production decisions. Kahane formalized Cooper's associate producer system with separate units under Pandro Berman, Kenneth MacGowan, Lou Brock, Richard A. Rowland, B. H. Fineman, Cliff Reid, Glendon Allvine and H. N. Swanson. The latter four supervised 'B' film operations, while Pandro Berman and company handled the top-drawer productions. Berman was the most valuable producer. Between 1935 and 1938, his Astaire–Rogers musicals were the only films to earn RKO a place in the industry's top grossing pictures. In the mid-1930s these Astaire–Rogers musicals grossed a consistent $2 million per film (**Top Hat** topped $3 million), earning RKO profits of at least $0.5 million per picture.

When in 1935 the Atlas Corporation bought into RKO and helped to install Leo Spitz as president, yet another executive team, headed by Samuel Briskin, was put in charge of feature film production at the Hollywood studio. Briskin made a significant

38. Fred Astaire in **Top Hat** (courtesy RKO General Pictures)

contribution right away by signing Disney to a distribution contract. This led to distribution fees from **Snow White and the Seven Dwarfs,** the top-grossing film of 1938. New producers, strictly feature film types, signed on, including Edward Small and Jesse Lasky. Briskin did not live up to this initial promise, in part because of losses generated by features planned by his predecessor. Katharine Hepburn, the studio's lone bankable star, went into a temporary career decline. The careers of Ann Harding and Richard Dix were ending. Technicolor spectacles such as **Daring Pirate** and Bobby Breen musicals lost money, as did prestige films **Mary of Scotland** and Maxwell Anderson's **Winterset.** RKO had profitable years in 1936 and 1937 only because its theaters participated in an upturn in movie attendance and the Astaire–Rogers musicals continued to earn millions.

RKO's downturn (toward years of losses in 1939 and 1940) led to Samuel Briskin's resignation in October 1937. Like Selznick before him, Briskin had waged almost continual warfare with the front office, in this case with Leo Spitz. Of course Spitz won, and appointed long-time RKO producer (and survivor) Pandro Berman as the next executive in charge of production. Berman had thrived as a unit producer under all administrations except Briskin's. He was an ace producer, but could not function as an administrator under Leo Spitz. Spitz and Berman managed to fritter away the few studio assets Briskin had kept. Katharine Hepburn left RKO only to appear two years later at better-managed MGM in **The Philadelphia Story.** Producers Edward Kaufman, Jesse Lasky and Edward Small took their leave. To Spitz's credit he did sign producer–directors Leo McCarey and Gregory La Cava, and promote George Stevens to producer status. In general, however, Spitz had decided to emphasize the 'B' film. The studio was able to develop only one long-running series, 'The Saint', featuring a suave private eye with style and wit. Actor Louis Hayward initiated the role; George Sanders made it famous. The original, **The Saint in New York,** proved that 'B' films could make as much money as most of RKO's 'A' features – on a quarter of the investment. Producer Lew Landers supervised eight 'B' films in 1938, all of which made enough money to cover RKO's losses on its 'A' films. Even **Carefree,** the penultimate RKO Astaire–Rogers musical, actually lost money.

As RKO began to move into the red, Leo Spitz resigned and George Schaefer took his place. This compromise candidate remained in charge for a turbulent three years. For a time, Schaefer let Pandro Berman run the studio while he reorganized the New York office. Then, in 1939, Schaefer moved west. After six months on the job Berman left for the luxury and stability of MGM. Schaefer reinstituted the unit production system, aiming to make top quality, prestige films and, he hoped, to turn RKO into another MGM. He looked to various sources for his new producers. Several came from Broadway. Theatrical impresarios

39. George Schaefer, Dolores Del Rio, Orson Welles and Elsa Maxwell outside Radio City Music Hall for the première of **Citizen Kane**

138

Max Gordon and Harry Goetz created **Abe Lincoln in Illinois** with Raymond Massey; Jed Harris, fresh from a string of successes on the stage in New York, signed a three-year contract to produce three films of his choice. British producer Herbert Wilcox relocated from London. In the long run, Schaefer's most sensational new finds, of course, were Orson Welles and his Mercury Theater Company.

Still, RKO did not give up totally on 'B' films. For the 1939–40 season RKO's $20 million production program included twelve 'A' films (costing about $800,000 each), six 'in-betweens' ($200,000 each), twenty 'Bs' ($125,000 each), and six George O'Brien westerns ($85,000). This array, topped by **The Hunchback of Notre Dame** and **Abe Lincoln in Illinois**, seemed solid. The stars were impressive: Charles Laughton, Carole Lombard, Ginger Rogers and Cary Grant. The top grossers turned out to be **Hunchback of Notre Dame, My Favorite Wife** (Garson Kanin, producer; Irene Dunne and Cary Grant, stars), and Disney's second animated feature, **Pinocchio.** Nonetheless, RKO lost money in both 1939 and 1940. Somehow Schaefer survived until 1942. Indeed, from 1940 to 1942 he ran the corporation single-handed. Conditions at the studio became somewhat chaotic. Fred Astaire and George Stevens left. To help sort things out Schaefer hired the former director of the Hays Office's Production Code Administration, Joseph I. Breen, as his personal assistant. Breen did not help and left within the year. On one positive note, Schaefer did initiate the signing of Samuel Goldwyn. Goldwyn had just ended a bitter lawsuit with his 'partners' at United Artists, and selected RKO to distribute his films. In Disney and Goldwyn, RKO now had two of the top independent producers in Hollywood – the core of what had been the profitable United Artists Corporation. However, attracting Goldwyn did not save Schaefer and in February 1942 he was replaced by Charles Koerner.

Koerner, a former theater executive, again changed studio gears, fully abandoning the idea of prestige films in favor of lower budget money-makers. He cancelled all the unit production deals and unceremoniously released all Schaefer's prestige films. The new administration sought to earn a small amount on all films, rather than risk millions on twelve 'A' films per year. Koerner instituted a policy of 'exploitation' films – cheaply made, concerned with topics of current interest and promoted heavily. Indeed, the top grossing RKO film of the highly successful 1942–3 season was **Hitler's Children,** an anti-Nazi melodrama which cost only $200,000 but grossed more than $3 million. RKO produced

40. Charles Koerner

Behind the Rising Sun as a sequel. More creative, but in the same vein, were the horror films of producer Val Lewton, initiated in 1942 with **The Cat People** (cost $80,000; gross $1 million). Lewton produced eleven horror film-thrillers in four years. Little of high quality could be found outside the Lewton products. Exceptions were Jean Renoir's **This Land is Mine,** Robert Siodmak's **The Spiral Staircase** and Alfred Hitchcock's **Notorious.** Leo McCarey brought Bing Crosby to RKO for one film, the smash hit, **The Bells of St Mary's.** But in general, RKO's biggest grosses for 'A' fare came from independent producer Samuel Goldwyn. His

41. **Hitler's Children**
(courtesy RKO
General Pictures)

140

North Star (1943 – Lewis Milestone, director, with Anne Baxter and Dana Andrews), **The Princess and the Pirate** (1944 – Bob Hope and Virginia Mayo), **Wonder Man** (1945 – Danny Kaye and Virginia Mayo), **The Kid from Brooklyn** (1946 – Kaye) and the much honored **The Best Years of Our Lives** (1946) accounted for nearly all RKO's top grossing mainline 'A' features of the Koerner era.

42. Myrna Loy and Fredric March in **The Best Years of Our Lives** (courtesy the Sam Goldwyn Company)

RKO's Golden Age ended when Koerner died on 2 February 1946. Dore Schary, an experienced writer and producer from MGM, took charge. Quickly he began to experiment with controversial films (**Crossfire**) and *films noirs* (Nicholas Ray's **They Live by Night** and Jacques Tourneur's **Out of the Past**). Almost overnight, RKO had become the boldest new studio in Hollywood, but no longer as profitable as under Koerner. Moreover, within a year Howard Hughes had seized control and begun to run RKO in his own quixotic manner. Schary was fired. Only Hughes' pet projects stood any chance of survival. So it surprised no one that, although producers Jerry Wald and Norman Krasna were brought in to make fifty films, they completed only four. The studio closed; reopened; closed again; and so on. During the final years of the studio era, RKO was able to create only one of the industry's sixty top grossing films, ranking with United Artists as the corporation with the poorest record among the Big Five and Little Three. Only by dismantling RKO was Hughes able to make a profit on his original investment.

With all its problems RKO was able to offer theater

owners short subjects and newsreels. The 1928 merger also proffered a shorts department. The studio produced and distributed several of the more popular series of shorts of the studio era. Moreover, several important directors were able to learn their craft in the shorts department. Mark Sandrich graduated to Astaire–Rogers musicals. (For the shorts unit, he directed **So This Is Harris,** a three-reeler which won the first Academy Award given for short subjects.) George Stevens also began in RKO's shorts unit. An alumnus of the Hal Roach lot, Stevens helped with the 'Blondes and Redheads' series. Variety was the watchword in RKO's shorts. During the 1930s RKO featured a wide selection of musical artists in its 'Headliners' series. Also quite popular were 'Information Please' (based on the popular radio show), 'Picture People' (behind the scenes of Hollywood productions, usually those at RKO), 'Flicker Flashbacks' (a comedy series based on silent film clips) and 'Sportscopes'. Finally, from August 1935 RKO distributed the famous 'March of Time' series (described in detail in the preceding chapter on Fox), until July 1942, when Time–Life, disgusted with RKO's frequent turnover in management, transferred to Fox. In response, in 1943 RKO created its own version 'This is America'. With 112 issues, it ran until 1951. It was RKO's low-cost alternative to 'March of Time' and was seen only in RKO theaters and non-affiliated houses.

However, RKO's stalwarts were comics Edgar Kennedy and Leon Errol. Kennedy, whose roots stretched back to the origins of silent comedy, created a seventeen-year series (1931–48) of more than 100 titles. His 'Average Man' began in April 1931, and progressed with a release every two months for nearly the length of the studio era. Each short regularly took only twenty days to shoot, so Kennedy could also appear in features. In 1948, when Kennedy died, RKO tried to perfect an updated replacement, 'The Newlyweds'. This precursor of situation comedy, which utilized the staff from the Kennedy unit as well as several of its players, lasted only four years. Leon Errol's career paralleled Kennedy's. Errol started on the burlesque circuit and eventually moved up to vaudeville and The Ziegfeld Follies (1911–15). Although he appeared in both silent and sound features, his motion picture career centered on the nearly one hundred two-reelers created at RKO between 1935 and 1951. Errol perfected the image of the 'henpecked husband', always in trouble with drink, another woman, the bill collector or some other threat to family tranquility. Early on in his career in comedy shorts, Errol had worked for Columbia, Paramount and Warners. He settled at RKO in 1935, producing one short every two months for the next sixteen years. Like the Kennedy series, the Leon Errol comedies ended with the star's death. Before he died in 1951, there was a plan to expand the series into a television situation comedy, but that was dropped.

RKO entered the newsreel business with the Pathé merger in 1931. Pathé had a long, distinguished history in newsreels beginning when Pathé Frères established an American branch in 1911. Centered in Jersey City, New Jersey, newsreels were originally released to the American market through the Keith-Albee vaudeville circuit. In the mid-1920s Charles Pathé sold off his motion picture empire and although the Pathé name survived, the American newsreel company was completely owned and operated by US interests. Not affiliated to a major studio, Pathé sold its product to independent, non-affiliated theaters. The link with RKO changed all that. In the 1930s, under former Fox Movietone executive Courtland Smith, Pathé emphasized sports coverage and occasional long editions focussing on one issue. The newsreel prospered throughout the studio era. Howard Hughes sold it in 1948 to Warner Bros. for $5 million cash.

The crown jewel in RKO's short subject offerings – from 1937 to 1954 – was animation from the Disney studio, but it was not always thus. During the early 1930s, RKO distributed cartoons created by the Van Beuren Studio. Amadee J. Van Beuren came to motion pictures in the late 1920s. For a time he teamed with Paul Terry to create 'Aesop's Fables' but the two split up in 1929. Terry left for Educational; most of his staff remained with Van Beuren, as did the 'Aesop's Fables' but the popularity of the series dropped off when Terry left and the newly-titled Van Beuren studio initiated a search for new animated stars. In 1931 Van Beuren tried Tom and Jerry, a Mutt and Jeff duo of human-life figures – not the MGM figures of a decade later. Van Beuren produced twenty-six 'Tom and Jerrys' with little success. Next came Cubby Bear, a Mickey Mouse clone. In 1934 the studio even tried an animated version of Amos 'n' Andy, using voices from the radio series. When Atlas bought into RKO in 1935 Floyd Oldum offered a favorable distribution deal to Disney. When the latter accepted, Van Beuren was out.

Disney came to RKO from United Artists. In 1936, when Mary Pickford became president of United Artists, her first major task was to renegotiate a renewal of the Disney contract. Disney, near the height of its critical and financial success, sought an improved deal including retention of any future television rights. Negotiations stalled and RKO stepped in and topped UA's offer on all counts. RKO had captured the most popular maker of

43. Roy and Walt
Disney stand behind an
Oscar and Mickey

animated films in the business, and through all the subsequent changes in ownership and management no one – not even Howard Hughes – ever contemplated axing Disney. Only when Hughes began to dismantle the corporation in 1954 did Disney set up its own distribution arm, Buena Vista.

When the Disney studio signed with RKO, it was already world-famous. With the coming of sound Disney created its first star in 1928 with Mickey Mouse. The 'Silly Symphonies', begun by Disney in 1929, pioneered the use of color in animated shorts. In 1932, Disney's **Flowers and Trees,** an entry in the 'Silly Symphony' series, won the first Oscar for a cartoon short. New stars quickly followed: Donald Duck, Goofy and Pluto. A lucrative merchandising sales force was set up, securing a percentage from all products utilizing a Disney character. But throughout the early 1930s, the Disney studio rarely earned profits of more than half a million dollars per annum. Walt Disney reinvested all earnings into more complex productions. When RKO agreed to top UA's distribution terms, it came as a welcome financial shot in the arm to the Disney operation.

RKO cashed in right away. Disney was on the verge of completing **Snow White and the Seven Dwarfs** when the Disney–RKO deal was consummated. That feature became the biggest hit of 1938, earning $8 million upon initial release. For a brief time it stood as the highest grossing film of all time. (**Gone With the Wind** took away that honor in 1939.) Disney seemed on a roll; all available money was poured into feature production. But although **Pinnochio** took in a lot, it cost even more. **Fantasia** lost a

144

44. **Snow White and the Seven Dwarfs** (courtesy Walt Disney Productions)

great deal of money and forced Disney in 1940 to go public to gather needed capital. The pressure of moving into a new studio and producing features and shorts produced a bitter strike in 1941. The result of the strike, settled in a matter of weeks, named the Screen Cartoonists Guild as the official negotiator for studio employees. This signaled the beginning of a rocky road for Disney during the rest of the studio era.

Disney did not prosper during the Second World War. **Bambi** in 1941 was the last major animated feature until the 1950 **Cinderella.** The Donald Duck, Pluto, Goofy and Mickey Mouse shorts continued (at the rate of one per month) throughout the 1940s, but were not enough to sustain the expanded overhead. The US government helped. Disney had negotiated government contracts prior to Pearl Harbor. From 1942 to 1946 the Disney studio produced numerous films for training and instruction. To 'boost wartime morale' and improve relations with Latin America, Disney produced two short, live–animated featurettes. **Saludos Amigos** (1943) grossed $1.2 million for a cost of $300,000; **The Three Caballeros** (1945) grossed $4 million for a cost of $2 million. But the expected post-war boom never took place. Profits stagnated; there were even losses in 1948 and 1949. It took Disney a decade to re-tool and turn to live features, television programs and amusement parks. However, no one should underestimate the importance of the Disney product to RKO. With it RKO always had one of the more attractive packages of shorts to offer theaters, and often the shorts helped sell the features – a situation unique among the Big Five.

145

All the same, RKO had the shortest, least profitable corporate life of any major motion picture corporation. What little success it did achieve was probably due to factors other than its production of feature films. RKO's theaters, though never a powerful circuit, continually made profits, except during the Great Depression. The corporation would not have survived had RKO owned no theaters. RKO did best during the Second World War boom. This Second World War prosperity came at a particularly useful time. The studio did make a handful of popular films, but what success it achieved in its 28 year life came from distribution of the features of Samuel Goldwyn and the shorts and features of the Disney studio. United Artists is remembered as the distributor of independent producers, but during the 1940s RKO ranked with UA as a home for independent producers.

7:

Universal

Universal, Columbia and United Artists constituted the studio era's Little Three. These three corporations were important industry participants but did not own any theaters and so lacked the profit potential and economic power of the Big Five. The largest of the Little Three was Universal Pictures Inc. This corporation could trace its origins as far back as Loew's, Paramount or Fox and had been in business for many years before Warners became important or RKO even existed. But Universal long suffered under poor management. The year 1930 was one of the best in movie history. Paramount made $25 million, Loew's nearly $15 million, Warners $7 million, Fox $6.5 million and RKO, only in business one year, credited $3.4 million. Remarkably, Universal lost money – $2.2 million to be exact (see Table 7.1). Universal, unlike the others, had not expanded in the 1920s. It had temporarily set up a theater circuit, but abandoned it, so, as the industry faced the Great Depression, Universal was ill-prepared, forced to the periphery of the studio system. As the Big Five rebounded during the 1930s, Universal continually suffered losses or earned tiny profits. For example, between 1936 and 1938, it lost $3.5 million as Loew's accumulated nearly $35 million in profits. Like RKO, Universal could not help but prosper during the Second World War but at a rate only a third to a fifth that of the Big Five, and as soon as economic conditions worsened after the war Universal's balance sheet quickly turned red. Universal did not do well as a corporation until after it was taken over by the Music Corporation of America (MCA) in 1959.

It was not always so. The Universal Film Manufacturing

Table 7.1: Universal's Balance Sheet

Year	Net Profit (millions of dollars)	Assets (millions of dollars)
1930	(2.2)	17.1
1931	0.4	15.2
1932	(1.7)	14.2
1933	(1.0)	13.6
1934	0.2	12.6
1935	(0.7)	11.6
1936	(1.8)	10.6
1937	(1.1)	11.8
1938	(0.6)	12.3
1939	1.2	14.9
1940	2.4	15.6
1941	2.7	19.5
1942	2.8	25.4
1943	3.8	27.6
1944	3.4	33.5
1945	4.0	31.7
1946	4.6	42.4
1947	3.2	53.9
1948	(3.2)	48.0
1949	(1.1)	45.0

Company was formed in June 1912 by a German immigrant, Carl Laemmle. Laemmle had come to the US in 1884. After a career in the clothing business, he opened a nickelodeon in Chicago in 1906. Soon after this he entered the distribution business in order to guarantee his growing chain of theaters a steady flow of films. Faced with the termination of his supply by virtue of his non-co-operation with the Motion Picture Patents Company, Laemmle formed the Independent Motion Picture Company of America (IMP) in 1909. By combining IMP production with releases from other independents a theater could operate outside the MPPC. Laemmle and IMP prospered and expanded. In 1910 IMP joined with several other independent producers to form the Motion Picture Distributing Sales Company. This association did not work out, so Laemmle tried again, and in 1912 formed

45. Will Hays, Mary Pickford, Carl Laemmle and Will Rogers at a ceremony marking the twenty-fifth anniversary of Laemmle's entry into motion pictures

Universal by combining the interests of six partners (IMP Films, Powers Motion Picture Company, Rex Motion Picture Company, Champion Film Company, Nestor Film Company, and the New York Film Company). This company also began to unravel as partners argued and disagreed, so a third try was necessary. Laemmle, with Robert H. Cochrane, his financial manager, formed the new Universal, the company which survived.

Universal had small studios in New York, New Jersey and Hollywood, but wanted to consolidate operations. So in 1914 it purchased the 230-acre Taylor ranch in North Hollywood for $165,000. For nearly a year laborers worked on the property. The new studio was the most modern in the world, with up-to-date electrical wiring and a massive open-air stage on which several films could be shot at the same time. Universal City had its gala opening on 15 March 1915 to a wave of national publicity. Thousands of tourists and native Californians helped with the celebration. Ironically, with this beginning Universal was near the peak of its power as a motion picture enterprise, a lofty position it would not again attain until the 1960s.

To reap the most from this investment, Universal went ahead to produce three brands of features, aiming to fill all of an exhibitor's time. Unfortunately, Universal sought in all three

149

cases to create inexpensive action-films and Westerns and let others (for example, Famous Players) go for quality stories with famous stars. Universal succeeded only in becoming the Woolworths of the movie production world. Consequently, producers, directors and performers started at Universal, only to move elsewhere for higher salaries and bigger budgets. For example, both the noted director John Ford and the famous producer Irving Thalberg started at Universal, but moved on by the mid-1920s – Ford to Fox and Thalberg to MGM. Universal's production strategy was aimed at rural and small-town exhibitors. Since Famous Players and Loew's had no interest in these subsequent-run houses, Universal had no trouble booking its 'Woolworth's' products throughout the 1920s, but while doing so, Universal missed its chance to acquire first-run picture palaces. Universal did try to start a theater circuit in 1925, but by then the Big Five (or their theater predecessors) had all the optimal situations locked up. Universal was left with no choice but to concentrate on production and distribution for small neighborhood and rural theaters. At its height, in 1928, Universal Theaters operated 315 houses in Canada, the District of Columbia and twenty states, principally Oklahoma, Texas, New York and Ohio. Universal did not have the economic muscle to wire these houses for sound, and so between 1929 and 1933 disposed of its circuit. In 1933 what remained of the Universal chain went into receivership and the remaining theaters were quickly sold.

In the 1920s prospects looked promising in the arenas of production and distribution. Not able to gain access to first-run theaters in the US, Universal organized substantial overseas operations. There seemed to be a profitable market in Europe for Universal's Westerns. Through these connections Universal tried to import leading European film-making talent to create prestige films. Carl Laemmle's son, Carl Laemmle Junior (also known as Junior Laemmle), assumed the post of head of production during the late 1920s and tried to push the studio into the realm of quality, high-cost, prestige motion pictures to compete with those of Loew's or Paramount. Consequently, Universal cut back on inexpensive productions and added a dozen expensive specials for the 1929–30 movie year. This was the season in which Universal created **All Quiet on the Western Front,** both a critical and financial success. Unfortunately, **The King of Jazz,** a $2 million Technicolor spectacle featuring Paul Whiteman, and **The Captain of the Guard** with John Boles and Laura LaPlante generated precious little revenue. Junior Laemmle was forced to cut back

46. Carl Laemmle,
Junior

and Universal entered the Great Depression unsure of its strategy as a producer.

Unlike the Big Five, Universal entered the studio era with a shrinking asset base, worth only $20 million (versus Paramount at $300 million and Loew's at $120 million). The Big Five held most of their assets as theaters; Universal's principal asset was its 230-acre California studio. Universal employed some 4000 people in production and distribution collected under six basic subsidiaries:

1. Universal Film Exchanges Inc. maintained distribution outlets in 30 US cities;
2. Motion Picture Export Corporation handled Universal films in all foreign countries except Britain and Canada;
3. Universal Pictures Ltd, a British corporation, handled distribution for the United Kingdom;
4. Canadian Universal Film Co. Ltd, a Canadian corporation, took care of distribution matters in Canada;
5. Motion Picture Realty Co. of California owned the studio. Universal's studio was also leased to independent producers;
6. Cellofilm Corporation owned land in Woodridge, New Jersey, for a plant which salvaged silver from obsolete positive prints.

On one level, distribution, Universal was the equal of the Big Five. It could distribute films in all markets of the world except the USSR; but Universal owned no US theaters after 1933. For a time in the 1930s it did hold on to control of two theaters in Berlin,

151

Germany, but these were sold before the start of the Second World War.

The first half of the 1930s was not a good period for Universal. Losses accumulated and assets fell (see Table 7.1). Not surprisingly, a great number of rumors of a sale or merger arose. In 1935 for example, reports had Warner Bros. taking over Universal for $7 million. Throughout the Depression Universal was always short of operating capital, and in November 1935, in order to finish two current specials, **Sutter's Gold** and **Show Boat,** Carl Laemmle Senior borrowed three-quarters of a million from Wall Street's Standard Capital Corporation, headed by J. Cheever Cowdin. A self-made millionaire, Cowdin had organized Standard Capital to seek out investments at deflated Great Depression prices. He had been seeking a way to enter the movie business ever since he formed Standard Capital. As part of the loan arrangement, Laemmle offered to sell Cowdin one-quarter of the company, but Cowdin naturally sought all or nothing. After some negotiation, Laemmle granted Standard Capital a 90-day exclusive option to acquire majority control of Universal for $5.5 million, of which $1.5 million would be paid to Laemmle in cash, the rest in eight annual instalments. Laemmle would be elevated to honorary chairman of the board.

Standard Capital exercised its option in March 1936, and in April of that year took control of more than 80 per cent of Universal's common stock. Long-time Laemmle associate R. H. Cochrane became president of the new Universal. Charles R. Rogers, a former executive at RKO, took charge of production, assisted by James E. Grainger, a former Fox executive. The new board of directors included several of Cowdin's Standard Capital associates. British movie man J. Arthur Rank represented a British consortium which put up a small portion of the purchase price.

The new management team was able to minimize losses, but red ink still accumulated to the extent of $3 million for 1936–7. So in December 1937 Cowdin and his associates voted Cochrane out of his short-lived presidency, severing the final management link with the Laemmle era. Nathan J. Blumberg became president. Unlike his predecessors, Blumberg had extensive experience in the exhibition end of the movie business. Ironically enough he had begun with the Universal chain in Racine, Wisconsin, then moved to an RKO vice-presidency in the early 1930s. Blumberg appointed William Scully, then head of the Eastern sales district for MGM, as his sales manager. Cliff Work was placed in charge of production in Hollywood and Rogers was

released. Work was another theater man who had worked for
Blumberg at RKO. The Blumberg administration definitely
turned things around. Universal's deficit in 1938 was the last
corporate red ink for a decade. In 1939, Universal actually turned
a $1.2 million profit, its largest since 1926. The Second World War
years saw the company averaging $3.3 million in profit, moving
past Columbia (and for a time even RKO) to a solid sixth position
in the industry hierarchy (though Warners still had twice Universal's average profits, Fox three times and Paramount and Loew's
four times). Operating revenues increased every year without
interruption. Universal's proportion of total film rental grew from
5 per cent to more than 10 per cent. The company even began to
retire debts and look forward to post-war expansion.

Universal's management planned to challenge the Big
Five as soon as the Second World War ended. Moreover, the day
of the 'B' Western, one of the cornerstones of Universal
production, would soon be over, what with the coming of
television and the new exhibition practices being demanded by
the US Department of Justice. Cowdin and Blumberg began to
look around for managers who could produce quality 'A' features
with popular stars. They found such a team in William Goetz and
Leo Spitz. Goetz, married to Louis B. Mayer's daughter Edith,
had long benefitted from his father-in-law's connections. In 1934
Mayer had helped Goetz to join Twentieth Century Pictures.
Goetz even took over 20th Century-Fox production when Darryl
F. Zanuck entered the Signal Corps during the Second World
War. With the return of Zanuck in 1943 Goetz moved on to form

47. Universal's
management team in
1946: (l. to r.) Cliff
Work, Nate Blumberg
and Leo Spitz

his own independent production partnership, International Pictures. Spitz, twenty years Goetz's senior, was an experienced attorney who helped to reorganize the Paramount theater chain and for a time served as president of RKO. With producers Nunnally Johnson and Clarence Brown and star Gary Cooper, Spitz and Goetz opened International in 1943. Universal would give International Pictures a permanent distribution outlet, permanent studio space and participation in cost savings only available to an integrated producer–distributor.

Universal-International was formed in August 1946. Goetz and Spitz supervised production in California while Cowdin and Blumberg continued to handle distribution and other business in New York. For a time it seemed that J. Arthur Rank would become a full partner, but that deal fell through. Instead, Universal-International negotiated a pact by which its films got first preference in Rank's 1000 British theaters. Universal-International did well for one year (1947), but as the studio system began to collapse, corporate red ink returned. Cowdin resigned in 1950, Spitz and Goetz in 1952. In 1952, Decca Records took control and promoted Nate Blumberg to an honorary post. Decca adjusted to the realities of television and brought consistent profits to Universal during the 1950s. In 1959 Decca merged with MCA and Universal, under former agent Lew Wasserman, became a true media conglomerate generating millions of dollars in profits a year (hundreds of millions by 1978).

Universal's strategy for film production during the studio era neatly divides into four eras: Laemmle (1930–5), Rogers (1936–7), Blumberg and Work (1938–45) and Spitz and Goetz (1946–50). As already noted, Junior Laemmle failed to produce prestige films profitably for the studio during the 1929–30 movie season. With only Lew Ayres and Margaret Sullavan as name stars, a new strategy was in order as the corporation headed into the Great Depression. Specialization in horror films filled part of the void, making good use of German talent under contract and leftover sets from **The Hunchback of Notre Dame** and **All Quiet on the Western Front.** Well-placed-lighting (or the lack thereof) and fine but economical art direction provided even more production economies. This horror film cycle began in 1930 when the studio signed Lon Chaney, Senior. He was to star in **Dracula,** from a recent Broadway play based on an 1897 Bram Stoker novel. Chaney died before production could start so Bela Lugosi, who created the role on Broadway, stepped in. Following this rare success at the box-office, Universal turned to another classic novel, Mary Shelley's **Frankenstein. The Mummy** came in

48. Bela Lugosi in **Dracula** (Universal 1931)

1932, **The Invisible Man** the following year and **The Bride of Frankenstein** in 1935. The cycle might have continued, but the Cowdin administration planned a new Universal.

The plan was to have new studio boss Charles Rogers turn Universal into an efficient, assembly-line movie factory. Rogers had been a producer of program pictures at RKO and Paramount. Universal would eliminate all prestige films and formally give up trying to break into the first-run exhibition market, returning to the rural, small town theater market. It is not surprising then that the lone star Universal developed in the

49. Deanna Durbin in **Mad About Music** (Universal 1938)

155

mid-1930s was an idealized virgin, Deanna Durbin. First seen in **Three Smart Girls** (1936), this teenaged 'girl-next-door' rendered semi-classical arias and popular tunes in a series of pre-Second World War hits: **One Hundred Men and a Girl** (1937), **Mad About Music** (1938), **That Certain Age** (1938), **Three Smart Girls Grow Up** (1939), **It's a Date** (1940) and **Spring Parade** (1940). None of these hits grossed less than twice production cost. Indeed **Mad About Music** and **That Certain Age** contributed $3.5 million to Universal's coffers, one-sixth of the studio's entire gross for 1938.

Apart from Durbin's films, Universal's low-cost strategy (as administered by Charles Rogers) never paid off. In January 1938, Nate Blumberg moved his assistant, Cliff Work, to Hollywood. Blumberg and Work trimmed overheads, expanded production and attempted to service more efficiently independent exhibitors. Between 1938 and 1941 this management team converted a $1 million loss into a $2 million profit. Universal brought to the lot W. C. Fields, Bing Crosby and Edgar Bergen and Charlie McCarthy, all radio stars. (Paramount adopted a similar strategy in the 1940s.) 'B' films were given some spice with Maria Montez and Jon Hall in Technicolor adventures and Basil Rathbone in the 'Sherlock Holmes' series. During the late 1930s and early 1940s, Universal seemed to have its greatest box-office success with comedies: W. C. Fields in **The Bank Dick, Never Give a Sucker an Even Break** and **My Little Chickadee** (with Mae West), and Bergen and McCarthy with Fields again in **You Can't Cheat an Honest Man.**

The linchpin of this new strategy emerged in the form of

50. Lou Costello (l.) and Bud Abbott (r.) in **Buck Privates** (Universal 1941)

156

Bud Abbott and Lou Costello. The duo started in burlesque and moved to radio in the late 1930s. They were signed by Universal in 1940. Success came in 1941 with **Buck Privates,** co-starring the Andrews Sisters. This minor production grossed millions. Quickly, the pair starred in **In the Navy** (1941), **Hold That Ghost** (1941), **Keep 'Em Flying** (1941), **Ride 'Em Cowboy** (1942), **Pardon My Sarong** (1942) and **Who Done It?** (1942). Universal coined extra money by lending the duo to MGM in 1942 for a re-make of **Rio Rita.** Abbott and Costello vaulted into third place in the poll for the ten most popular stars, the first Universal stars even to be ranked. (The poll was begun in 1930.) In 1942 the pair ranked first and earned nearly $800,000. Wall Street analysts noted the trend, upgrading their appraisal of Universal as a stock purchase as a result of the hits of this one pair of stars. Abbott and Costello were a true Second World War phenomenon, dropping out of the list of top ten stars in 1945 and returning to minor status for the remainder of their careers.

Universal benefitted from the Second World War boom, generating its best years at the box-office since the 1920s. Even non-Abbott and Costello films did well. Universal City was renovated; two new sound stages were constructed. Big budget films returned: René Clair's **The Flame of New Orleans** with Marlene Dietrich, Alfred Hitchcock's **Shadow of a Doubt,** with Teresa Wright and Joseph Cotten, **Pittsburgh** with John Wayne and Randolph Scott and **The Suspect** with Charles Laughton. To his credit, Nate Blumberg recognized the artificiality of this surge in popularity and began to hoard funds to use after the war. That is, he and Cowdin went out and got Spitz and Goetz, much as Sidney Kent had located Joseph Schenck and Darryl Zanuck for Fox ten years earlier.

Spitz and Goetz set out a new strategy for Universal–International in 1946. Out went Abbott and Costello, Deanna Durbin, 'B' films, westerns and serials. Universal–International, instead, sought independent producers; it became the home for Diana Productions (Walter Wanger, Joan Bennett and Fritz Lang) with **Scarlet Street** (1946) and **Secret Beyond the Door** (1948), and a unit headed by Mark Hellinger for **The Killers** (1946), **Brute Force** (1947), and **The Naked City** (1948). Average budgets rose to $1 million. Universal seemed headed toward the big time. Unfortunately, Spitz and Goetz initiated a big-budget studio strategy just as that practice had lost its viability. The success of **The Egg and I** (1947) notwithstanding, losses piled up during 1948 and 1949. In 1949, Universal City temporarily closed. Executives conferred and decided the era of multi-million dollar

51. Percy Kilbride and Marjorie Main in **Ma and Pa Kettle** (Universal 1949)

production was over. Universal then returned to a low-cost, assembly-line strategy aimed at creating films for small-town exhibitors. Profits returned in 1949 with Marjorie Main and Percy Kilbride in **Ma and Pa Kettle,** a 75-minute feature costing $200,000 which grossed $2.5 million. The successful 'Francis the Talking Mule' series with Donald O'Connor also appeared that same year. Universal was again back with rural programmers, seeking profits in areas which would not get television until 1955 and 1956. Decca continued such a strategy as it turned the studio into a factory for television production.

Universal produced a specialized form of feature film throughout the 1930s and 1940s – the serial. Universal began with serials in 1914, even before Pathé's **The Perils of Pauline.** By the mid-1920s Universal was creating seven new serials per year. With the coming of sound, Pathé pulled out of serial production, leaving only Universal and a fly-by-night studio, Mascot Productions (see Chapter 9). Universal regularly produced four serials per year, delivering one new episode per week. Success in the early 1930s came with westerns starring Buck Jones and Johnny Mack Brown. When Columbia entered the serials market in 1937 Universal countered with **Flash Gordon,** which cost a record $150,000 (three times the average). Quick to take advantage of a trend, Universal created **Flash Gordon's Trip to Mars** (1938), **Buck Rogers** (1939) and **Flash Gordon Conquers the Universe** (1940), all starring Buster Crabbe. Universal took other heroes from the comics: **Jungle Jim, Radio Patrol, Secret Agent X–9** and **The Green Hornet.** The Second World War became the subject of

Don Winslow of the Navy and **Don Winslow of the Coast Guard.**
When Spitz and Goetz joined Universal in 1946 they terminated
serials production, leaving the market to Republic (which had
taken over Mascot) and Columbia.

Throughout all management and ownership changes,
Universal also distributed newsreels, cartoons and other short
subjects, principally to subsequent-run theaters in rural and
small-town locations not serviced by the Big Five. Universal was
the lone non-Big Five movie corporation to offer newsreels. Many
newsreel services were already in business when Universal started
in 1913. By 1925 only four remained, Universal among them. The
coming of sound shook up the newsreel field, but Universal hung
on, competing with Fox, MGM (linked to Hearst), Paramount
and the RKO-supported Pathé News. In the 1930s Universal
alone serviced the independent theater market. Not as well-
financed as its fours competitors, Universal did not maintain a
network of world-wide stringers and so relied heavily on whatever
silent footage it could merge with studio-produced sound effects,
music and narration. The organization gathered some scoops, but
generally offered lower cost as its distinct comparative advantage.
Decca and MCA kept the service going until 1967, when this last
distributor of newsreels closed up shop.

Universal also distributed animated short subjects. In
the mid-1920s Universal featured cartoons from producer Charles
Mintz, starring Oswald the Lucky Rabbit. Originally Mintz
sub-contracted the shorts from Disney. Later in the 1920s Mintz
set up a shop of ex-Disney staffers headed by his brother-in-law,
George Winkler. In 1929 Universal established its own operation
under one of the former Disney staffers, Walter Lantz. This
in-house studio supplied twenty-six Oswalds per year. In 1932
Lantz added a second 'star', Pooch the Pup; in 1934 came a color
series called 'Cartune Classics', yet another imitation of Disney's
'Silly Symphonies'. When the Cowdin group took over Universal
in 1936, Lantz struck a deal to form an independent unit and
distribute through Universal.

Finally on his own, Walter Lantz sought out animals not
yet developed as cartoon stars. Starting in 1936 there were brief
experiments with a trio of monkeys (Meany, Minny and Moe),
Snuffy the Skunk and Andy Panda. Success finally came in 1941
with Woody the Woodpecker. (Woody at this point strongly
resembled Warner Bros' successful Bugs Bunny.) Along with
'Swing Symphonies' (one-shot cartoons based on popular songs of
the day) Woody Woodpecker constituted Universal's cartoon
output through 1948. Costs were low ($15,000 per short versus

Disney's $35,000 average), but quality high enough to ensure constant sales. When the new Universal management of 1946 wanted more Lantz left and went to United Artists. Universal–International reissued older Lantz products to fill its schedule. In 1950 Lantz returned. With the coming of television, the Lantz studio laid off artists and simplified drawings. Lantz continued to create cartoons for Universal until 1972, when he finally halted production, the last in-house animation shop left from the studio era.

Lantz cartoons did not supply all Universal's short subjects. The studio also created a continuous series of moderately popular comedy shorts starring, among others, Slim Summerville, Billy Gilbert and James Gleason. The studio also had two other popular series. John Hix produced 'Strange as It Seems', a second-rung 'Ripley's Believe It or Not'. The studio's most successful series were its variously titled big-band reels. These were simple recordings of the famous bands of the era: Stan Kenton, Woody Herman, Jimmy Dorsey, Duke Ellington, Les Brown, Desi Arnaz and Lawrence Welk. Indeed, they were so popular that Universal–International's new management did not try to ax them in its quest for studio quality. 'Name-Band Musicals' continued to be issued – one per month – well into the 1950s. Decca, of course, had a major stake in this series, since many of the shorts promoted new Decca releases.

All in all, Universal remained a marginally profitable motion picture corporation throughout the studio era. Two factors contributed to relative prosperity during the 1940s. First, new management located a niche in the market in which Universal could compete freely. The Big Five did not much care about subsequent-run theaters; Universal did well in this market. Second, the Second World War boom extended to all existing companies. Universal – with Abbott and Costello – took advantage of an increase in audience demand for movies. The post-war years were not kind to Universal because management picked the wrong time to try to imitate the Big Five. Once Universal returned to productions for subsequent-run houses, it did relatively well. (By 1957 it exceeded the mighty MGM in profits.) One other factor helped Universal to make a successful transition to television- and movie-production. Since Universal owned no theaters, it could more quickly adjust to a new world of popular entertainment. When it became a media conglomerate in the television age, Universal finally surpassed the former Big Five, and captured millions of dollars of profits. At last this once former member of the Little Three had made it into the big time.

8:

Columbia

In the early 1920s there were a great many small Hollywood film producers distributing films through states-rights organizations. All aspired to grow, someday even to challenge the mighty Famous Players. Only two did. The more famous was Warner Bros. Less spectacular in its growth was Columbia Pictures. By the Great Depression, this formerly independent company had grown to match Universal and had become a member of the industry's Little Three. Whereas the Great Depression crippled Warners, Paramount and Fox, Columbia, which was not dragged down by an ailing theater circuit, continuously sustained profits – the only corporation, except for mighty Loew's, to do so (see Table 7.1). The Second World War boom enabled the studio to prosper and to double its assets in five years. The company never lost money until founders Harry and Jack Cohn passed out of the picture in 1958. By then, with its television division – Screen Gems – and sponsorship of independent producers, Columbia had moved up to become a major studio.

Columbia formally incorporated on 10 January 1924, developed from a partnership, CBC Film Sales Company, by the two Cohn brothers, Jack and Harry, and Joseph Brandt. The Cohn brothers were products of New York's popular entertainment world of the turn of the century. Harry Cohn had started as a vaudeville performer and song-plugger in the New York environs, beginning in 1912. Older brother Jack started as a $7 a week laboratory assistant for Carl Laemmle's IMP Company and worked his way up from editor to newsreel producer for the growing Universal Pictures. By their late teens, the two Cohns and lawyer Brandt all worked for Universal. In 1919, the three ventured on their own with the CBC company. Brandt handled legal affairs, Jack Cohn sales and Harry Cohn production. As with many such independent companies of the time, CBC rented its New York offices and Hollywood studio space in special areas of New York and Hollywood spilling forth with rival, shoe-string producer/states-rights firms.

Table 8.1: Columbia's Balance Sheet

Year	Net Profit (millions of dollars)	Assets (millions of dollars)
1930	1.0	5.8
1931	0.6	6.4
1932	0.6	6.0
1933	0.7	6.6
1934	1.0	7.9
1935	1.8	9.4
1936	1.5	13.5
1937	1.3	14.8
1938	0.2	15.7
1939	0.0	15.8
1940	0.5	15.9
1941	0.6	16.7
1942	1.6	19.9
1943	1.8	22.6
1944	2.0	24.6
1945	1.9	29.0
1946	3.4	38.0
1947	3.7	39.5
1948	0.6	43.1
1949	1.0	41.9

When the Cohns and Brandt formed Columbia in 1924, they, like executives at Warners and Fox, knew that their corporation needed to expand if it was not to be eliminated by Loew's and Famous Players. The first step was for Columbia to establish its own system for distribution. Its initial exchange was in

place in 1926. Within four years, Columbia had a complete network in the United States and Canada. Columbia's success with talkies enabled it to set up an international distribution system by 1931, but this new distribution apparatus needed a continuous flow of films in order to remain cost-efficient. In 1926 Columbia purchased its own studio lot, a property around the corner on Gower Street from the one it was currently renting. The new studio included two stages and an office building. In 1928, Columbia – through merger – acquired Screen Snapshots Inc., Hall Room Boys Photoplays Inc., and Starland Revue Inc., all producers of short subjects. To finance this expansion, Columbia issued its first stock in March 1929.

Although such growth was quite extraordinary, pushing corporate assets over $3 million in 1930, Columbia did not have the resources to become a vertically-integrated corporation. Unlike rivals Universal and United Artists, it never ventured into theater ownership. This would severely limit corporate flexibility in the studio era. Columbia spent a great deal of time trying to convince the 'Big Five' to book its products in choice first-run theaters. Columbia could not offer smaller theaters a complete package of filmed entertainment as could Universal. In 1930 it had neither a serials unit nor newsreel production. What differentiated Columbia were its shorts, especially its comic shorts. By the mid-1930s, production of shorts surpassed two per week, and kept at that pace until the Second World War boom era.

A significant change in Columbia's management came about in the early 1930s. Joseph Brandt withdrew, selling his shares to Harry Cohn for a reported $0.5 million. Harry Cohn assumed the presidency of Columbia and retained his position of chief of production; throughout Hollywood's studio era he was the only studio boss to hold both positions. Brother Jack Cohn remained in New York in charge of distribution. The brothers continued to control this family enterprise, with this particular division of labor, until Jack Cohn's death in 1956. Columbia and Warner Bros. were the only studios with continuity of management by the founders.

Columbia entered the 1930s as a growing independent corporation with assets of $5.8 million. It grew steadily throughout the 1930s, temporarily passing Universal in size in 1936 to become the motion picture industry's sixth largest corporation. Universal passed Columbia again in 1941, remaining about 10 per cent larger through the remainder of the studio era. Columbia's principal asset was its Hollywood studio. The corporation employed 2500 people throughout the world in four subsidiaries:

1. Columbia Pictures Corporation of California Ltd. was organized in California in 1930 to engage in the production of motion pictures. This subsidiary handled all production activities from Hollywood;
2. Columbia Pictures Distributing Company Inc. was organized in Delaware in June 1926 to take in all foreign and domestic distribution of Columbia products, except in Louisiana;
3. Columbia Pictures of Louisiana Inc., organized in Delaware, handled distribution in Louisiana;
4. William Horsley Film Laboratories Inc. processed 400,000 feet of film per day for Columbia and other independent producers.

Like all members of the Big Five and Little Three, Columbia maintained distribution offices in thirty-two key cities in the United States. But there were only twenty-eight branch offices throughout the world – about half the number maintained by giants Loew's and Paramount. Still, Columbia was well-represented in Europe (UK, France, Belgium, Sweden, Denmark, Norway, Italy, Spain, Germany), South America (Argentina, Chile, Brazil, Columbia, Peru, Venezuela), Mexico, Cuba, Puerto Rico, British West Indies and the Far East (China, India, Philippines) and Australia. Other offices completed the girth of the globe, although some closed because of the Second World War.

The early 1930s were trying times for all motion picture corporations. Although Columbia did suspend dividends from late-1931 until mid-1934, and cut salaries in 1933, it prospered in comparison with some members of the Big Five. Through the early 1930s Columbia continuously made profits, albeit small ones, while all members of the Big Five except Loew's were losing millions. Columbia did not have to go to court to save its theaters. The corporation, frugal even with its expansion in the late 1920s, had no funded debt. Crude as he was in his public persona, Harry Cohn was a skillful corporate manager. He kept production costs low and was even able to expand production during the Depression. Brother Jack was as adroit in his New York operations. In 1929 Columbia occupied one floor of offices in a seventeen-story building which served as the New York center for independent-states-rights film producers. By 1925, Columbia had taken over more than four floors, becoming the largest tenant in the building.

Wall Street noticed. The corporation recorded its best year in 1934; profits in 1935 topped the former record set in 1929 which was considered the best year for the movie business to that date. Stock-market analysts cited two reasons for this success. First, there were the popular films. For example, in 1934, Columbia recorded two major hits – films pulling in as much money as top MGM and Paramount products. **It Happened One Night** received the Academy Award for best picture, actor, actress, direction and adaptation – a stunning achievement for a non-Big Five product. Not as honored but nearly as successful was **One Night of Love,** starring opera singer Grace Moore. Second, during the early 1930s, Columbia's features cost less than $200,000; MGM's averaged more than twice that much. Even **It Happened One Night** – with two major stars, Clark Gable and Claudette Colbert – reportedly cost less than $300,000.

Harry Cohn kept costs low by using a variety of methods. Columbia took on few long-term contracts with stars, instead borrowing or signing actors and actresses (writers and directors too) to short-term contracts for one, two or at most three films. Harry Cohn, for example, pulled a coup by obtaining Gable from MGM and Colbert from Paramount for **It Happened One Night.** This policy towards talent coupled flexibility with reduced overhead. A shrewd producer like Cohn could pick and choose his trends, taking full advantage when a cycle seemed on top, abandoning it on its decline. Cohn also kept executive salaries low. In 1935, he earned $3500 a week as president, Jack Cohn $2000 week as vice-president and treasurer, Sam Briskin, Harry Cohn's top production assistant, $2750 a week and Abe Schneider (Briskin's brother-in-law), second in command in New York, collected $650 per week. These were high salaries for American

53. Clark Gable and
Claudette Colbert in **It
Happened One Night**
(courtesy Columbia
Pictures Industries
Inc.)

business as a whole, but low by motion-picture industry standards. In a 1939 Securities and Exchange Commission poll Columbia had only fifteen of the top 550 salary earners in the movie
industry (executives and stars included). Finally, Cohn kept a
tight rein on book-keeping practices. Production costs for feature
films were written off by 98 per cent within one year, shorts and
westerns by 90 per cent per annum. Consequently, any re-releases
(or later television releases) simply generated pure profit. Columbia also kept itself very liquid, not significantly expanding its
physical plant until 1935 when it acquired the first forty acres (of
an eventual eighty) for location shooting in nearby Burbank.

To generate continuous profits, Columbia had to turn
out a few big hits each year. Shorts and westerns, steady
producers of income, provided a strong base. Columbia added
serials in 1937 to make optimal use of its new studio ranch in
Burbank, but in order to grow the studio had to produce its
successive 'A' film hits. The late 1930s were not as kind to the
studio as earlier years in that decade. Profits fell steadily from a
$1.8 million high in 1935, reaching zero in 1939. (Columbia made
precisely $2000 that year.) Part of the reason was that Frank
Capra did not continue to create a string of films as popular and
profitable as **It Happened One Night.** For every **Mr Deeds Goes to
Town** (1936) and **You Can't Take It With You** (1938), there were
losers like **Broadway Bill** (1934) and **Lost Horizon** (1937).
Moreover, Capra was making fewer films at greater and greater
costs. Columbia needed money-makers every few months, not
once a year. Columbia never seemed to develop other hits to go

54. Gary Cooper in **Mr Deeds Goes to Town** (courtesy Columbia Pictures Industries Inc.)

with Capra's films. A promising start was **The Awful Truth** in 1937, unusual in that it starred three of the studio's contract players (Irene Dunne, Cary Grant and Ralph Bellamy). Unfortunately, director Leo McCarey soon left for another studio. A number of significant producer–directors, potential Capra replacements, came and went in the late 1930s: Howard Hawks, John Ford and Josef von Sternberg. In the late 1930s it was not possible for Harry Cohn to remain as flexible as he had been in the early 1930s. So he turned more and more to 'B' films. Indeed, in 1938, the average length of a Columbia feature came to only 66 minutes (ninth among the studios, far below MGM's 90-minute average). Series such as 'Blondie', 'Lone Wolf', 'Boston Blackie' and 'Crime Doctor' had become the rule rather than the exception.

In an effort to bolster sliding profits, Harry Cohn decided to reverse Columbia's strategy completely. At the time some 70 per cent of the studio's features were either cheap westerns or 'B' films. Cohn kept that percentage, but took money from 'B' films and poured it into a few quality 'A' features per year. Profits began to rise, pulled up again by a few big hits. In 1940-1, six 'A's brought in $500,000; by 1941-2 their contribution neared $2 million. **Here Comes Mr Jordan** was a top comedy of 1941. George Stevens produced and directed his first of three for Columbia, **Penny Serenade,** that same year; **Talk of the Town** followed in 1942 and **The More the Merrier** in 1943. The year 1942 saw Fredric March and Loretta Young in **Bedtime Story**, Joan Crawford and Melvyn Douglas in **They All Kissed the Bride** and

167

55. Gene Kelly, Rita Hayworth, Phil Silvers and Edward Brophy in **Cover Girl** (courtesy Columbia Pictures Industries Inc.)

Rosalind Russell and Janet Blair in **My Sister Eileen.** Columbia's biggest star during the Second World War boom was Rita Hayworth in **You'll Never Get Rich** (1942), **You Were Never Lovelier** (1942) and **Cover Girl** (1944).

Profits from 'A' films continued after the war. Indeed, 1946 and 1947 were the best years for the studio up to that time. The driving force for 1946 was **The Jolson Story,** the studio's biggest single grosser to date. The sequel **Jolson Sings Again** (1949) improved on that record, becoming the industry's top grossing film of the year. But when the post-war decline in movie

56. Larry Parks with Evelyn Keyes in **The Jolson Story** (courtesy Columbia Pictures Industries Inc.)

attendance came, Columbia began to reissue a number of older films (fully reaping the profits of these completely amortized products), sought more efficient ways to extract revenues from overseas markets and looked more to independent producers to supply films. All these strategies worked in the long run, and eventually propelled Columbia into full parity with Fox, Loew's, Warner Bros. and Paramount one decade later.

Feature film success pushed Columbia up and down a roller-coaster of profitability. What kept the studio on solid ground, year-in and year-out, were its westerns, shorts and serials. Westerns began in 1930 with the acquisition of a permanent studio and became solidly entrenched in 1937 with the purchase of the Burbank ranch. Columbia's westerns represented a solid middle-line product, not as slick as RKO 'B' features, but not as primitive as those of marginal operators such as Monogram and Republic. In the early 1930s Columbia's stars were Buck Jones and Tim McCoy. When Tim McCoy left in 1935 Columbia added Ken Maynard, Bob Allen and Charles Starrett series. In the 1940s yet another cycle began with the signing of Tex Ritter and Russell Hayden. Probably Columbia's greatest success with westerns came at the end of the studio era when it signed Gene Autry. In exchange, Autry gained more autonomy and publicity than he had at Republic. This signaled the peak of Autry's post-war popularity. However, the era for westerns was soon over; in the early 1950s Autry, Maynard and others moved to television.

Columbia produced many other 'B' films. They were cheap, predictable in the market-place and a useful way to test potential new stars and directors. For example, Rita Hayworth was first used in the 'Blondie' series. 'B' films lasted at Columbia until the mid-1950s, when television took over the market. Whenever possible Columbia tried to develop series to be sold in blocks with its westerns. Columbia was quite successful in developing long-run series, typically based on popular characters from other media:

1. there were twenty-eight 'Blondie' films (1938–51), all starring Arthur Lake and Penny Singleton, based on the comic strip;
2. there were ten 'Crime Doctors' (1943–8), starring Warner Baxter, based on a radio show;
3. there were thirteen 'Boston Blackie' films (1941–9), starring Chester Morris, based on a radio show;
4. there were fourteen 'Lone Wolf' films (1935–49), first starring Melvyn Douglas, then Warren William, based on a novel;

5. there were eight 'The Whistler' films (1944–7), starring Richard Dix, based on a radio series;
6. there were sixteen 'Jungle Jim' films (1948–54), starring Johnny Weismuller, based on a radio series.

Columbia did not get into serials until 1937, after it had acquired its location ranch in Burbank. It produced fifty-six different serials until it quit – the last studio to do so – in 1956. Columbia relied on ties to the comics (**Batman** 1943, and **Terry and the Pirates** 1940), and radio (**The Shadow,** 1940). The studio's greatest financial success with serials came during the final studio era years. In 1947 Columbia lured director Spencer Gordon Bennet from Republic. This former stunt man, whose career began with Pearl White, oversaw twenty of Columbia's final twenty-one productions. Adopting Republic budget-cutting techniques, Bennet centered whole series on stock footage already fully amortized. So in **Riding with Buffalo Bill** (1954) the hero altered his costume to match footage from **Deadwood Dick** (1940) and **The Valley of Vanishing Men** (1942). A whole serial of this type could be worked out in less than two weeks, half the usual production time. Columbia turned to new subjects in the 1950s, especially outer space series, for example **The Lost Planet** (1952) and **Captain Video** (1951), but ended, appropriately enough, with a western, **Blazing the Overland Trail,** in 1956.

Short subjects constituted Columbia's strongest offerings. Live features were more successful than animated work. But this was not always the case. In 1929, Columbia picked up Disney's new productions, the Mickey Mouse cartoons. Until 1932, the Disney product flowed through Columbia distribution channels. The oft-imitated 'Silly Symphonies' series began in 1929. Other famous Disney stars began with Columbia: Pluto in 1930 and Goofy in 1932. However, Disney wanted a larger distribution network, and moved to United Artists in 1932. Columbia found a replacement in Charles Mintz's 'Krazy Kat' series, a spin-off from a comic strip character. Mintz moved over from Paramount in 1929 when the latter studio settled on Fleischer cartoons. Unfortunately 'Krazy Kat' never approached Disney's success. In 1930, the Mintz unit came up with Scrappy, a cute little human boy with large round eyes, a button nose, and a curly forelock. Scrappy and Krazy Kat lasted with Columbia until 1940 when producer Mintz died at the age of 44.

From 1940 to 1948 there were seven different regimes at Columbia's animated shop. The most dramatic move took place in 1941 when Frank Tashlin, who had been with Disney, joined

Columbia first as a writer, then production supervisor. The animation studio had closed its doors for a time to be completely reorganized. Most of the Mintz artists left. Tashlin replaced them with Disney strikers, but no successful cartoons came forth and this experiment was terminated after only one year. Dave Fleischer from Paramount came next. 'Fox and the Crow' were 'stars', again with little success. In 1946, Columbia tried a handful of ex-Warners people, headed by Henry Binder, Ray Katz and Bob Clampett. They too were gone after only a short while. Dissatisfied, Columbia turned to outside sources in 1948. Independent producer Steve Bosustow of United Productions of America, famous for Mr. Magoo and Gerald McBoing Boing, finally provided Columbia with profitable output. UPA produced for Columbia until 1959.

A more stable profit contribution came from traditional short subjects. 'Screen Snapshots', one of the first CBC, then Columbia, products, provided the film equivalent of the fan magazine with glimpses of behind-the-scenes in movieland. This series lasted from 1920 until 1958. Columbia could produce these shorts very cheaply because stars were glad to gain the free publicity. In the 1930s, Columbia covered its own stars and many from radio. USO tours and Army performances provided new sources of footage.

During the early 1930s comedy shorts production was consolidated under veteran producer Jules White. White picked up stars from other studios and the vaudeville stage. Andy Clyde and Leon Errol came first. In 1934 the Three Stooges (who stayed on until 1959), Harry Langdon and Buster Keaton joined Columbia. Columbia practised extreme economies with its comedy shorts units. White, who remained in charge until 1959, became one of Harry Cohn's trusted lieutenants. Both sought profits, not fame or prestige. Shorts were filmed in three to five days. Experimentation was kept to a minimum; remakes were common. For example, during the 1940s Shemp Howard of 'The Three Stooges' remade most of the Charley Chase comedies of the 1930s. During the 1950s Columbia turned more and more to television production and closed its shorts unit in 1959. Until then non-animated short subjects had provided the corporation with a consistent base of sales, especially to non-affiliated exhibitors.

Columbia was the lone example in the studio era of a small producer–distributor which could consistently make profits. Neither of the other members of the Little Three (Universal and United Artists) could. Indeed, only Loew's of the Big Five matched Columbia's profit consistency. Columbia was unique in another way. Its management and ownership, the brothers Cohn, was one and the same from well before to well after the studio era. Even the Warner brothers did not hold on as long. Finally, Columbia illustrates the importance of shorts and serials to a small company. Hit feature films were hard to generate, but a consistent if small amount of money could be made from shorts and serials. Columbia would only truly challenge the Big Five in the 1950s when no competitor was allowed to own theaters. Columbia travelled a rocky road in the 1950s and 1960s, with especially good years in 1955–6 and 1976–7, and poor years in 1958–9 and 1971–4 (a total loss of some $85.3 million). Purchased by Coca-Cola in 1981, a revitalized Columbia Pictures has diversified into cable and pay television.

9:

Specialized Studios

Economic power and profit in the Hollywood studio system flowed through the vertically-integrated corporations with their first-run theaters. Columbia and Universal did not own theaters, and more often than not had to be satisfied servicing subsequent-run, independently owned theaters. Even further on the fringe were a number of smaller, specialized operations. United Artists (hereafter UA) tried to provide a mechanism for the distribution and release of independently-produced features. During the studio era UA persevered, but never took away significant profits from the Big Five. At the other end of the production scale were Monogram, Republic and a host of other small producers who came to life in the 1930s with the rise of the double feature. Possibly thirty fringe producers came and went during the studio era. Only Republic and Monogram survived for an extended period of time. Specialized studios in the shorts field were far greater in number, but all important ones have been mentioned in preceding chapters because they released through one of the Big Five, Universal or Columbia.

United Artists

The most important specialized studio and the final member of the Little Three was United Artists. This corporation was a unique Hollywood enterprise, created for independent producers who sought a distribution network outside the Big Five. Throughout the studio era UA handled features for its founders Mary Pickford, Charlie Chaplin, Douglas Fairbanks and D. W. Griffith

57. Joseph M. Schenck

as well as Samuel Goldwyn, Howard Hughes, Darryl Zanuck and
Alexander Korda. Despite some limited success during the late
1920s, United Artists was never able to maintain a consistent
output of 'A' features. Usually, UA was forced to work closely
with the Big Five in order to gain bookings in first-run theaters.
When Joseph Schenck, brother of Loew's president Nicholas
Schenck, was president of UA such access was no problem. But
after Schenck's departure in 1935 (and the loss of Samuel
Goldwyn to RKO in 1941) UA went steadily downhill. Remarkably, it lost money during the Second World War boom – the only
member of the Big Five or Little Three to do so (see Table 9:1).
When the Big Five took on independent producers after the war,
UA lost its tiny comparative advantage and neared bankruptcy.
In 1951, a syndicate headed by Arthur Krim and Robert
Benjamin purchased the private corporation, signed up new
independent producers, went public and turned UA into one of
the giants of the American motion picture business.

United Artists was organized in 1919 by Pickford,
Chaplin, Fairbanks and Griffith to gain direct control over their
own films and profits. William Gibbs McAdoo, former US
Secretary of Treasury, took over management of the new
enterprise. All the stock was privately held by the four principals

and McAdoo. Its principal assets were exclusive five-year contracts to distribute the films of the founders. The corporation
owned no studio lot. The four principals worked through their
own production corporations. Within two years, United Artists
established a network of exchanges in the United States and
throughout the rest of the world. A former Famous Players
executive, Hiram Abrams, was taken on to run UA's distribution
apparatus.

Table 9.1: United Artists' Balance Sheet

Year	Net Profit (millions of dollars)	Features distributed	Shorts distributed
1930	0.4	15	–
1931	0.9	14	–
1932	(0.3)	13	14
1933	0.1	16	19
1934	1.1	20	17
1935	1.5	18	18
1936	0.9	16	17
1937	0.8	25	8
1938	0.3	18	–
1939	0.4	18	–
1940	0.2	20	–
1941	0.1	22	–
1942	0.1	26	–
1943	1.0	28	–
1944	(0.3)	20	–
1945	0.6	17	–
1946	0.4	19	–
1947	0.5	26	–
1948	(0.5)	26	–
1949	(0.2)	20	–

Announced with great fanfare, the corporation did not
get off to a very good start. The original plan called for the release
of one film per month, the four principals each promising three
films per year. They did not deliver. Chaplin, Pickford and

Griffith still owed films to First National under prior contracts. Only Fairbanks was free to contribute his films to United Artists. The new corporation had to find another source of product to capitalize initial investments. Hiram Abrams, fully in charge in 1921 after a sudden departure by McAdoo, began to seek out other independent producers. Several deals were formulated and even a picture or two released, but this avenue of expansion never worked out. Indeed, with Griffith's departure in 1924 the problem got worse. UA pressed an alternative plan. It would seek out a strong manager to develop films to draw the new enterprise out of the red.

Joseph Schenck had had a long history in the motion picture industry. He and his brother Nicholas joined up with Marcus Loew in 1910. He resigned from Loew's in 1917 to promote the career of his new wife, actress Norma Talmadge. In the 1920s, Schenck expanded his production company to include Fatty Arbuckle and Talmadge relatives, his sister-in-law Constance and brother-in-law Buster Keaton. In 1934 UA brought Schenck in as a full partner, made him chairman of the board and empowered him to revitalize the company. Schenck's first step was to create a new production unit, the Art Finance Corporation. Capitalized at more than half a million dollars, Art Finance

58. Rudolph Valentino with Vilma Banky in **The Son of the Sheik** (courtesy UA)

boosted UA's prospects right away since Schenck assigned it his exclusive contract with Rudolph Valentino. This major star's initial UA release, **The Eagle,** was a moderate success; his second (and last) was a major hit. Not released until after Valentino's death, **The Son of the Sheik** grossed millions. Next, Schenck signed Gloria Swanson as a UA partner. Unhappy at Famous Players, Swanson wanted to manage her own career; Art Finance would back her pictures.

But in the long run Schenck's greatest success for UA came with his deal with Samuel Goldwyn. Another industry veteran, Goldwyn had started with the original Famous Players, but had become an independent who liked to make and profit from his own deals. He left his own company in 1922. (It later merged into MGM, without Goldwyn.) With the proceeds from that company, Goldwyn began to function as an independent producer. He needed a distributor and so joined UA.

After Hiram Abrams' death in 1926, Joseph Schenck took on full corporate authority. UA began to prosper, entering a corporate golden age. Schenck committed himself to delivering ten films per year from yet another new subsidiary, Art Cinema Corporation. With underwriting of more than $2 million, Art Cinema took up headquarters at the Pickford–Fairbanks studio in Hollywood, signed stars and contracted for films from producer Howard Hughes and director-star Buster Keaton. Schenck's reorganization efforts began to make an impact on the profit ledger in 1928. UA began the year with a $1 million deficit, and ended it with more than $1.5 million surplus. In 1928 and 1929 the corporation accumulated nearly $3 million in profits. Hits that year were found in Chaplin's **The Circus,** the Pickford–Fairbanks production of **The Taming of the Shrew,** Goldwyn's **Bulldog Drummond** (with Ronald Colman) and Swanson's **The Trespasser.**

But UA still struggled to have its growing list of films reach first-run theaters. There seemed to be no shortage of alternative plans of action. On the one hand, the company could ally itself with one of the Big Five. A natural alliance would have been with Loew's, allowing the Schenck brothers to join forces again but UA's partners feared they would lose their autonomy and vehemently objected. UA's other major alternative was to initiate its own theater circuit, and so the United Artists Theater Circuit was formed in June 1926. It was never a formal subsidiary, connected only through common stockholders Schenck, Pickford, Fairbanks and Goldwyn. To minimize risk, UA Theaters sought partnerships with the Big Five in new downtown picture palaces. Only in Detroit, Chicago and Los Angeles did UA Theaters own its houses outright. In Pittsburgh, Baltimore and Louisville, UA Theaters purchased half interest in seven theaters owned by Loew's. In New York City and Hollywood partnerships were struck with Paramount and Sid Grauman (the Egyptian and the Chinese) respectively. Realizing that UA was serious about theater expansion, the Big Five agreed to book UA films if UA Theaters would expand no further. Nicholas Schenck, who had ascended to the presidency of Loew's Inc. in 1927, sought a compromise. He stepped forward and agreed to play UA films in Loew's theaters. Similar deals were set up with Publix, RKO and Warner Bros. The Schencks had cleverly created a place for United Artists' high-cost features.

UA's golden age coincided with the coming of sound, but such a glowing corporate record masked serious problems. By 1930 United Artists was really a two-unit production company: Schenck and Goldwyn. Chaplin produced a hit only every four or five years; Swanson, Pickford, Fairbanks, and Griffith added even less. All were near the end of their careers. The Great Depression began an unraveling of United Artists which went on for the next twenty years. Gradually, in fits and starts, United Artists came apart. Headstrong independent producers dropped out, seeking better deals with other companies. The Big Five lost their tolerance for accommodating the place of United Artists, especially after Joseph Schenck left in 1935. Only the addition of Disney's highly popular short subjects in 1932 added any new luster, but even Disney's eighteen Mickey Mouse cartoons, and thirteen Silly Symphonies for the 1932–3 season could not prevent a loss in 1932.

Yet remarkably 1934 and 1935 were two of the better years in UA history, certainly the best pair during the studio era. The reason was UA's short-term alliance with the most successful new production company of the 1930s – Twentieth Century Pictures, founded by the disgruntled executive from Warner Bros.,Darryl Zanuck. Schenck recognized Zanuck's talents and proposed that the two should team up, distributing through United Artists. Considering the economic climate of the times, Twentieth Century started off in grand style. Fully nine of its first twelve films were money-makers. Zanuck and Schenck felt that the new company ought to be made a full partner in the UA venture, but Chaplin, Pickford, Goldwyn and Fairbanks – for a variety of different reasons – opposed direct infusion. Zanuck and Schenck haggled for a short time, but in the end withdrew from UA. Schenck tendered his resignation in May 1935; one month later he severed all relations by selling his stock as part of a deal by which he took over United Artists Theaters. Soon after, Twentieth Century merged with Fox (see Chapter 4).

United Artists was never the same again. Profits fell, at first somewhat gradually but eventually turning into steady losses. In 1935 UA needed films to distribute. Alexander Korda signed a sixteen-picture contract and became a partner. David O. Selznick agreed to provide eight pictures. Former Paramount producer Walter Wanger also joined UA. Although UA seemed to be headed onward and upward, little progress was made because partners and producers began to feud. There were two camps: active producers (Goldwyn and Korda) and inactive owners (Chaplin, Pickford and Fairbanks). Korda sought support from UA, but received little. Goldwyn, like Disney before him, wanted to renegotiate a better distribution deal. He felt he was producing the majority of company profits, only to see them disappear into the pockets of his inactive partners in the form of dividends. For a time in 1937 it seemed that Goldwyn and Korda might team together to buy United Artists, but Korda was too deeply in debt to hold up his end in such a deal. Goldwyn tried to manipulate the board, with little success, and so, after a lengthy court fight, sold all his UA stock and in 1941 moved to RKO. The other major producers also left (Korda in 1942; Wanger in 1941; Selznick in 1945).

Replacements were, at best, competent producers. Hal Roach, Edward Small, Sol Lessor, Richard Rowland and David Loew could not consistently provide profitable films. By 1943 UA had become desperate. When it learned that Paramount might need an outlet to distribute some 'overflow' films, UA signed on. Along with Hal Roach's 'Streamliners', Paramount's second-rung product constituted the bulk of UA's releases for 1943 and 1944. It is no wonder that UA was the only major movie corporation actually to lose money during the Second World War. In its continual quest for profitable films, UA courted numerous independent producers: Benedict Bogeaus, Samuel Bronston, Lester Cowan, Jules Levey, Charles R. Rogers (not the one who was Mary Pickfords husband), Andrew Stone and Hunt Stromberg. James Cagney, fresh from his Academy Award performance in **Yankee Doodle Dandy,** came on board in 1943. Selznick even produced three films; but there was no consistent pattern of distribution. Sometimes months went by with no releases. None of the new producers could match Goldwyn and Schenck's record of profit production.

After the war UA had little ability to adjust to the new

era of popular entertainment. When it suited them the Big Five simply took away independent productions. UA desperately needed a buyer. After a couple of years of offers and counter-offers, UA's remaining partners finally sold out to Arthur Krim and Robert Benjamin, two New York entertainment lawyers. By this time UA was losing a reported $100,000 per week. In February 1951 Krim and Benjamin took control and worked fast. UA took the films from a minor company, Eagle–Lion, and added **High Noon** and **The African Queen** to create a steady flow of features for distribution. Later UA worked out a contract with the Mirisch brothers to distribute for Billy Wilder, John Sturges, Robert Wise and Norman Jewison. Stanley Kramer and Fred Zinnemann would work for UA. The 'James Bond' series, starting with **Dr No** (1962), proved to be a consistent money-maker. In 1967 Krim and Benjamin sold out to a giant conglomerate, Transamerica. In 1981 a revitalized MGM bought UA from Transamerica and formed MGM/UA. This new corporation continues to release films and has planned ventures in pay and cable television.

Monogram

United Artists was the most famous of the specialized movie corporations. Before the Great Depression there were dozens of small production companies trying to make a go of it: Allied, Big 5, Christie, Chesterfield, Continental, Invincible, Liberty, Majestic, Mascot, Mayfair, Monogram, Pioneer, Tiffany and Worldwide, to cite the largest. The Depression forced nearly all to fold. Two significant problems plagued all these small companies: the cost of the transition to sound, and inadequate distribution. Operating on wafer-thin profit margins, all utilized inferior 'bootleg' sound-equipment and had to rely on states-rights distributors. Exhibitors preferred the products of the Big Five and Little Three, which had superior sound and reliable release schedules. (Small producers often promised films, but less frequently delivered.) Only subsequent-run houses, with their own slim profits, would risk booking films from the aforementioned producers, and even that small market barely survived in the Depression. The double feature was the only way the independent theater could keep going. In this difficult environment, it is not surprising that only two, Monogram and Republic, could last long enough to be able to participate in the boom times of the Second World War.

59. W. Ray Johnston

Monogram was founded in 1929 by veteran film producer W. Ray Johnston. In the film business since 1914, Johnston had
worked in distribution for Syndicate, Thanhouser and Amkins. In
1924, Johnston and producer Trem Carr organized Rayart
Pictures. Johnston handled the financial end while Carr supervised production. A set of independent exhibitors, formed into a
co-operative, guaranteed outlets for the films. In only its first year
Rayart was able to release sixty-two films, forty of which were
westerns. In five years Johnston ran his initial investment of
$10,000 to $1,250,000 and so in the heady days of 1929 Johnson
and Carr transformed Rayart into Monogram. Monogram was
unique among the small companies, for it consisted of a production studio and a national distribution network with offices in
thirty-three cities across the USA.

In the 1930s, Monogram sought to take advantage of its
ability to supply 'B' films to double-feature theaters. The average
budget per film was $20,000, less than one-tenth that of Para-
mount or MGM. Films were shot in eight days and a profit of
$3–4000 per film was considered a job well done. In 1933
Monogram produced a version of **Oliver Twist** which received an
award from *Parents* magazine and made money. As a consequence Monogram produced several classics in 1934, including
Black Beauty and **Jane Eyre.** Budgets for these specials reached a
record $100,000. By 1935, *Motion Picture Herald* referred to
Monogram as 'the ninth national producing and distributing
structure'. However, the corporation had accumulated sizeable
debts, one of which was to the Consolidated Film Laboratory, a

film-processing laboratory which handled work for many small firms. Consolidated forced the issue, took over Monogram and folded it into its own subsidiary, Republic Pictures. Johnston and Carr left and formed a new Monogram in 1936. They gradually built a completely new system for production and distribution just in time for the prosperous years of the Second World War. Stephen Broidy, a former Universal and Warner Bros. sales executive, became president in 1945. (Johnston became chairman of the board.) Otherwise the management of the new Monogram remained the same until 1953. New managers were brought in, the corporation was renamed Allied Artists, and John Huston, Billy Wilder and William Wyler were signed to create big-budget films. Wilder's **Love in the Afternoon** and Wyler's **Friendly Persuasion** followed. Later Allied Artists moved into television production, while continuing with some feature film production – for example, **Cabaret** (1972).

The new Monogram of 1936 had produced 'B' films, one per week, for the second half of double bills. These programmers were its sole product until 1947. It concentrated on westerns and stars included Tom Keene, Bob Steele, Tim McCoy, Tex Ritter, Rex Bell and Jack Randall. Buck Jones and Raymond Hatton joined in the 1940s for the 'Rough Riders' series. Later Johnny Mack Brown became the studio's big star while Jimmy Wakely functioned as its singing cowboy. But Monogram made more than cheap westerns. Other series were developed, the most famous of which included the 'Bowery Boys' (thirty-two films), 'Charlie Chan' (sixteen) and 'The Cisco Kid' (seven). During the boom Second World War years Monogram prospered. As a consequence the studio expanded in all genres. There were comedies (the 'Snuffy Smith' and 'Jiggs and Maggie' series), adventure series ('Bomba the Jungle Boy'), aviation films and horror films (the 'Mysterious Mr Wong' series featured Boris Karloff and Bela Lugosi). The Second World War inspired intrigue and crime tales, as well as detective films. Musicals were rarely produced since their budgets were too high.

Republic

Monogram's principal rival in the 'B' film market was Republic Pictures. Founder Herbert J. Yates first entered the movie business in 1913 when he helped finance several Fatty Arbuckle shorts. In 1915 he became associated with Hedwig Laboratories, a film-processing concern. After two years of study and experi-

60. Herbert J. Yates

mentation Yates established his own firm, Republic Film Laboratories. Republic expanded rapidly after the First World War. In 1924 Yates drew together several film-processing corporations and established Consolidated Film Laboratories. In the Great Depression many small producers, including the original Monogram, accumulated debts with Consolidated. Gradually Yates bought each one and in 1935 merged them into Republic Pictures. Two units constituted the core of the new studio. The first was the original Monogram. From this concern Yates was able to set up Mascot Pictures, which had been formed in 1927 by Nat Levine to produce serials. Mascot brought Republic its first star, singing cowboy Gene Autry.

Republic grew quickly. Its initial output was released under the banners of the original companies. For $2 million Republic could create twenty-two features including eight John Wayne westerns, eight Gene Autry westerns and four serials. By 1940, total budgets had increased to $9 million and profits edged toward half a million. Features were created in three categories:

1. *Jubilees* – westerns with a seven-day shooting schedule and a $30,000 budget.
2. *Anniversaries* – westerns, action films or musicals with a

fourteen-day shooting schedule, and budgets up to $200,000 each.

3. *Deluxes* – various genres with a twenty-one-day shooting schedule and a $300,000 to $500,000 budget.

Republic did so well during the Second World War boom that its production budget doubled, reaching $20 million in 1945. At that point Yates added a fourth category of features, 'Specials', with budgets sometimes approaching more than $1.5 million.

In 1945 Republic reached its peak, with profits topping $1 million for the only time in the studio era. Resident stars included John Wayne, Roy Rogers, Gene Autry, Ann Dvorak and Yates' protégé (later spouse) Vera Hruba Ralston. In 1945 Yates merged the three businesses he headed into one company, Republic Pictures Corporation. Yates' other properties included Consolidated Film Laboratories, Consolidated Moulded Products (plastics), a munitions factory in Scranton, Pennsylvania and Setay Inc. (Yates backwards), an investment-real estate concern. During the late 1940s, Republic's Consolidated Film Laboratories, along with E. I. DuPont, processed most of the raw film stock in the United States. Consolidated had plants in Fort Lee, New Jersey and Hollywood, which together could process 40 million feet of film per month. In the 1940s, Consolidated unsuccessfully tried to develop Trucolor to rival then then-dominant Technicolor. Closely tied to Republic were Yates' interests in the Grumman Aircraft Company and a sizeable amount of real estate in Southern California in addition to the studio (the former Mack Sennett lot with its dozen sound stages).

Motion picture serials constituted the core of Republic's productions from 1935 to 1950. Republic produced an episode per week, falling into one of five categories:

1. westerns, for example, **The Lone Ranger** (1938);
2. jungle adventures, for example, **Jungle Girl** (1941);
3. outer space, for example, **King of the Rocket Men** (1949);
4. detectives, for example, **Dick Tracy** (1937);
5. costume drama, for example, **Ghost of Zorro** (1949).

Republic's production of serials was fast and efficient. Working from the suggestions of exhibitor clients, Republic fashioned ideas a year in advance. In the preceding spring the four titles for the forthcoming season were announced. Supervisors then worked with a three-month production schedule. The serial's twelve chapters always incorporated stock footage and existing sets.

Special effects (by the well-known Lydecker brothers) were utilized whenever possible to save costs of location shooting. Completed products ran from three to five hours, and cost from $100,000 to $200,000.

Republic serials relied on commercial tie-ins with newspaper comics and radio. In 1937, it was **Dick Tracy**, hero of the comics. The next year saw the release of **The Lone Ranger**, which had begun on radio in 1934. The latter was a big hit, playing in Loew's New York houses and going out abroad in ten different languages. Republic took on any connections that promised free publicity, so All-American Football's Sammy Baugh starred in **King of the Texas Rangers** (1941) and FBI head, J. Edgar Hoover provided a spoken prologue to **Spy Smasher** (1942). The Second World War inspired changes. In 1943, 'The Masked Marvel' of comics fame posed as an insurance investigator to fight Japanese espionage activities. A decade later Republic released **Canadian Mounties Versus Atomic Invaders**, an anti-communist tract. Republic drew inspiration from whatever sources were available. **The Vigilantes Are Coming** (1936), for example, was a reworking of a Rudolph Valentino silent film, **The Eagle.** 'Zorro' became a Republic staple years before Disney made it a hit on television.

But it was the western series with which Republic garnered its most loyal audience. Made in batches of six to eight, most small neighborhood and rural theaters rotated them on a weekly basis. Over the years, Republic produced nearly 400 such westerns starring Bob Steele (sixteen), Johnny Mack Brown (eight), John Wayne (eight), Don 'Red' Barry (twenty-nine), Wild Bill Elliott (twenty-four), Allan Lane (fifty-one), Sunset Carson (fifteen), Monte Hale (nineteen) and Rex Allen (nineteen), among others. Wayne was the only one to go on to become a big star with other studios, but even so, his last Republic westerns were released after his success with **Stagecoach** (1939). Where Republic clearly differentiated this product, and made most of its money, was with its singing cowboys Gene Autry and Roy Rogers. Nat Levine of Mascot had brought Autry to Hollywood (from radio in Chicago) and into Republic with the 1935 merger. Autry quickly established himself as one of the top attractions in the field, ranking in the poll of top ten western stars from 1936 to 1942 and from 1946 to 1952 (the interruption being for Army service). More important for Republic, he vaulted into the top ten list of all movie stars in 1940 (4), 1941 (6) and 1942 (7). The 57-minute **Tumbling Tumbleweeds** (1935) established his successful formula. With his 'wonder horse' Champion, and sidekick, Smiley Burnette, Autry would in Frank-Capraesque

61. Gene Autry (with guitar) in **Tumbling Tumbleweeds** (courtesy Republic)

fashion rescue an innocent victim from an evil exploitive business-man in the 'modern' west, complete with cars, radios and airplanes. Anywhere from five to eight times per film, Autry would break into song, often regardless of narrative logic. Autry completed eight programmers in 1936 and 1937, each costing between $50,000 and $75,000. Each usually grossed more than $500,000.

In 1938, Autry demanded a higher salary. In response, Republic introduced a replacement, Roy Rogers. (Autry eventually received nearly a 1000 per cent rise in pay plus a percentage of the growing sale of licensed products using his name. Republic made some of this money back in 1940 when in an unusual move it *lent* Autry to 20th Century-Fox). Roy Rogers also came to the movies from a career in what was then called 'hillbilly' music, as a member of the Sons of the Pioneers. In films Rogers maintained a traditional western hero image. He stuck to the motifs and narratives of the classical western story. When Autry went into the Army in 1942, Rogers moved to become the number one money-making western star in the annual *Motion Picture Herald* poll. Surprisingly, he held that spot until 1954, long after Autry had returned. In 1948, Autry left Republic for Columbia. Both turned to television in the 1950s.

Republic made more than serials and westerns. Its 1938–41 comedy series, 'The Higgins Family', tried to compete with the Hardy family at MGM and Jones family at 20th Century-Fox. The Republic version began with a real-life father, mother, and son: James, Lucille, and Russell Gleason. There were nine episodes in the series (not all with the Gleasons). Republic's Weavers series (1938–43) created a rural family.

Famous on radio as the 'Arkansas Travelers', the Weavers were noted for their home-spun humor. Judy Canova created yet another rural series, retelling the Cinderella story over and over again. Her 'B' comedies were punctuated with musical interludes.

As often as it could, Republic imitated the Big Five. For example, to match popular musicals Republic offered its **Hit Parade** (1941, 1943, 1947 and 1951). There were also two Earl Carroll musicals (1945 and 1946) and several Sonja Henie ice spectaculars, starring Vera Ralston. Republic constantly drew inspiration from radio; there were two 'Ellery Queen' mysteries and three 'Mr District Attorney' films, both from the highly-rated radio shows. In short, Republic banked on proven material which it could tender to small town theaters at rock-bottom costs. All these short-lived series supplemented Republic's staples – its serials and westerns.

The Second World War boom pushed Republic's 1945 profits over $1 million. Flush with success, in 1946 Republic began to create a few prestige films each year. It drew John Ford, Fritz Lang and Frank Borzage to the lot. Ford's **Rio Grande** (1950) was the first of three at Republic for that famous director. He enjoyed a thirty-two day shooting schedule and a budget of more than $1.2 million. Similarly, Borzage created **Moonrise** (1948), Lang **Secret Beyond the Door** (1949), Orson Welles **Macbeth** (1948) and Allan Dwan **Sands of Iwo Jima** (1949). Ford's **The Quiet Man** (1952) won Republic two Oscars. Unfortunately, these prestige films rarely made money. Profits declined to less than half a million dollars a year. The 1950s saw even smaller profits eventually dwindle into losses. Republic was in the red by more than $1 million in 1957 and closed up shop in 1958. Herbert J. Yates returned to his original venture, Consolidated Film Laboratories.

Others

Republic and Monogram were not the only small corporations to open up in the 1930s: they were simply the most long-lived and most profitable. In 1936 came Grand National. It took over the former Educational Studios lot and announced thirty-four productions, two of which starred Warner's defector, James Cagney. Cagney did release the two features, but then the company went broke. It was reorganized in 1938, and absorbed into Educational.

Producers Releasing Corporation (PRC) came next. It set its sights on the market for westerns and a few exploitation productions. For example, PRC released **Hitler, Beast of Berlin**

62. **Minstrel Man**
(courtesy PRC)

soon after Warners' **Confessions of a Nazi Spy.** PRC, unlike
Grand National, was able to stay in business long enough to
participate in the Second World War boom. By 1942 production
reached one film per week. A gangster film, **Paper Bullets,** even
received bookings in several Fox and Warner theaters. PRC
spread out to all genres. Buster Crabbe became **Jungle Man. The
Lone Rider** rode the range. The teenage audience saw Dickie
Moore in the musical **Jive Junction.** Comedy was available in **My
Son, The Hero** starring Patsy Kelly and Roscoe Karnes. **Minstrel
Man** (1944) preceded even Columbia's hit **The Jolson Story,** but as
soon as the war boom ended, PRC fell into a sea of red ink. In
1947 it was absorbed by Eagle–Lion, a distribution company
owned by the Rank Organization in England. Four years later,
United Artists absorbed Eagle–Lion.

PRC became but another footnote in Hollywood history
linked to a list which would include Supreme Pictures (1934–6),
Mayfair Pictures (1932–5), Screen Guild (1946–9) and Lippert
Pictures (1949–55). None survived. Television took away all
opportunities to enter the movie business through a combination
of westerns and 'B' films. The new popular entertainment
economics provided incentives for drive-in products in the 1950s
and television work thereafter. Specialized studios would have to
seek out fringe profits wherever they seemed to be found.

10:

Conclusion

The studio era stands as one of the three major epochs in the history of the American cinema. From the time that film was first used to generate mass entertainment (and profit) it took thirty years for a multi-million dollar industry to form. That defined the first epoch. The studio era defined the second. We are still in the third, where independent productions shot on location represent the norm and movie-going is not a national habit but largely confined to young people attending during school vacations (Christmas and the summer months). Indeed, since the studio era most 'movie-going' occurs on television, be it through pay-cable, a network or a local station. What remains from the studio era is the dominance in distribution by the major companies (except RKO) throughout the world. We still see films brought to us by corporations which came to prominence during the studio era, and which have been analyzed in this book.

The individual chapters in **The Hollywood Studio System** have stressed the traits which made each corporation different from the rest. In no way, however, should this be interpreted as a 'studio-as-*auteur*' argument. These were giant corporations trying to differentiate their product and thus garner the largest share of a predetermined profit pie. Each corporation adopted slightly different business strategies, but in the end all were inexorably linked through essential arrangements in distribution and exhibition. Corporate differences, therefore, should best be seen as traits of an industrial whole, characteristics of a smoothly-running economic system.

Certain corporations earned greater long-run profits than others, of course. Loew's dominated in the 1930s, while

Paramount rose to the top during the 1940s. For the studio era as a whole, Paramount made the most money. It did this for three specific reasons. First, it owned and operated the most theaters. This meant that in weak economic times (the early 1930s) the corporation would flounder badly, but with prosperity during the Second World War boom, no corporation did better. Indeed Paramount's profits of some $39.2 million in 1946 stood as a record until well into the television era of the 1970s. (Loew's in the 1930s never came to more than one-half of that record total.) Second, led by Barney Balaban, Paramount was far and away the most progressive motion-picture corporation in terms of technological change. Despite repeated claims, this major movie corporation did not hide from television, but embraced the new medium. Finally, Paramount prospered not as the most 'European' of studios (under Ernst Lubitsch), but as the most dependent on the American media of all the film factories. Judiciously it plucked stars from radio and vaudeville and placed them in Paramount films. Its greatest years came with Bob Hope and Bing Crosby's **Road to . . .** films, not Lubitsch comedies.

Loew's production arm, Metro-Goldwyn-Mayer, has been credited with producing corporate prosperity. Certainly Loew's corporation earned profits when few others did – during the Great Depression, but this was as much due to the lack of theaters as it was to popular films. Loew's did well because it had been so cautious during the 1920s and purchased so few theaters, but its small chain caused Loew's problems during the boom 1940s. By 1946 Paramount was making twice as much money as Loew's. (Indeed the difference at that point surpassed the total profits of Loew's best year of the 1930s.) MGM's laudable image of elegance seems to be based on those films of the 1930s supervised by the 'boy wonder', Irving Thalberg, but for box-office power MGM never fully relied on a style of elegance. The corporation always tried to produce as many different types of films as possible, spreading its risk. Its stars reflected a broad appeal – from Clark Gable to Spencer Tracy, from Mickey Rooney to Greer Garson, from Esther Williams to Van Johnson. It took the coming of Dore Schary in 1948 to change this, and bring on what some consider MGM's true Golden Age with the Freed musicals.

20th Century-Fox and Warner Bros. never achieved the magnitude of long-run profits as did Paramount and Loew's. 20th Century-Fox was created out of what was the most devastated major movie corporation. Gradually, Fox climbed to move past Loew's into second place in the industry by 1946. This corporate movement was engineered by Joseph Schenck (former president of United Artists), Sidney Kent (former vice-president of Paramount), Spyros Skouras (veteran theater executive), and Darryl F. Zanuck (former chief of production at Warner Bros.). That is, it took men with experience and ties to existing corporations to save Fox, not outside bankers or industrialists. Indeed, the key connection in this case was not to a bank, but to Loew's through brothers Nicholas and Joseph Schenck. At first the new 20th Century-Fox developed several important stars. Fox, not MGM, dominated the list of top ten stars during the late 1930s with Shirley Temple, Sonja Henie, Alice Faye, Jane Withers and Tyrone Power, all top-ten stars. During the war years the corporation further differentiated its product with Technicolor. Fox clearly led the industry with color spectacles, creating twice as many as its next closest competitor. The cornerstone of this corporate strategy was the Betty Grable musical. In terms of pure economic power, Betty Grable was the most important female star of the studio era.

Warner Bros. is continually portrayed as the 'working-class' movie corporation, the lone studio which dealt with controversial subjects. Certainly many of its films of the 1930s did treat sensitive subjects, but the impact on the corporation was only to help it to lose money. It was during the late 1940s, especially 1947–9, when the corporation prospered, moving past Loew's into third place in the industry. Warners suffered during the early 1930s because, like Paramount, it owned too many highly leveraged mortgages. Warners had not only taken on several hundred theaters, but also interests in music publishing and radio broadcasting. Through the 1930s and early 1940s Warners shed most of its non-motion picture assets, and stream-lined its operations. It never had the stars to match Paramount, Loew's or Fox, and so turned to assorted genres during the 1940s. In the end Warners, more so than even Paramount, relied on its theater circuit to boost overall profits. As a movie producer connected to a major circuit it could always generate a marginal profit for all films produced.

The other four major motion picture corporations – RKO, Universal, Columbia and United Artists – never came close to matching the profits of Paramount or Loew's. RKO, with its small theater chain, hovered in fifth place, and never moved up despite numerous changes in ownership and management. It is no wonder that RKO created some of Hollywood's more interesting films, for it alone had both the resources to fund such projects and get them into theaters, all the while continually having new production executives looking for differentiable products. One long-run strength – not often enough linked to RKO – was its long-term association with key independent producers such as Walt Disney and Samuel Goldwyn.

Universal owned no theaters and so managed to lose money nearly half the time. Like Warners, Universal's main reputation (as a producer of horror films) coincides with its least profitable years. Universal, though in a small way, prospered during the Second World War when Abbott and Costello reached the top of the star poll in 1942, but success was short-lived and the corporation returned to red ink at the end of the studio era.

Columbia's surprising strength lay with the Cohn brothers. This pair steered Columbia to twenty years of con-tinuous profits, a record unmatched except by Loew's. Jack Cohn, the invisible brother, should be credited for booking Columbia films into the best possible theaters, always owned by others. Harry Cohn has come to represent the archetypal crude, cigar-smoking movie mogul, but year after year he presided over successful slates of Columbia productions. Frank Capra receives much of the credit for this profit production, but Cohn kept the record intact long after Capra moved on. With only one real star (Rita Hayworth) but an ability to jump on trends (for example, the post-Second World War nostalgia boom with **The Jolson Story**) Harry Cohn certainly deserves credit as one of the studio era's more skillful production executives. He certainly did more with less.

None of the specialized corporations matched Columbia or Universal. United Artists provided a distribution haven for independent producers, most notably Samuel Goldwyn, but Paramount's best year (1946) generated nearly four times more profit than United Artists did for the whole studio era. When Paramount, Fox and Warners began to take on independent producers regularly during the late 1940s it signaled the downfall of UA. Monogram and Republic emerged with the innovation of the double feature during the mid-1930s, the only ones among the small independents to survive the shakeout which occurred during the coming of sound. Neither found a great deal of money to be made in the markets (principally in rural America) that the majors ignored. The prosperity of the Second World War guaranteed limited success; the coming of television guaranteed their demise. During the studio era the specialized studios served constantly to remind anyone considering entering the film industry that the majors allowed few profits to escape their corporate coffers.

The Hollywood Studio System has argued for an alternative image to be adopted for the major move corporations. More importantly, however, it has stressed that the system always overrode all differences. As noted throughout, but especially in Chapter 1, co-operation in distribution and exhibition guaranteed that the eight majors were able to dominate American film production, distribution and exhibition for twenty years. With this system they could survive a world war, a Great Depression, a ten-year anti-trust suit, the coming of unions and new technologies, and still keep out all potential competitors. Profits went up and down, but the corporations which took in those profits remained the same. The eight major corporations defined American movies.

The implications of this successful system are many – too many to be concisely summarized in a few paragraphs. Indeed, all scholars of the American cinema of the 1930s and 1940s must in some way grapple with the effects of the studio system. I want to stress, however, that we need to emphasize the importance of film distribution and exhibition. Theaters, especially the first-run houses owned by the Big Five, took in the money which gave rise to any profits. Production of films was only one part of the overall profit-making system. Historians' interest in competition for maximum box-office revenues (i.e. the differences between films) has only served to ignore the total and necessary corporate cooperation which existed on the levels of distribution and exhibition. The inordinate interest in production has also focussed too much attention on Hollywood as the center for movies, when in reality throughout the studio era officials in New York 'called the shots'. So when Loew's profits declined, Nicholas Schenck hired a replacement for his much more famous employee, Louis B. Mayer. And of course the money from the box-offices throughout the world always flowed to New York to be counted and banked.

Each year the New York office decided how much money would be allocated for production, and then it became the production executive's job to bring in popular fare within the dictated constraint. New York officers hoped to regularize returns from the corporation's theaters and so discouraged producers from experimentation. Their aim was to stabilize the product, and so we have the familiar genres, stars, narratives and other formulaic elements associated with the studio era. Likewise, the major corporations banded together to eliminate any elements which might be offensive to a large interest group in society by means of the so-called Production Code. Throughout the studio era film production was seen as a risky business, one

193

which needed careful monitoring. When profits fell, new management teams were brought in to stabilize production and begin again creating popular products. Meanwhile, distribution and exhibition rolled on, with few changes in management, operating in a manner quite similar to branches of a mass-retailing operation such as Woolworths.

Perhaps the concept 'Hollywood' was the greatest corporate creation of the studio system. The behavior of its participants became an ideological construct known throughout the world. 'Going to the movies' during the studio era came to represent a chance for audiences to partake in the unique world 'Hollywood' represented. Products rolled out continuously, not linked to any one film or any one star. Hollywood encouraged patrons to see a film as soon as it arrived in town. Economic factors helped to define the types and quantity of films produced, although the system, remarkably flexible, at times opened internal contradictions, a space for other factors to come into play, so that in the end an understanding of the motion picture industry as an economic system cannot answer all historical questions raised about the cinema of the studio era. Nevertheless, a grasp of its essentials is a necessary preliminary to any discussion of Hollywood.

Bibliographic Guide

This guide seeks to fulfill two functions. First, it lays out the resources used to research this book, and second it provides suggestions for further reading, organized by the subject matter of individual chapters.

The organization of this book emerged from a framework suggested by Richard Caves, **American Industry: Structure, Conduct, Performance** (Englewood Cliffs, New Jersey: Prentice Hall, 1982, 5th ed.) and Alfred D. Chandler, **The Visible Hand: The Managerial Revolution in America** (Cambridge, Massachusetts: Harvard University Press, 1977). A similar approach was taken to the history of the American photography industry in Reese V. Jenkins, **Images and Enterprise: Technology and the American Photographic Industry 1839 to 1925** (Baltimore: The Johns Hopkins University Press, 1975). This book includes a chapter on Eastman Kodak's relationship to the motion picture industry.

For decades, primary documents generated by the major motion picture corporations were unavailable to outside researchers. Within the past ten years important collections have been opened: United Artists at the University of Wisconsin in Madison, RKO at the University of California in Los Angeles, Warner Bros. at Princeton University and the University of Southern California and Disney at the studio in Burbank, California.

To supplement this material the researcher turns to three types of indirect sources. The richest of this type are usually the records provided during an action in a civil or criminal court case. The major motion picture corporations, fortunately, were in court quite often during the studio era. Several thousand cases are listed in Dennis Hartman, **Motion Picture Law Digest: Indexing All Court Decisions from 1900 to June 1947** (Los Angeles: privately printed, 1948). The case which produced the most useful material was the ten-year anti-trust proceeding United States *v.* Paramount Pictures 334 US 131 (1948). This case's records fill nearly three full reels of microfilm. A first-rate study of the actions in and impacts of this particular legal struggle can be found in Michael Conant, **Antitrust in the Motion Picture Industry** (Berkeley: University of California Press, 1960).

Other government agencies also interacted with the film industry during the studio era. In 1933 the US federal government passed the National Recovery Act. Toward administering that law two studies surveying the state of film production, distribution and exhibition in the United States were completed (see Daniel Bertrand, 'The Motion Picture Industry', Work Materials no 34, Industry Studies Section, Division of Review, Office of National Recovery Administration, Washington, DC, February 1936, and Daniel Bertrand, 'The Motion Picture Industry', Evidence Study no 25, Division of Review, National Recovery Administration, Washington, DC, November 1935). For background on this valuable material see Louis Nizer, **New Courts of Industry: Self-Regulation Under the Motion Picture Code** (New York: The Longacre Press, 1935) and Douglas Gomery, 'Hollywood, the National Recovery Administration and the Question of Monopoly Power', **Journal of the University Film Association**, XXXI, no. 2 (Spring 1979) pp. 47-52, reprinted in the Kindem anthology noted below.

Another important governmental study was commissioned in 1940 as part of the US federal government's massive study of monopoly in America. The National Economic Committee devoted one of forty-three reports solely to the film industry. See US Temporary National Economic Committee, **The Motion Picture Industry: A Pattern of Control,** Monograph 43 (Washington, DC: 1941). Arno Press has reprinted this valuable document.

A second set of indirect evidence concerning the film industry was generated throughout the 1930s and 1940s by Wall Street and the investment community. Basic data on ownership and assets, profits and losses were published yearly in **Moody's Manual of Industrials** for publicly-held corporations. Since only United Artists was privately owned at the time, **Moody's** provides a year-by-year portrait of nearly all the major motion-picture corporations and even includes Republic and Monogram. Luckily for us, the one inaccessable corporation, United Artists, has deposited its financial records at the University of Wisconsin in Madison. This mountain of material has been summarized by Tino Balio in his **United Artists: The Company Built By the Stars** (Madison: University of Wisconsin Press, 1976) pp. 283–8. But what stockmarket players wanted were clear and concise analysis of the state of the publicly-held movie companies and recommendations as to whether to invest or not. Such analysis was widely disseminated throughout the studio era in such publications as **The Annalist, Barrons, Business Week, Fortune** and **The Magazine of Wall Street.** Easy access to articles in these and other business publications is available through the annual **Industrial Arts Index.** The articles in **Fortune,** in particular, were detailed and insightful and the major ones are noted later.

A third indirect source provides the greatest volume of useful information on the film industry. These were its own trade papers: **Variety** (1905 to date), **Daily Variety** (1933 to date), **Motion Picture Herald** (1930–72), **Film Daily** (1922–70), **Hollywood Reporter** (1930 to date) and **Box Office** (1932 to date). Each, to a different audience, provided reports about production (**Daily Variety, Hollywood Reporter**), exhibition (**Motion Picture Herald, Box Office**), and the industry as a whole (**Variety, Film Daily**). Throughout the period the Quigley organization, publishers of **Motion Picture Herald,** issued a year book in the **Motion Picture Almanac;** the **Film Daily** corporation made up and sold the rival **Film Daily Yearbook.** Each is indispensable for study of the studio era.

Further reading about the studio era should begin with several important studies by social scientists of the period. Only rarely during the 1930s and 1940s did scholars apply their analytical tools to the film industry. The best of these studies is by economist Mae D. Huettig in her **Economic Control of the Motion Picture Industry** (Philadelphia: University of Pennsylvania Press, 1944). For a description of the industry at the beginning of the studio era by a professor of business at Harvard see Howard T. Lewis, **The Motion Picture Industry** (New York: D. Van Nostrand, 1933). Twenty-five writers looked at the state of the industry in November 1947 in a special issue of **The Annals of the American Academy of Political and Social Science.** Be forewarned that more than half the material in this 172-page collection dealt with the effects of censorship on industry conduct. Arno Press has reprinted this volume.

There is only one other book-length history of the studio system besides the volume you are now reading. That is Roy

Pickard, **The Hollywood Studios** (London: Frederick Muller, 1978), a rehash of stories of the stars and their tyrannical bosses. Much more useful are two collections of articles about the history of the US movie industry: Tino Balio (ed.) **The American Film Industry** (Madison: University of Wisconsin Press, 1984), revised ed.), and Gorham Kindem (ed.) **The American Movie Industry** (Carbondale: Southern Illinois Press, 1982). In the Balio anthology are two Gomery essays, one of which analyzes the coming of sound to the American cinema, while the other traces the rise of movie exhibition before 1930. Three more Gomery essays are reprinted in Kindem's volume, examining film exhibition, corporate relations among the Big Five, and the interaction of the major movie corporations with the US federal government. In addition Balio reprinted material from Conant and Huettig, already noted, plus several pieces from **Fortune**. Both Balio and Kindem provide first-rate bibliographies. A third collection, **The Hollywood Film Industry,** edited by Paul Kerr, will be published in 1986 in the British Film Institute/Routledge & Kegan Paul series: Readers in Film Studies.

The Paramount corporation has inspired little scholarly work. Two picture-book overviews are I. G. Edmonds and Reiko Mimura, **Paramount Pictures and the People Who Made Them** (San Diego: A. S. Barnes, 1980) and Leslie Halliwell, **Mountain of Dreams: The Golden Years at Paramount Pictures** (New York: Stonehill Publishing Co., 1976). The best material on the studio can still be found in two articles in **Fortune:** 'Paramount Pictures', 15 (March 1937) pp. 87–96+, and 'Paramount: Oscar for Profits', 35 (June 1947) pp. 90–4+. An almost useless tool is Adolph Zukor's autobiography (written with Dale Kramer) **The Public Is Never Wrong** (New York: G. P. Putnam's Sons, 1953). A good deal of production information can be gleaned from James Curtis: **Between Flops: A Biography of Preston Sturges** (New York: Harcourt Brace Jovanovich, 1982).

In contrast, Loew's has inspired a great deal of work. For an overview and list of all the MGM features made before 1975, see John Douglas Eames, **The MGM Story: The Complete History of Over Fifty Roaring Years** (New York: Crown, 1976). All other data about Loew's usually originates with Bosley Crowther, **The Lion's Share: The Story of an Entertainment Empire** (New York: Dutton, 1957). MGM's production bosses Irving Thalberg and Louis B. Mayer have generated several book-length studies. See Bosley Crowther, **Hollywood Rajah: The Life and Times of Louis B. Mayer** (New York: Holt, Rinehart & Winston, 1960); Gary Carey, **All The Stars in Heaven: Louis B.**

Mayer's M-G-M (New York: Dutton, 1981) and Samuel Marx, Mayer and Thalberg: The Make-Believe Saints (New York: Random House, 1975). Two valuable case studies of well-known MGM productions are Aljean Harmetz, The Making of The Wizard of Oz (New York: Alfred A. Knopf, 1981) and Donald Knox, The Magic Factory: How MGM Made An American in Paris (New York: Praeger, 1973). A nice collection of popular magazine articles about Loew's and MGM can be found in BFI Dossier Number 1 – MGM (London: BFI Publishing, 1980). Fortune provided two important business analyses during the 1930s in 'Metro-Goldwyn-Mayer', 6 (December 1932), pp. 51–8+, and 'Loew's Inc.', 20 (August 1938) pp. 69–72+. Both are reprinted in the Balio anthology and the BFI Dossier.

There has been precious little of substance written about 20th Century-Fox. Start with a complete list of all features, 1935 to 1979, in Tony Thomas and Aubrey Soloman, The Films of 20th Century-Fox: A Pictorial History (Secausus: The Citadel Press, 1979). For information on Fox before the Twentieth Century merger, see Glendon Allvine, The Greatest Fox of Them All (New York: Lyle Stuart, 1969). An informative book on Fox production chief Darryl F. Zanuck is Mel Gussow, Don't Say Yes Until I Finish Talking (New York: Doubleday, 1971). Less informative is Carlo Curti's gossipy Skouras: King of Fox Studios (Los Angeles: Holloway House, 1967). The best source on this corporation remains yet another Fortune article, this one written at the time of the merger: '20th Century-Fox', Fortune 12 (December 1935) pp. 85–93+.

A great deal has been written about Warner Bros. For a comprehensive list of features see Clive Hirschhorn, The Warner Bros. Story (New York: Crown, 1979), and Arthur Wilson, The Warner Bros. Golden Anniversary Book (New York: Dell, 1973). An adequate studio history can be found in Charles Higham, Warner Brothers (New York: Charles Scribner's Sons, 1975). To learn more about the brothers as Hollywood mogul types see Michael Freedland, The Warner Brothers (London: Harrap, 1983). This portrait concentrates on the flamboyant Jack Warner, drawing a great deal of information from Jack Warner's rather self-serving autobiography, My First Hundred Years in Hollywood (New York: Random House, 1964). The Velvet Light Trap has devoted two complete issues, numbers 1 and 15, to studies of the studio, its stars and directors. My own work has concentrated on the corporation's adoption of sound. For two overviews see 'The Coming of the Talkies: Invention, Innovation, and Diffusion', in the aforementioned Balio anthology, and 'Warner Bros.

Innovates Sound: A Business History', in Gerald Mast (ed.), **The Movies In Our Midst: Documents in the Cultural History of Film in America** (Chicago: University of Chicago Press, 1982) pp. 267–81. **Fortune** provided a vivid portrait of the production process in 'Warner Brothers', **Fortune** 16 (December 1937) pp. 110–13+. Indeed Warners has inspired numerous analyses of its working conditions. A first-rate overview can be found in Nick Roddick, **A New Deal in Entertainment: Warner Brothers in the 1930s** (London: British Film Institute, 1983). See also Hal Wallis and Charles Higham, **Starmaker: The Autobiography of Hal Wallis** (New York: Macmillan, 1980). The University of Wisconsin Press has issued sixteen original scripts of classic Warners films; thirty more are promised. The introductions to these volumes tell a great deal about Warners' production methods. A complete list of Warners' animation output can be found in Will Friedwald and Jerry Beck, **The Warner Brothers Cartoons** (Metuchen, New Jersey: The Scarecrow Press, 1981).

Many have been curious about RKO, the studio which issued **Citizen Kane** and **King Kong.** For basic information read a picture book which includes a fine studio history within its covers: Richard Jewell with Vernon Harbin, **The RKO Story** (New York: Arlington House, 1982). See also Russell Merritt, 'R.K.O. Radio: The Little Studio That Couldn't', in **Marquee Theater** (Madison: WHA-Television, 1972). **Fortune**'s treatment of the studio came as Howard Hughes was taking it out of business. See 'RKO: It's Only Money', **Fortune** 47 (May 1953) pp. 122–7, reprinted in Richard Austin Smith, **Corporations in Crisis** (Garden City, New York: Doubleday, 1966). **The Velvet Light Trap** devoted issue number 10 to RKO. There is a popular overview in Ron Haver, 'The Mighty Money Machine', **American Film** 3, no. 2 (November 1977) pp. 55–61. Probably the most writing concerning the corporation has come as a part of the mountain of material written about the eccentric Howard Hughes. For biographies see Donald L. Bartlett and James B. Wilson, **Empire** (New York: W. W. Norton, 1979); John Keats, **Howard Hughes** (New York: Random House, 1966); Noah Dietrich and Bob Thomas, **Howard: The Amazing Mr Hughes** (Greenwich, Connecticut: Fawcett, 1972) and Albert B. Gerber, **Bashful Billionaire** (New York: Lyle Stuart, 1967). Other RKO owners have inspired far less interest but see Eugene Lyons, **David Sarnoff** (New York: Harper & Row, 1966); Carl Dreher, **Sarnoff: An American Success** (New York: Quadrangle, 1977) and Floyd B. Odlum, **Selected Speeches of Floyd B. Odlum, 1930 to 1960** (New York: Random House, 1960).

For two overviews of Disney the man and his studio see Leonard Maltin, **The Disney Films** (New York: Crown, 1973) and Bob Thomas, **Walt Disney: An American Original** (New York: Simon & Schuster, 1976). A coffee-table tome, which adds little, is Christopher Finch, **The Art of Walt Disney: From Mickey Mouse to the Magic Kingdom** (New York: Harry N. Abrams, 1973). Debunking the Disney myth provides the focus for Richard Schickel, **The Disney Version** (New York: Simon & Schuster, 1968). **Fortune** supplied 'The Big Bad Wolf', **Fortune** 10 (November 1934), pp. 88–95+. A bibliography, *circa* 1977, of some 700 references to all aspects of the man and his studio (plus a complete filmography) can be found in Elizabeth Leebron and Lynn Gartley, **Walt Disney: A Guide to References and Resources** (Boston: G.K. Hall, 1979).

Universal is well-served by a listing of all its productions which can be found in Clive Hirschhorn, **The Universal Story** (New York: Crown, 1983). An inadequate substitute is Michael G. Fitzgerald, **Universal Pictures: A Panoramic History in Words, Pictures and Filmographies** (New Rochelle: Arlington House, 1977). For an article-length interpretative history of the studio see Richard Koszarski, **Universal Pictures 65 Years** (New York: The Museum of Modern Art). For a flattering biography of founder Carl Laemmle see John Drinkwater, **The Life and Adventures of Carl Laemmle** (New York: Putnam, 1931). A survey history of Universal in the 1910s and 1920s is the subject of I. G. Edmonds, **Big U: Universal in the Silent Days** (New York: A. S. Barnes, 1977).

There is a picture history of Columbia in Rochelle Larkin, **Hail Columbia** (New Rochelle: Arlington House, 1975). A useful survey can be found in Ed Buscombe's probing, 'Notes on Columbia Pictures Corporation, 1926–1941', *Screen,* 15, no. 1 Autumn 1975, pp. 65–82, reprinted in the forthcoming anthology edited by Paul Kerr. Bob Thomas' biography has too long served as the lone source of detailed information: Bob Thomas, *King Cohn* (New York: G. P. Putnam's Sons, 1967). A fair amount of production information can be gleaned from Frank Capra's **The Name Above the Title** (New York: Macmillan, 1971).

United Artists is the lone corporation served by a comprehensive history based on primary documents. See Tino Balio, **United Artists: The Company Built By The Stars** (Madison: University of Wisconsin Press, 1976). **Fortune** did a good job surveying the studio in 'United Artists: Final Shooting Script', **Fortune** 22 (December 1940) pp. 95–102+. See also Arthur Mayer, 'The Origins of United Artists', in **Films in Review** 5, no. 4

(April 1954) pp. 389–399, and Gaizka S. Usabel, **The High Noon of American Films in Latin America** (Ann Arbor: UMI Research Press, 1982).

Information on the specialized studios is hard to find. For a start see Richard Maurice Hurst, **Republic Studios: Between Poverty Row and the Majors** (Metuchen: The Scarecrow Press, 1979); Gene Fernett, **Poverty Row** (Satellite Beach, Florida: Coral Reef Publications, 1973), Todd McCarthy and Charles Flynn (ed.) **Kings of the Bs** (New York: E. P. Dutton, 1975) and Tom Onosko, 'Monogram: Its Rise and Fall in the 1940s', in **The Velvet Light Trap**, 5 (1972), pp. 5–9.

Index

British Film Institute Cinema Series
Edited by Ed Buscombe

The British Film Institute Cinema Series opens up a new area of cinema publishing with books that will appeal to people who are already interested in the cinema but want to know more, written in an accessible style by authors who have some authority in their field. The authors write about areas of the cinema where there is substantial interest, but as yet little serious writing, or they bring together for a wider audience some of the important ideas which have been developed in film studies in recent years.

Published:

Thomas Elsaesser: **New German Cinema**
Jane Feuer: **The Hollywood Musical**
Douglas Gomery: **The Hollywood Studio System**
Colin MacCabe: **Godard: Images, Sounds, Politics**
Steve Neale: **Cinema and Technology**

Forthcoming:

Pam Cooke: **Feminism,
Authorship and Cinema**
Richard Dyer: **The Stars**
Maria Kornatowska: **Contemporary Polish Cinema**
Christopher Williams: **Film and Marxism**